the Wonder Weeks

"Portrait of the first author, Hetty van de Rijt, created by her grandson Thomas on September 12, 1998, when he was 23 months old. Grandson and Grandma had a very close relationship and during her last seven years he was the sunshine in Hetty's life, which was restricted by disease.

On September 29, 2003, Hetty passed away. Till the very last moment she worked on the extended edition of this book in Dutch. When she died, the first draft of the last chapter was ready. Through her life's work Hetty hoped to empower parents and give them peace of mind and self-confidence in their role as upbringer and socializer in such a way that they could enjoy their little sunshine."

the wonder weeks

How to stimulate your baby's mental development
and help him turn his 10 predictable, great, fussy
phases into magical leaps forward

Hetty van de Rijt, Ph.D.,
and
Frans Plooij, Ph.D.

To our children, Xaviera and Marco,
and to our grandchildren,
Thomas, Victoria and Sarah,
from whom we have learned so much

© 2008–2010 by Kiddy World Promotions B.V.

First published in 1992 as Oei, ik groei! by Zomer & Keuning Boeken B.V., Ede and Antwerp

Kiddy World Promotions B.V. 1992, 2010

Hetty van de Rijt and Frans Plooij assert the moral right to be identified as the authors of this work.

Translation by Stephen Sonderegger and Gayle Kidder
Book design by Convorm Ontwerp, Niels Terol
Illustrations by Jan Jutte

van de Rijt, Hetty 1944 – 2003
Plooij, Frans X. 1946 –
    [Oei, ik groei! English]
    The wonder weeks : how to stimulate your baby's mental development and help him
    turn his 10 predictable, great, fussy phases into magical leaps forward
    / Hetty van de Rijt and Frans Plooij.
    480 p. 24 cm.
    Includes index.
    ISBN 978-90-79208-04-3
    1. Infant psychology 2. Infants - Development 3. Child rearing. 4. Baby books.
    5. Life change events. 6. Emotions in infants. 7. Attachment behavior in infants.
    8. Cognition in infants. 9. Parenting.
    I. Title II. How to stimulate your baby's mental development and help him
    turn his 10 predictable, great, fussy phases into magical leaps forward.

BF719 .V3613 2010
649'.122-dc21
v. 0212

Kiddy World Promotions B.V.
Zijpendaalseweg 73
6814 CE Arnhem
The Netherlands

Contents

About this Book ix

Introduction 1

Leap Alarm 8

Chapter 1: Growing Up: How Your Baby Does It 9

Chapter 2: Newborn: Welcome to the World 19

Chapter 3: Wonder Week 5:
The World of Changing Sensations 37

Chapter 4: Wonder Week 8:
The World of Patterns 55

Chapter 5: Wonder Week 12:
The World of Smooth Transitions. 83

Chapter 6: Wonder Week 19:
The World of Events 109

Chapter 7: Wonder Week 26:
The World of Relationships 147

Chapter 8: Wonder Week 37:
The World of Categories 197

Chapter 9: Wonder Week 46:
The World of Sequences 231

Chapter 10: Wonder Week 55:
The World of Programs 269

Chapter 11: Wonder Week 64:
The World of Principles 305

Chapter 12: Wonder Week 75:
The World of Systems 371

Postscript: Countless Wonders 443

Further Reading .447

Index 450

Internet 465

about this book

Having completed our studies in Educational Psychology, Physical Anthropology and Behavioral Biology, and just married, my wife Hetty van de Rijt and I left for the Gombe National Park, Tanzania, East-Africa to study chimpanzees with Jane Goodall. The particular research project we had prepared for proved impossible under the prevailing circumstances, so we had to change topic. There and then we realized that there was no place on Earth where one could observe freeliving newborn chimpanzee babies at such close range. We did not have any theory or hypothesis at hand for testing, but we were trained in systematic, direct observation of animal behavior in the field, in the tradition of Nobel Laureate Niko Tinbergen. So that is what we did for nearly two years.

When we returned to Europe to work in Robert Hinde's Medical Research Council-unit on the Development and Integration of Behavior, University Sub-department of Animal Behavior in Madingley, Cambridge, England, we had to analyze reams of data. Out of this analysis emerged the notion of regression periods—difficult periods where the baby clings more closely to the mother. Previously, such regression periods had been found by others in no less than 12 other primate species. The results of the data analysis also supported the idea that in the course of early ontogeny a hierarchical organization emerges in the central nervous system that underlies the behavioral development of the freeliving chimpanzee babies and infants.

It was only after we had analyzed our data and discerned a hierarchical organization that our friend and colleague Lex Cools, a neurobiologist, suggested that we compare our findings about the capabilities of infants at the different stages of development to the levels of perception spelled out by Hierarchical Perceptual Control Theory (PCT) developed by William T. Powers. PCT turned out to explain our findings very well. In the following years, the core postulates of PCT have been further tested by other researchers and results published in the scientific literature. Readers who are interested can go to the website www.livingcontrolsystems.com for an overview of PCT.

Once we had earned our Ph.D. degrees in Cambridge, England (Hetty) and Groningen, the Netherlands (Frans), we moved on to observe and film human mothers and infants in their home environment. These studies demonstrated clearly that human babies, too, go through difficult, age-linked regression periods in a similar way. With each difficult period, babies make a leap in their mental development. Each time another layer of perceptual control systems is superimposed onto the already existing, hierarchically organized layers of perceptual control systems.

Based on our research, Hetty and I wrote the original Dutch version of *The Wonder Weeks*, published in 1992 and followed in subsequent years by German, French, Swedish, Italian, Danish, Spanish, English, Japanese, Korean, and Russian editions. Our original research in The Netherlands has been replicated and confirmed by other researchers in Spain, Britain and Sweden. For information about the research upon which *The Wonder Weeks* is based, and about editions in various languages, see www.thewonderweeks.com.

Unfortunately, Hetty contracted a rare tropical disease during our stay in Tanzania and following a long, brave battle with the disease, she passed away in 2003. Hetty's legacy is alive and well as her life's work continues to bear fruit and *The Wonder Weeks* continues to make life easier for parents and contribute to the healthy development of children.

Frans Plooij
Arnhem, The Netherlands

introduction

*J*olted from a deep sleep, the new mother leaps from her bed and runs down the hall to the nursery. Her tiny infant, red-faced, fists clenched, screams in his crib. On instinct, the mother picks up the baby, cradling him in her arms. The baby continues to shriek. The mother nurses the baby, changes his diaper, then rocks him, trying every trick to ease his discomfort, but nothing seems to work. "Is there something wrong with the baby?" the mother wonders. "Am I doing something wrong?"

Parents commonly experience worry, fatigue, aggravation, guilt, and sometimes even aggression toward their inconsolable infants. The baby's cries may cause friction between the parents, especially when they disagree on how to deal with it. Well-meant but unwelcome advice from family, friends, and even strangers only makes things worse. "Let him cry, it's good for his lungs" is not the solution mothers wish to hear. Disregarding the problem does not make it go away.

The Good News: There Is a Reason

For the past 35 years, we have studied the development of babies and the way mothers and other caregivers respond to their changes. Our research was done in homes, where we observed the daily activities of mothers and children. We gleaned further information from more formal interviews.

Our research has shown that from time to time all parents are plagued by a baby who won't stop crying. In fact, we found that, surprisingly, all normal, healthy babies are more tearful, troublesome, demanding, and fussy at the same ages, and when this occurs they may drive the entire household to despair. *From our research, we are now able to predict, almost to the week, when parents can expect their babies to go through one of these "fussy phases."*

During these periods, a baby cries for a good reason. She is suddenly undergoing drastic changes in her development, which are upsetting to her. These changes enable the baby to learn many new skills and should therefore be a reason for celebration. After all, it's a sign that she is making wonderful progress. But as far as the baby is concerned, these changes are bewildering. She's taken aback—everything has changed overnight. It is as if she has entered a whole new world.

It is well known that a child's physical development progresses in what we commonly call "growth spurts." A baby may not grow at all for some time, but then she'll grow a quarter inch in just one night. Research has shown that essentially the same thing happens in a child's mental development. Neurological studies have shown that there are times when major, dramatic changes take place in the brains of children younger than 20 months. Shortly after each of them, there is a parallel leap forward in mental development.

This book focuses on the ten major leaps that every baby takes in her first 20 months of life. It tells you what each of these developments mean for your baby's understanding of the world about her and how she uses this understanding to develop the new skills that she needs at each stage in her development.

What This Means for You and Your Baby

Parents can use this understanding of their baby's developmental leaps to help them through these often confusing times in their new lives. You will better understand the way your baby is thinking and why he acts as he does at certain times. You will be able to choose the right kind of help to give him when he needs it and the right kind of environment to help him make the most of every leap in his development.

This is not a book about how to make your child into a genius, however. We firmly believe that every child is unique and intelligent in his own way. It is a book on how to understand and cope with your baby when he is difficult and how to enjoy him most as he grows. It is about the joys and sorrows of growing with your baby.

All that's required to use this book is:
- One (or two) loving parent(s)
- One active, vocal, growing baby
- A willingness to grow along with your baby
- Patience.

How to Use This Book

This book grows with your baby. You can compare your experiences with those of other mothers during all stages of your baby's development. Over the years, we've asked many mothers of new babies to keep records of their babies' progress and also to record their thoughts and feelings as well as observations of their babies' behavior from day to day. The diaries we've included in this book are a sample of these, based on the weekly reports of mothers of 15 babies—eight girls and seven boys. We hope you will feel that your baby is growing alongside those in our study group and that you can relate your observations of your baby to those of other mothers.

However, this book is not just for reading. Each section offers you the opportunity to record the details of your baby's progress. By the time a baby has grown into middle childhood, many mothers yearn to recall all of the events and emotions of those first all-important years. Some mothers keep diaries, but most mothers—who are not particularly fond of writing or who simply lack the time—are convinced they will remember the milestones and even the minor details in their babies' lives. Unfortunately, later on these mothers end up deeply regretting the fact that their memories faded faster than they could ever have imagined.

You can keep a personal record of your baby's interests and progress in the "My Diary" sections provided throughout this book. They offer space for you to record your thoughts and comments on your child's growth and budding personality, so that you can easily turn this book into a diary of the development of your baby. Often, a few key phrases are enough to bring memories flooding back later on.

The next chapter, "Growing Up: How Your Baby Does It" explains some of the research on which this book is based and how it applies to your baby. You will learn how your baby grows by making "leaps" in her mental development and how these are preceded by stormy periods when you can expect her to be fussy, cranky, or temperamental.

"Chapter 2: Newborn: Welcome to the World" describes what a newborn's world is like and how she perceives the new sensations that surround her. You will learn how nature has equipped her to deal with the challenges of life and how important physical contact is to her future development. These facts will help you get to know your new baby, to learn about her wants and needs, and to understand what she is experiencing when she takes the first leap forward.

Subsequent chapters discuss the Wonder Weeks—the ten big changes your baby undergoes in the first 20 months of life, at around 5, 8, 12, 19, 26, 37, 46, 55, 64 and 75 weeks. Each chapter tells you the signs that will let you know that a major leap is occurring. Then they explain the new perceptual changes your baby experiences at this time and how your baby will make use of them in his development.

Each leap is discussed in a separate chapter, consisting of four sections: **"This Week's Fussy Signs"** describes the clues that your baby is about to make a developmental leap. Reflections from other mothers about their babies' troublesome times offer sympathetic support as you endure your baby's stormy periods.

In this section, you'll also find a diary section titled "Signs My Baby Is Growing Again." Check off the signs you've noticed that indicate your baby is about to experience a big change.

"The Magical Leap Forward" discusses the new abilities your baby will acquire during the current leap. In each case it's like a new world opening up, full of observations she can make and skills she can acquire.

In this section, you will find a diary section, "How My Baby Explores the New World," which lists the skills that babies can develop once they have made this developmental leap. As you check off your baby's skills on the lists, remember that no baby will do everything listed. Your baby may exhibit only a few of the listed skills at this time, and you may not see other skills until weeks or months later. How much your baby does is not important—your baby will choose the skills best suited to her at this time. Tastes differ, even among babies! As you mark or highlight your own baby's preferences, you will discover what makes your baby unique.

"What You Can Do to Help" gives you suggestions for games, activities, and toys appropriate to each stage of development which will increase your baby's awareness and satisfaction—and enhance your playtime together.

"After the Leap" lets you know when you can expect your baby to become more independent and cheerful again. This is likely to be a delightful time for parents and babies, when both can appreciate the newly acquired skills that equip the baby to learn about and enjoy her world.

This book is designed to be picked up at any point in your baby's first 20 months when you feel you need help understanding her current stage of development. You do not have to read it from cover to cover. If your baby is a little older, you can skip the earlier chapters.

What This Book Offers You

We hope that you will use this knowledge of your child's developmental leaps to understand what he is going through, help him through the difficult times, and encourage him as he takes on the momentous task of growing into a toddler. Also, we hope that this book helps provide the following.

Support in times of trouble. During the times that you have to cope with crying problems, it helps to know that you are not alone, that there is a reason for the crying, and that a fussy period never lasts more than a few weeks, and sometimes no longer than several days. This book tells you what other mothers experienced when their babies were the same age as yours. You will learn that all mothers struggle with feelings of anxiety, aggravation, and a whole range of other emotions. You will come to understand that these feelings are all part of the process, and that they will help your baby progress.

Self-confidence. You will learn that you are capable of sensing your baby's needs better than anyone else. You are the expert, the leading authority on your baby.

Help in understanding your baby. This book will tell you what your baby endures during each fussy phase. It explains that he will be difficult when he's on the verge of learning new skills, as the changes to his nervous system start to upset him. Once you understand this, you will be less concerned about and less resentful of his behavior. This knowledge will also give you more peace of mind and help you to help him through each of these fussy periods.

Hints on how to help your baby play and learn. After each fussy period, your baby will be able to learn new skills. He will learn faster, more easily, and with more pleasure if you help him. This book will give you insight into what is preoccupying him at each age. On top of that, we supply a range of ideas for different games, activities, and toys so that you can choose those best suited to your baby.

A unique account of your baby's development. You can track your baby's fussy phases and progress throughout the book and supplement it with your own notes, so that it charts your baby's progress during the first 20 months of his life.

We hope that you will use this knowledge of your child's developmental leaps to understand what he is going through, help him through the difficult times, and encourage him as he takes on the momentous task of growing into a toddler. Also, we hope you will be able to share with him the joys and challenges of growing up.

Most of all, we hope you will gain peace of mind and confidence in your ability to bring up your baby. We hope this book will be a reliable friend and an indispensable guide in the crucial first 20 months of your baby's life.

leap alarm

A mother sent us this letter:

Dear Frans and Hetty,

... I always noticed that my baby was difficult for a few days before I realized that he was making a leap. I was irritated for a few days, but kept the feeling to myself until the proverbial straw broke the camel's back. At that point, I became very angry with him sometimes, and my own reaction scared me. When this had happened three times, I wrote down all the leaps in my calendar. That way, I can read the next chapter in time for the next leap. It may seem crazy, but I think I can handle his difficult periods much better now. I know what will happen before it does. I won't be surprised any more.

Sincerely, Maribel

To us, this was a very special letter. Maribel described what many mothers feel—their baby's leaps can be overwhelming!

This is why we developed the Leap Alarm. Using it is easy. Just enter your data (due date, not birth date!) at www.thewonderweeks.com. Each email will feature a short description of your baby's imminent leap in mental development. And of course, this service is completely free!

chapter 1

Growing Up:
How Your Baby Does It
One small step back and a
giant leap forward

Watching their babies grow is, for many parents, one of the most interesting and rewarding experiences of their lives. Parents love to record and celebrate the first time their babies sit up, crawl, say their first words, feed themselves, and a myriad of other precious "firsts."

But few parents stop to think about what's happening in their babies' minds that allows them to learn these skills when they do. We know that a baby's perception of the world is growing and changing when she suddenly is able to play peek-a-boo or to recognize Grandma's voice on the telephone. These moments are as remarkable as the first time she crawls, but even more mysterious because they involve things happening inside her brain that we cannot see. They're proof that her brain is growing as rapidly as her chubby little body.

But every parent discovers sooner or later that the first 20 months of life can be a bumpy road. While parents revel in their children's development and share their joy as they discover the world around them, parents also find that at times baby joyfulness can suddenly turn to abject misery. A baby can seem as changeable as a spring day.

At times, life with baby can be a very trying experience. Inexplicable crying bouts and fussy periods are likely to drive both mother and father to desperation, as they wonder what's wrong with their little tyke and try every trick to soothe her or coax her to happiness, to no avail.

Crying and Clinging Can Simply Mean He's Growing

For 35 years, we have been studying interactions between mothers and babies. We have documented—in objective observations, from personal records, and on videotape—the times at which mothers report their babies to be "difficult." These difficult periods are usually accompanied by the three C's: **Clinginess, Crankiness, and Crying.** We now know that they are the telltale signs of a period in which the child makes a major leap forward in his development.

It is well known that a child's physical growth progresses in what are commonly called "growth spurts." A child's mental development progresses in much the same way.

Recent neurological studies on the growth and development of the brain support our observations of mother and baby interactions. Study of the physical events that accompany mental changes in the brain is still in its infancy. Yet, at six of the ten difficult ages we see take place in the first 20 months, major changes in the brain have been identified by other scientists. Each major change announces a leap forward in mental development of the kind we are describing in this book. We expect that studies of other critical ages will eventually show similar results.

It is hardly surprising, when you think of the number of changes that your baby has to go through in just the first 20 months of life, that he should occasionally feel out of sorts. Growing up is hard work!

The Fussy Signs that Signal a Magical Leap Forward

In this book, we outline the ten major developmental leaps that all babies go through in the first 20 months of their lives. Each leap allows your baby to assimilate information in a new way and use it to advance the skills she needs to grow, not just physically but also mentally, into a fully functioning, thinking adult.

Each leap is invariably preceded by what we call a fussy phase or clingy period, in which the baby demands extra attention from her mother or other caregiver. The amazing and wonderful thing is that all babies go through these difficult periods at exactly the same time, give or take a week or two, during the first 20 months of their lives.

These ten developmental leaps that infants undergo are not necessarily in sync with physical growth spurts, although they may occasionally coincide. Many of the common milestones for a baby's first 20 months of development, such as cutting teeth, are also unrelated to these leaps in mental development.

Milestones in mental development may, on the other hand, be *reflected* in physical progress, although they are by no means limited to that.

Signs of a Leap

Shortly before each leap, a sudden and extremely rapid change occurs within the baby. It's a change in the nervous system, chiefly the brain, and it may be accompanied by some physical changes as well. In this book we call this a "big change." Each big change brings the baby a new kind of perception and alters the way that she perceives the world. And each time a new kind of perception swamps your baby, it also brings the means of learning a new set of skills appropriate for that world. For instance, at approximately 8 weeks, the big change in the brain enables the baby to perceive simple patterns for the first time.

During the initial period of disturbance that the big change always brings, you may already notice new behaviors emerging. Shortly thereafter, you most certainly will. In the 8-week example, your baby will suddenly show an interest in visible shapes, patterns, and structures, such as cans on a supermarket shelf or the slats on her crib. Physical developments may be seen as well. For example, she may start to gain some control over her body, since she now recognizes the way her arms and legs work in precise patterns and is able to control them. So, the big change alters the perception of sensations inside the baby's body as well as outside it.

The major sign of a big change is that the baby's behavior takes an inexplicable turn for the worse. Sometimes it will seem as if your baby has become a changeling. You will notice a fussiness that wasn't there in the previous weeks and often there will be bouts of crying that you are at a loss to explain. This is very worrisome, especially when you encounter it for the first time, but it is perfectly normal. When their babies become more difficult and demanding, many mothers wonder if their babies are becoming ill. Or they may feel annoyed, not understanding why their babies are suddenly so fussy and trying.

The Timing of the Fussy Phases

Babies all undergo these fussy phases at around the same ages. During the first 20 months of a baby's life, there are ten developmental leaps with their corresponding fussy periods at onset. The fussy periods come at 5, 8, 12, 15, 23, 34, 42, 51, 60 and 71 weeks. The onsets may vary by a week or two, but you can be sure of their arrival.

In this book, we confine ourselves to the developmental period from birth to just past the first year and a half of your baby's life. This pattern does not end when your baby has become a toddler, however. Several more leaps have been documented throughout childhood, and even into the teenage years.

The initial fussy phases your baby goes through as an infant do not last long. They can be as short as a few days—although they often seem longer to parents distressed over an infant's inexplicable crying. The intervals between these early periods are also short—3 or 4 weeks, on average.

Later, as the changes your infant undergoes become more complex, they take longer for her to assimilate and the fussy periods may last from 1 to 6 weeks. Every baby will be different, however. Some babies find change more distressing than others, and some changes will be more distressing than others. But every baby will be upset to some degree while these big changes are occurring in her life.

Every big change is closely linked to changes in the developing infant's nervous system, so nature's timing for developmental leaps is actually calculated from the date of conception. In this book, we use the more

Your Baby's 10 Great Fussy Phases

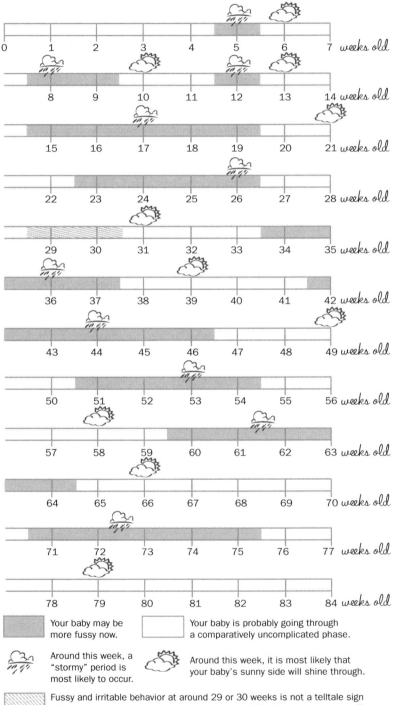

Your baby may be more fussy now.		Your baby is probably going through a comparatively uncomplicated phase.

Around this week, a "stormy" period is most likely to occur.

Around this week, it is most likely that your baby's sunny side will shine through.

Fussy and irritable behavior at around 29 or 30 weeks is not a telltale sign of another leap. Your baby has simply discovered that his mommy can walk away and leave him behind. Funny as it may sound, this is progress. It is a new skill: He is learning about distances.

Not a Single Baby Gets Away

All babies experience fussy periods when big changes in their development occur. Usually calm, easygoing babies will react to these changes just as much as more difficult, temperamental babies do. But not surprisingly, temperamental babies will have more difficulty in dealing with them than their calmer counterparts. Mothers of "difficult" babies will also have a harder time as their babies already require more attention and will demand even more when they have to cope with these big changes. These babies will have the greatest need for mommy, the most conflict with their mothers, and the largest appetite for learning.

conventional calculation of age from a baby's birth date. Therefore, the ages given at which developmental leaps occur are calculated for full-term babies. If your baby was premature or very late, you should adjust the ages accordingly. For example, if your baby was born 2 weeks late, her first fussy phase will probably occur 2 weeks earlier than we show here. If she was 4 weeks early, it will occur 4 weeks later. Remember to make allowances for this with each of the ten developmental leaps.

The Magical Leap Forward

To the baby, these big changes always come as a shock, as they turn the familiar world he has come to know inside out. If you stop to think about this, it makes perfect sense. Just imagine what it would be like to wake up and find yourself on a strange planet where everything was different from the one you were used to. What would you do?

You wouldn't want to calmly eat or take a long nap. Neither does your baby.

All she wants is to cling tightly to someone she feels safe with. To make matters more challenging for you and your baby, each developmental leap is different. Each gives the baby a new kind of perception that allows him to learn a new set of skills that belong to the new developmental world— skills he could not possibly have learned at an earlier age, no matter how much encouragement you gave him.

We will describe the perceptual changes your baby undergoes in each developmental leap, as well as the new skills that then become available to him. You will notice that each world builds upon the foundations of the previous one. In each new world, your baby can make lots of new discoveries. Some skills he discovers will be completely new, while others will be an improvement on skills he acquired earlier.

No two babies are exactly the same. Each baby has his own preferences, temperament, and physical characteristics, and these will lead him to select things in this new world that he, personally, finds interesting. Where one baby will quickly sample everything, another will be captivated by one special skill. These differences are what makes babies unique. If you watch, you will see your baby's unique personality emerging as he grows.

What You Can Do to Help

You are the person your baby knows best. She trusts you more and has known you longer than anyone else. When her world has been turned inside out, she will be completely bewildered. She will cry, sometimes incessantly, and she will like nothing better than to be simply carried in your arms all day long. As she gets older, she will do anything to stay near you. Sometimes she will cling to you and hold on for dear life. She may want to be treated like a tiny baby again. These are all signs that she is in need of comfort and security. This is her way of feeling safe. You could say that she is returning to home base, clinging to mommy.

When your baby suddenly becomes fussy, you may feel worried or even irritated by her troublesome behavior. You will want to know

Quality Time: An Unnatural Whim

When a baby is allowed to decide for himself when and what sort of attention he prefers, you'll notice this differs from one week to the next. When a big change occurs within a baby he will go through the following phases.

- A need to cling to mommy
- A need to play and learn new skills with mommy
- A need to play on his own.

Because of this, planned playtimes are unnatural. If you want your baby's undivided attention, you have to play when it suits him. It is impossible to plan having fun with a baby. In fact, he may not even *appreciate* your attention at the time you had set aside for "quality time." Gratifying, tender, and funny moments simply *happen* with babies.

what's wrong with her, and you will wish that she would become her old self again. Your natural reaction will be to watch her even more closely. It's then that you are likely to discover that she knows much more than you thought. You may notice that she's attempting to do things you have never seen her do before. It may dawn on you that your baby is changing, although your baby has known it for some time already.

As her mother, you are in the best position to give your baby things that she can handle and to meet her needs. If you respond to what your baby is trying to tell you, you will help her progress. Obviously, your baby may enjoy certain games, activities, and toys that you, personally, find less appealing, while you may enjoy others that she does not like at all. Don't forget that mothers are unique, too. You can also encourage her if she loses interest or wants to give up too easily. With your help, she will find the whole play-and-learn process more challenging and fun, too.

When your baby learns something new, it often means that she has to break an old habit. Once she can crawl, she is perfectly capable of fetching her own playthings, and once she can walk quite confidently on her own, she can't expect to be carried as often as before. Each leap forward in her development will make her more capable and more independent.

This is the time when mother and baby may have problems adjusting to one another. There is often a big difference in what baby wants and what mother wants or thinks is good for the baby, and this can lead to anger and resentment on both sides. When you realize what new skills your baby is trying to exercise, you will be better equipped to set the right rules for each developmental stage and alter them as needed as she grows.

After the Leap

The troublesome phase stops just as suddenly as it started. Most mothers see this as a time to relax and enjoy their babies. The pressure to provide constant attention is off. The baby has become more independent, and she is often busy putting her new skills into practice. She is more cheerful at this stage, too. Unfortunately, this period of relative peace and quiet doesn't last long—it's just a lull before the next storm. Nature does not allow babies to rest for long.

chapter 2

Newborn:
Welcome to the World

Watch any new mother when she holds her baby for the first time. Chances are she'll follow this particular pattern: First she'll run her fingers through his hair. Then she'll run a finger around his head and over his face. After this, she'll feel his fingers and toes. Then she'll slowly move toward his middle, along his arms, legs, and neck. Finally, she'll touch his tummy and chest.

The *way* in which mothers generally touch their newborn babies is often very similar, too. First a new mother will touch her infant with her fingertips only, stroking and handling him very gently. Slowly but surely, as she becomes more comfortable, she'll use all of her fingers and may sometimes squeeze him. Finally, she'll touch him with the palm of her hand. When she eventually dares to hold him by the chest or tummy, the new mother will be so delighted that she may exclaim what a miracle it is that she has produced something as precious as this.

Ideally, this discovery process should happen as close to birth as possible. After a mother's first encounter with her baby, she will no longer be afraid to pick him up, turn him around, or put him down. She will know how her little one feels to the touch.

Every baby looks and feels different. Try picking up another baby if his mother will allow it, and you'll find that it's a strange experience. It will take a minute or two to get used to the other infant. This is because you have become so accustomed to *your* baby.

Take Charge Early

The sooner a mother becomes confident handling her baby, the quicker she can begin responding sensitively to his needs. A baby shouldn't be dumped in his mother's arms; she should be allowed all the time she needs to take her baby into her arms herself. This sort of tuning-in to the new

Those Important First Hours

A mother is usually extremely perceptive to her newborn baby in the first hours after birth. Try to have your baby with you at this critical time to get to know each other. Your newborn baby is often wide awake during this period. She is aware of her surroundings, she turns toward quiet sounds, and she fixes her gaze on the face that happens to hover above her. Most mothers love it if the father is there, too, so they can share this experience as a brand-new family.

baby is easily interrupted if others don't give the mother space at the birth. If the new mother feels that things are not under her control, she may feel powerless and even afraid to handle her baby.

Take control of the situation as soon as you are able, and get to know your baby as soon as you can. Even if the baby has to be placed in an incubator, spend as much time with him as you can and look after as many aspects of his care as you are able. Talk to him to let him know you are there when you are not able to touch him.

Be sure to speak up. If you want to have your baby near you, or if you want to be alone with him for a while, say so. *You* decide how often you want to pick him up and cuddle him.

The majority of mothers whose early contact with their newborns was thwarted by hospital procedures or others around them say that they regret not having spent more time alone with their babies during this period. Many mothers feel resentful about this for quite some time. The maternity period wasn't like they imagined. Instead of enjoying a well-earned rest, they felt harassed. They had wanted to have their babies near them all the time, especially when the little ones were crying. If they were not allowed to hold their babies, the new mothers felt disappointed and annoyed.

They felt as if they were being treated like immature, helpless children who were incapable of deciding for themselves what was best for them and their babies. These feelings have also been expressed by fathers, too, who felt overwhelmed by hospital rules and frustrated by meddling from others.

"I had to do as I was told. I wasn't just told *how* to sit during nursing, but also when I could nurse, and for how long. I also had to allow my baby to cry whenever it wasn't "his time" yet. I was annoyed most of the time, but I didn't want to be rude, so I nursed him in secret. I just couldn't stand hearing him cry, and I wanted to comfort him. My breasts kept swelling and shrinking all day long. I'd really had more than I could take. I was the one who had given birth, and I wanted my baby. I was so angry that I just started crying. But of course they had a name for that, too—'maternity tears.' That was the last straw. All I wanted was my baby and a bit of peace and quiet."

Paul's mom

"I had a long delivery. Our baby was taken away from us immediately. For hours, we assumed we'd had a baby boy. When I got my baby back later on, it turned out to be a girl. We were shocked. It wasn't that we didn't want a girl, but we had started getting used to the idea that we had a son."

Jenny's mom

"When I nursed my baby, I liked to snuggle up to her and get nice and close. But the maternity nurse wouldn't let me. She made me lean back into the cushions on the sofa. It felt so unnatural—detached and unemotional."

Nina's mom

When mothers have problems with their babies shortly after the birth, they often say this is because they don't feel completely confident. They are afraid of dropping them or holding them too tightly. They haven't learned to assess their babies' needs and responses to certain situations. They feel they are failing as mothers.

Some mothers think this has to do with the fact that they saw so little of their babies just after the birth. They would have loved to have spent more time with their babies back then, but now they feel relieved when the babies are back in their cribs. They've become afraid of motherhood.

"Because I had a difficult birth, we had to stay in the hospital for 10 days. I was only allowed to see my baby during the day, at nursing times. Nothing was the way I had imagined it would be. I'd planned to breastfeed, but sometimes the staff gave my baby a bottle on the sly, to make things easier for themselves. At night, they always gave her bottles. I wanted to have her near me more often, but they wouldn't allow it. I felt helpless and angry. When I was allowed to go home, I felt that they might as well keep her. By that time, she felt like a stranger, like she wasn't mine."

Juliette's mom

Do Remember

Cuddle, rock, caress, and massage your baby when she is in a good mood, since this is the best time to find out what suits her and what relaxes her most. When you know her preferences, you will be able to use these methods to comfort her later on when she is upset. If you cuddle, rock, caress, and massage her only when she is in a bad mood, the "comfort" will cause her to cry even longer and louder.

"The maternity nurse was a nuisance. She stayed when I had company, did most of the talking, and went on and on telling everyone about every case she'd been on that had ever gone just the slightest bit wrong. For some reason, she was overly concerned that my healthy baby would turn yellow. She would check on her every hour, sometimes every 15 minutes, and tell me she thought she'd seen the first signs of jaundice. It made me so nervous. When I tried to breastfeed, the nurse kept interrupting by whisking my hungry baby off to be weighed. This upset me every time, and my baby didn't seem too pleased about it, either. She wriggled around on the scales, so it would take even longer for the nurse to see whether she had taken 1.4 or 1.5 ounces of milk. Meanwhile, my baby's desperate screams made me even more nervous, so I finally decided to stop breastfeeding. When I look back on it, I feel terrible. I would have liked so much to nurse my little girl."

Emily's mom

"With my second child, we were determined to do everything exactly the way we wanted. When the baby started crying, I would simply feed her a little. For nearly 2 weeks, we had been told to let our eldest cry and go hungry—for no reason, as it later turned out. With the first baby, you tend to take advice from everyone. The second time, I listened only to myself."

Eve's mom

Getting to Know and Understand Your Baby

In some ways, you already know your baby. After all, she was with you day and night for 9 months. Before she was born, you wondered what kind of baby you would have and whether you would recognize any traits you thought she had while in your womb. But once she's born it's different —totally different, in fact. You see your baby for the first time, and your baby also finds herself in completely new surroundings.

Most mothers look for familiar traits in their tiny newborns. Is she the peaceful little person she expected her to be? Does she kick at certain times of the day like she did before she was born? Does she have a special bond with her Dad? Does she recognize his voice?

Often mothers want to "test" their babies' reactions. They want to find out what makes their children happy and contented. They will appreciate advice, but not rules and regulations. They want to get to know their babies and see how their babies respond to them. They want to find out for themselves what is best for their children. If they're right about their likes and dislikes, they feel pleased with themselves, as it shows how well they know their babies. This increases their self-confidence and will make them feel they are perfectly able to cope after they take their infants home.

Seeing, hearing, smelling, and feeling your baby during those first few days has a tremendous impact on your relationship with your baby. Most mothers instinctively know how important these intimate "parties" are. They want to experience everything their babies do. Just looking at them gives them enormous pleasure. They want to watch them sleep and listen to them breathe. They want to be there when they wake up. They want to caress them, cuddle them, and smell them whenever they feel like it.

"My son's breathing changes whenever he hears a sudden noise or sees a light. When I first noticed this irregular breathing, I was really concerned, but then I realized he was just reacting to sound and light. Now I think it's wonderful when his breathing changes, and I don't worry about it anymore."

Bob's mom

Your Baby Gets to Know and Understand You

When a new parent gazes down into her baby's face, it often seems as if the baby, gazing steadily back with wide, astonished eyes, is thinking, "What a strange and wonderful world this is!"

Indeed, a newborn baby's world is an astonishing place of new and strange sensations. Light, sound, motion, smells, the sensations on his soft skin—it is all so new that he can't even separate them one from another yet. Sometimes, snuggled tightly up against his mother's breast, it all feels so wonderfully good. He feels full, warm, sleepy, and soothed by the softness around him.

At other times, his whole world seems utterly shattered, and he can't figure out what's making him feel so miserable. *Something* is wet, cold, hungry, noisy, blindingly bright, or just desperately unhappy, and all he can do is wail.

During the first 5 weeks of your baby's life, he will slowly become familiar with the world around him. You and he will get to know each other more intimately than anyone else in your shared world at this time. Soon he will make the first major leap in his development.

But before you are able to understand what your baby will experience when he is 5 weeks old and takes his first leap forward, you need to know what your newborn baby's world is like now and how he is equipped to deal with it. Also, to help him meet his new challenges, you need to know how important physical contact is and how to use it.

Your New Baby's World

Babies are interested in the world around them from the moment they are born. They look and listen, taking in their surroundings. They try very hard to focus their eyes as sharply as possible, which is why babies frequently look cross-eyed as they strain to get a better look. Sometimes they tremble and gasp from sheer exhaustion in the effort. A newborn often looks at you as if he is staring, transfixed with interest.

Your new baby has an excellent memory, and he is quick to recognize voices, people, and even some toys, such as an especially colorful stuffed animal. He also clearly anticipates regular parts of his daily routine, such as bath-time, cuddle-time, and nursing-time.

Even at this age, a baby mimics facial expressions. Try sticking your tongue out at him while you sit and talk to him, or open your mouth wide as if you are going to call out. Make sure that he's really looking at you when you try this, and give him plenty of time to respond. Most of your baby's movements are very slow by adult standards, and it will take him several seconds to react.

A young baby is able to tell his mother just how he feels—whether he is happy, angry, or surprised. He does this by slightly changing the tone of his murmuring, gurgling, and crying and by using body language. You will rapidly get to know what he means. Besides, the baby will make it perfectly clear that he expects to be understood. If he isn't, he will cry angrily or sob as if heartbroken.

Your newborn baby has preferences even at this tender age. Most babies prefer to look at people, rather than toys. You will also find that if presented with two playthings, he is able to express a preference by fixing his gaze on one of them.

Your new baby is quick to react to encouragement. He will adore being praised for his soft baby fragrance, his looks, and his achievements. You will hold his interest longer if you shower him with compliments!

Even though your baby's senses are in complete working order, he is unable to process the signals his senses send to his brain in the same way adults do. This means that he isn't able to distinguish among his senses. Babies experience their world in their own way, and it's quite different from ours. We *smell* a scent, *see* the flower spreading it, *touch* its soft, velvety petals, *hear* a bee buzzing toward it, and know we are *tasting* honey when we put it into our mouths. We understand the difference among each of our senses, and so we are able to distinguish the differences.

(continued on page 31)

Your New Baby's Senses

Young babies can already see, hear, smell, taste, and feel a variety of things, and they are able to remember these sensations. However, a newborn baby's perception of these sensations is very different from the way she will experience them as she gets older.

WHAT BABIES SEE

Until recently, scientists and doctors believed that new babies were unable to see. This is not true. Mothers knew all along that newborns love to look at faces, although it is true that vision is the last sense to reach full capacity. Your newborn can see most clearly up to a distance of about a foot. Beyond this, her vision is probably blurred. Sometimes she will also have difficulty focusing both eyes on whatever she is looking at, but once she has, she can stare at the object intently. She will even stop moving briefly. All her attention will be focused on the object. If she is very alert, she will sometimes be able to follow a moving toy by moving her eyes, turning her head, or sometimes by doing both together. She can manage to do this whether the object is moved horizontally or vertically. The important thing is that the object must be moved very slowly and deliberately. If she loses track after a few moments, pick up her gaze again and try it even more slowly.

The object that your baby will follow best is a simple pattern with the basic characteristics of a human face—two large dots at the top for the eyes and one below for the mouth. Babies are able to do this within an hour of birth. Many of them have their eyes wide open and are very alert. Fathers and mothers are often completely fascinated by their newborn baby's big, beautiful eyes. It is possible that babies are attracted to anything that even vaguely resembles a human face when they are this young.

Your baby will be particularly interested in sharp contrasts—red and white stripes will probably hold her attention longer than green and blue ones. The brighter the color contrasts, the more interested she will be. Black and white stripes actually hold a baby's attention longest because the contrast is strongest.

WHAT BABIES HEAR

At birth, your new baby can already clearly distinguish between different sounds. She will recognize your voice shortly after birth. She may like music, the hum of an engine, and soft drumming. This makes sense, because these sounds are already familiar to her. In the womb, she was surrounded by the constant thump, rustle, grumble, wheeze, and squeak of heart, veins, stomach, lungs, and intestines. She also has a built-in interest in people's voices and finds them soothing. By and large babies will feel comfortable in environments similar to those that they were used to in the womb. For example, a baby whose mother spent a lot of time in noisy surroundings while she was pregnant may be quite upset by a room that is too quiet.

Your baby recognizes the difference between deep and high-pitched voices. High-pitched sounds will draw her attention more quickly. Adults sense this and speak to babies in high-pitched voices, so there is no need to be ashamed of your "oochykoochy-cooing." Your baby is also able to differentiate between soft and loud sounds and does not like sudden, loud noises. Some babies are easily frightened, and if this is so for your baby, it is important that you do nothing that will frighten her.

WHAT BABIES SMELL

Your new baby is very sensitive to smells. She does not like pungent or sharp odors. These smells will make her overactive. She will try to turn away from the source of the smell, and she may start to cry, too.

(continued)

Your baby can smell the difference between your body scent and breast milk and those of other mothers. If she is presented with several items of worn clothing, she will turn toward the article that you have worn.

WHAT BABIES TASTE

Your baby can already distinguish between several different flavors. She has a distinct preference for sweet things and will dislike anything that tastes sour or acidic. If something tastes bitter, she will spit it out as fast as she can.

WHAT BABIES FEEL

Your baby can sense changes in temperature. She can feel heat, which she puts to good use when searching for a nipple if it is not put in her mouth, since the nipple is much warmer than the breast. She simply moves her head in the direction of the warmest spot. Your baby can also sense cold. But if she is allowed to become cold, she will be unable to warm herself, because at this age she can't shiver to get warm as a means of controlling her own body temperature. Her parents need to consider her bodily warmth. For instance, it's not very sensible to take a baby for a long walk through snow and ice, no matter how well wrapped up she is, because she may become too cold and show signs of hypothermia. If your baby shows distress of any kind, hurry inside where it is warm.

Your baby is extremely sensitive to being touched. Generally, she loves skin contact, whether it's soft or firm. Find out what your baby prefers. She will usually enjoy a body massage in a nice warm room, too. Physical contact is simply the best possible comfort and amusement for her. Try to find out what kind of contact makes your baby sleepy or alert, since you can put this knowledge to good use in troublesome times.

Your new baby is not yet able to make this distinction, however. He experiences the world as all one universe—a mish-mash of sensation that changes drastically as soon as a single element changes. He receives all these impressions but cannot distinguish among them. He does not yet realize that his world is made up of signals from individual senses and that each sense conveys messages about a single aspect of it.

To make matters even more confusing for your infant, he cannot yet make a distinction between himself and his surroundings, and he is not yet aware of being an independent person. Because of this, he also is unable to make a distinction between sensations that have their origin within his own body and those that come from outside it. As far as he is concerned, the outside world and his body are one and the same. To him, the world is one big color-cuddle-smell-and-sound sensation. What his body feels, he assumes everyone and everything else feels.

Because a newborn baby perceives the world and himself as one and the same, it is often difficult to discover the reason why he is crying. It could be anything inside or outside of him. No wonder his crying fits can drive his parents to distraction.

Your New Baby's Tool Kit

If you were to experience the world in the same way your baby does, you too would be incapable of acting independently. You would not know that you have hands to grasp things with and a mouth to suck with. Only when you understand these things will you be able to do things deliberately.

This does not mean, however, that newborn babies are completely incapable of reacting to the world. Fortunately, your baby comes equipped with several special features to compensate for these shortcomings and help him survive this initial period.

His Reflexes Tell Him What to Do

Babies have several reflex reactions to keep them safe. For example, a new-born baby will automatically turn his head to one side to breathe freely when lying face down. In some ways, this reflex is similar to the way a puppet reacts to its strings being pulled. He does not stop to think, "I'm going to turn my head." It simply happens. As soon as a baby learns to think and respond, this reflex disappears. It is a perfect system. (Of course, when it's time for your baby to go to sleep, be sure to place him on his back.)

Newborn babies also turn their heads toward sound. This automatic reaction ensures that a baby will shift his attention to the place of interest closest by. For many years, doctors overlooked this reaction because the newborn's response to sound is delayed. It takes 5 to 7 seconds before the baby starts to move his head, and it takes another 3 to 4 seconds to complete the movement. This reflex disappears somewhere between the 5th and 8th week after birth.

Here are some of your baby's other reflexes.

As soon as the mouth of a hungry newborn comes in contact with an object, his mouth will close around it, and he will start to suck. This reflex provides the baby with an incredibly strong sucking ability. It disappears as soon as a baby no longer needs to suckle.

Babies also have a strong gripping reflex. If you want your baby to grasp your finger, just stroke the palm of his hand. He will automatically grab your finger. If you do the same with his feet, he'll use his toes to grab your finger. This gripping reflex is thought to date back to prehistoric times, when hominid mothers were covered with thick body hair. Because of this reflex, babies were able to cling to their mothers' hair shortly after birth. A baby will use this gripping reflex during the first 2 months of life, especially if he senses you want to put him down when he would much rather stay with you!

A baby shows a reaction called the *Moro reflex* when he is frightened. He looks as if he is trying to grab at something during a fall. He arches his back, throws his head back, and waves his arms and legs about, outward

Babies Get Bored, Too

Your tiny infant is not yet able to amuse herself. Lively, temperamental babies in particular make no secret about wanting some action as soon as they are awake.

Here are some ways to keep your baby entertained.

- Explore the house with her. Give her the opportunity to see, hear, and touch whatever she finds interesting. Explain the items you come across while exploring. No matter what it is, she will enjoy listening to your voice. Pretty soon, she will start recognizing objects herself.

- Have a quiet "chat." Your baby enjoys listening to your voice. But if you also have a radio playing in the background, she will have difficulty in concentrating on your voice only. Although young babies are able to make a distinction between different voices when they hear them one at a time, they cannot distinguish one from the other when hearing them simultaneously.

- Place interesting objects in convenient places for your baby to look at when she is awake. At this age she won't be able to search for them herself, so for her it's "out of sight, out of mind."

- Experiment with music. Try to discover her favorite music and play it to her. She may find it to be very soothing.

In all activities, let your baby's responses guide you.

at first, then inward, before crossing them across his chest and stomach.

All of these baby reflexes disappear when they are replaced by voluntary responses. But there are other automatic reflexes that remain for life, such as breathing, sneezing, coughing, blinking, and jerking back a hand from a hot surface.

His Cries Get Your Attention

The reflexes mentioned above are your new baby's way of restoring an uncomfortable situation to normal. Sometimes these reflexes are not enough—for instance, if he is too hot or cold, if he is not feeling well, or if he is bored. In these cases, the baby employs another strategy: He wails until *someone else* rectifies the situation. If no one helps him, the baby will cry incessantly until he is completely exhausted.

"My son's crying fits started in his second week. He yelled day and night, even though he was nursing well and growing steadily. When I took him to the clinic for his regular checkup, I mentioned that perhaps he was bored. But the pediatrician said that was impossible because babies keep their eyes closed for the first 10 days, and even if my baby had his eyes open, he still wouldn't be able to see anything. Last week, I put a rattle in his crib anyway. It seems to be helping. He's certainly crying less. So he was bored after all!"

Paul's mom, 4th week

His Appearance Melts Your Heart

In order to survive, your baby has to rely on someone else to attend to his every need, morning, noon, and night. Therefore, nature has supplied him with a powerful weapon that he continually puts to use—his appearance.

Nothing is cuter than a baby. His extraordinarily large head makes up almost one third of his total length. His eyes and forehead are also "too big," and his cheeks are "too chubby." Furthermore, his arms and legs are "too short and too plump." His cute looks are endearing. Designers of dolls, cuddly toys, and cartoons are quick to copy them. This look sells! This is exactly how your baby sells himself, too. He is sweet, tiny, and helpless—a little cutie, just begging for attention. He will charm you into picking him up, cuddling him, and taking care of him.

Throughout the world, babies have been seen smiling before they are 6 weeks old. Smiling babies have even been filmed in the womb. Even so, this is a very rare occurrence in babies this young. Nevertheless, you may be one of the lucky parents who has witnessed an early smile. Newborn babies smile when touched, when a breath of fresh air brushes their cheeks, when they hear human voices or other sounds, when they see faces hovering over their cribs, or simply when they are full of milk and feeling content. Sometimes they even smile in their sleep.

Your New Baby's Biggest Need

Even before she was born, your baby perceived her world as one whole. At birth, she left her familiar surroundings and for the first time was exposed to all kinds of unknown, completely new things. This new world was made up of many new sensations. Suddenly, she's able to move freely, sense heat and cold, hear a whole range of different and louder noises, see bright lights, and feel clothes wrapped around her body. Besides these impressions, she also has to breathe by herself and get used to drinking milk, and her digestive organs have to process this new food, too. All these things are new to her. Because she suddenly has to cope with these enormous changes in lifestyle, it's easy to understand why she needs to feel safe and secure.

Close human contact is the best way of imitating your baby's secure world inside the womb. It makes her feel safe. After all, your womb hugged her body, and your movements kneaded it, as far back as she can remember. It was her home. She was part of whatever took place in there—the rhythmical beating of your heart, the flow of your blood, and the rumbling of your stomach. Therefore, it makes perfect sense that she will enjoy feeling the old, familiar physical contact and hearing those well-known sounds once more. It is her way of "touching base."

Touch: Simply the Best Comfort

Besides food and warmth, nothing is more important to your infant than snuggling close to you during the first 4 months of her life. As long as she experiences lots of physical contact, her development will not be delayed, even if you don't have much opportunity to play with her.

A young baby generally loves lying close to you and being carried around. At the same time, this is also a good opportunity for her to learn to control her body.

Another idea is to give her a relaxing massage. Make sure the room is warm. Pour some baby oil into your hands and softly massage every part of her naked body. This is a nice way of helping her to grow accustomed to her body, and it will make her wonderfully drowsy.

At this age, a baby loves to be picked up, cuddled, caressed, and rocked. She may even enjoy soft pats on her back. She cannot get enough physical contact now. Don't worry about whether you're doing the right thing—she'll soon let you know what she likes best and what comforts her most. In the meantime, she is learning that she has a wonderful home base to which she can safely return when she is upset.

chapter 3

Wonder Week 5:
The World of Changing
Sensations

For much of the last 4 or 5 weeks, you have watched your infant grow rapidly. You have become acquainted with each other, and you have learned all of his little ways. His world at this time is hard for adults to imagine. It's in soft focus and its qualities are undefined—in some ways it has not been so different from his life in your womb.

Now, before the mists that envelop his infant world part and allow him to start making sense of all the impressions that he has been busy absorbing in the last few weeks, he will need to go through his first major developmental leap. At about 5 weeks, and sometimes as early as 4, your baby will begin to take the first leap forward in his development.

New sensations bombard your baby inside and out, and he is usually bewildered by them. Some of these new things have to do with the development of his internal organs and his metabolism. Others are a result of his increased alertness—his senses are more sensitive than they were immediately after birth. So it is not so much the sensations themselves that are changing, but rather the baby's perceptions of them.

This rapidly changing world is very disturbing at first. Your baby's first reaction will be to want to return to the safe, warm, familiar world he so recently left, a world with mommy at its center. Suddenly, your infant may seem to need more cuddles and attention than he did before. While eating and sleeping and being well-looked after physically were enough to lull him with a sense of well-being before, he now seems to need something more from you. Although your baby has been very close to you since his birth, this may be the first time you think of him as fussy or demanding. This period may last only a day, but with some babies it lasts a whole week.

As this clinginess begins to ease, you will notice that your baby is just a little more grown-up in some way that you find it hard to put your finger on. He seems more alert and aware of the world around him.

Do Remember

> If your baby is fussy, watch him closely to see if he is attempting to master new skills.

 this **Week's Fussy Signs**

Even very young babies of 5 weeks can sense the changes occurring inside their tiny bodies. Having so newly gotten used to a world outside the warm embrace of your body, your baby is now finding her world changing for a second time. It's important to understand that although everything seems the same to you, to her everything she sees, feels, hears, smells, or tastes is different somehow. She may like some of these changes, but she may dislike others because she doesn't yet know how to cope with them. She is still too young to turn to you for help, and she certainly can't ask you what is going on.

How You Know It's Time to Grow

Even though your baby can't form the words to tell you what's going on, she is able to communicate quite a bit. Here are some signs that she is preparing to make her first leap.

She May Be Highly Upset

At this time, it's very likely your baby will yell, cry, scream, and refuse to go to sleep in her crib until she has driven the entire household crazy. These are the clues that your baby is about to make her first leap! With a

bit of luck, her distress will make you run toward her, pick her up, hold her tight, and let her snuggle up.

She May Crave Closeness with You

If she's even luckier, after you pick her up, you may also let her nurse. Sometimes she will drift off to sleep only if she's snuggled up to mommy in the closest way possible—latched onto the breast. Providing this sort of physical comfort with breast or bottle may be the only way to create the safe world she is so desperate for at this time.

> "Normally, my baby is very easy, but she suddenly started crying non-stop for almost 2 days. At first I thought it was just stomach cramps. But then I noticed she stopped whenever I had her on my lap, or when I let her lie in between us. She fell asleep right away then. I kept asking myself if I was spoiling her too much by allowing it. But the crying period stopped just as suddenly as it started, and now she's as easygoing as she was before."
>
> Eve's mom, 5th week

How This Leap May Affect You

As these major changes in your baby affect her, they're bound to have an affect on you as well. Here are some emotions you may feel.

You May Feel Insecure

All mothers want to find out why their babies are being troublesome and restless so that they can make it better for them. Usually, they will first try to see if the baby is hungry. Then they check if the diaper has come loose. They change her diaper. They try to comfort her with all the love and soothing they can muster in those trying moments. But it isn't easy. Pretty soon they discover that all the best care and comfort doesn't really stop the little bundle from resuming her relentless crying.

Most mothers find a sudden change in their babies' behavior to be a miserable experience. It undermines their confidence and is very distressing.

> "My son wanted to be with me all of the time, and I either held him against my chest or on my lap, even when we had company. I was terribly concerned. One night I hardly slept at all. I just spent the whole night holding and cuddling him. Then my sister came and took over for a night. I went in the other bedroom and slept like a log the whole night. I felt reborn when I woke up the next day."
>
> Bob's mom, 5th week

You May Feel Very Concerned

Often, mothers are afraid that something is wrong with their tiny screamers. They think that she's in pain, or that she may be suffering from some abnormality or disorder that has gone undetected until now. Others worry that the milk supply from breastfeeding alone is not sufficient. This is because the baby seems to crave the breast constantly and is always hungry. Some mothers take their babies to doctors for checkups. Of course, most babies are pronounced perfectly healthy and the mothers are sent home to worry alone. (When in doubt, always consult your family doctor or go to the childcare clinic.)

> "My daughter was crying so much that I was afraid something was terribly wrong. She wanted to breastfeed constantly. I took her to see the pediatrician, but he couldn't find anything wrong with her. He said she just needed time to get used to my milk and that many infants went through a similar crying phase at 5 weeks. I thought that it was a strange thing to say, because she hadn't had any problems with my milk until then. Her cousin, who was the same age, kept crying, too, but he was being bottle-fed. When I told the doctor that, he pretended he hadn't heard. I didn't push the subject, though. I was happy enough just knowing it wasn't anything serious."
>
> Juliette's mom, 5th week

Because your baby senses something changing, she feels insecure and has a greater need for close skin-to-skin contact. This close embrace seems to be the most powerfully calming type of physical contact when she is upset. Give her all the cuddling she needs and all the contact you feel you can handle at times like these. She needs time to adjust to these new changes and grow into her new world. She's accustomed to your body scent, warmth, voice, and touch. With you, she will relax a little and feel contented again. You can provide the tender loving care she really needs during this trying period.

> "Sometimes my daughter will nurse for half an hour and refuse to come off the breast. 'Just take her off after 20 minutes, and let her scream. She'll soon learn,' is the advice people give me. But secretly I think, 'They can say what they like; I decide what's best.'"
>
> Nina's mom, 5th week

You may notice that close physical contact will help during these crying fits, and that a noisy little creature will respond better and quicker when she is with you. Try carrying your baby around in a sling if you can while you go about your chores, or keep her on your lap while you read or do other sedentary activities. A gentle massage or stroking can be helpful, too.

> "When my baby was crying all the time, she seemed so lost. I had to massage her for a long time before she calmed down a bit. I felt exhausted but extremely satisfied. Something changed after that. It doesn't seem to take as long to soothe her now. When she cries now, I don't find it such an effort to put her world to rights again."
>
> Nina's mom, 4th week

Mothers who carry their babies around whenever they are in a fussy mood may label them "extremely dependent." These babies like nothing

Soothing Tips

When you want to comfort a tiny baby, a gentle rhythm can play a very important role. Hold your baby close to you, with his bottom resting on one arm while your other arm supports his head resting against your shoulder. When he's in this position, he can feel the soothing beat of your heart.

Here are a few other mom-recommended methods to soothe a tiny screamer.

- Cuddle and caress him.

- Rock him gently in your arms, or sit in a rocking chair with him.

- Walk around slowly with him.

- Talk or sing to him.

- Pat him gently on the bottom.

Not all of these ideas will suit your baby personally, so if you don't succeed at first, keep trying until you find out what works for him. The most successful way of comforting a crying baby is to do the things he enjoys most when he's in a cheerful mood.

better than lying quietly against their mothers and being stroked, rocked, or cuddled. They may fall asleep on their mothers' laps, but start to cry again as soon as furtive attempts are made to sneak them back into their cribs.

Mothers who stick to feeding and sleeping schedules often notice that their babies fall asleep during feeding. Some wonder if this is because the babies are so exhausted from crying and lack of sleep that they have no energy left to nurse. This may seem logical, but it may not be the whole story. It's more likely that the baby falls asleep because she's where she wants to be. She's finally with mommy, and she's content, so she is able to fall asleep.

How to Make a Sling

Slings are extremely easy to make and cozy for you and your new baby. A sling will help to give your arms a break by supporting your baby's weight and make your baby feel safe and secure. Plus, they cost only a few dollars to make. Your baby can use a sling almost immediately after birth since it allows him to lie flat. Here's how to make one.

Use a sturdy piece of material, 1 yard by 3 1/2 yards. Drape the cloth over your left shoulder if you are right-handed, or over your right shoulder if you are left-handed, and knot the ends together at the opposite hip. Turn the knot toward your back. Check to see if the length of the sling feels right. If it does, the sling is ready for use. Pop your baby inside and support her with your hands. It's that easy!

"The first 2 days my son cried so much. I was doing my best to stick to the proper bedtimes, but it turned out to be a total disaster. It drove us both up the wall. Now I keep him on my lap for as long as he wants without feeling guilty. I feel good about it. It's nice and warm and cozy. It's obvious he loves it. The feeding schedule's gone out the window, too. I didn't stick to it. Now he just lets me know when he's hungry. Sometimes he nurses for a long time, but sometimes he doesn't. He's much more contented now, and I am, too."

Steven's mom, 5th week

A number of indications in babies of approximately 4 to 5 weeks show that they are undergoing enormous changes that affect their senses, metabolism, and internal organs. This is when the first leap occurs—the baby's alertness in the world of sensations increases dramatically. At this point your baby is losing some of his newborn skills. He will no longer follow a face with his eyes or turn toward a sound. There are signs that these early skills were controlled by primitive centers in the lower brain, and that they disappear to make way for developments in the higher levels of the brain. Soon you will see similar behaviors emerge, but this time they

Sleeping Tips

A baby with sleeping problems will often fall asleep more quickly when he is with you. The warmth of your body, your gentle movements, and your soft sounds will help to soothe him. Here are some tips on the best ways to get him to sleep.

- Give him a warm bath, put him on a warm towel, and then massage him gently with baby oil.

- Breast or bottle-feed him, since sucking will help to relax and soothe him.

- Walk around with him, either in a sling or baby carrier.

- Push him around in his stroller.

- Take him for a ride in the car.

- Pop him into bed beside you.

will seem to be much more under your baby's control. At this age, your baby is also likely to outgrow problems that he may have had initially with his digestive system.

Between 4 and 5 weeks old, your baby goes through a whole set of changes that affect his senses—the way he experiences the world, the way he feels, even the way he digests his food. His whole world feels, looks, smells, and sounds different. Some of these changes have direct consequences that you can see. For example, this may be the first time that you notice him crying real tears. He may stay awake for longer periods and seem more interested in the world around him. Just after birth, he was only able to focus on objects that were up to a foot away, but now he can focus at a longer distance. It's not surprising, therefore, that a baby feels it's time for some action.

Five to six-week-old babies are even prepared to *work* in order to experience interesting sensations. In a laboratory experiment, babies showed that they could adjust the focus of a color movie by sucking harder on a pacifier. As soon as the baby stopped sucking, the picture blurred. Babies at this age have difficulty sucking and watching at the same time, so they could keep this up only for a few seconds. To check that this was really what they were trying to do, the babies were then required to stop sucking in order to bring the picture into focus. They could do this, too!

Babies can also start using their smile in social contact to influence their experiences. Your baby's smiles change from something superficial,

Brain Changes

At approximately 3 to 4 weeks, there is a dramatic increase in a baby's head circumference. His glucose metabolism, in the brain, also changes.

My Diary

How My Baby Explores the New World of Changing Sensations

Check off the boxes below as your baby changes. Stop filling this out once the next stormy period begins, heralding the next leap.

HIS INTEREST IN HIS SURROUNDINGS

❑ Looks at things longer and more often

❑ Listens to things more often and pays closer attention

❑ Is more aware of being touched

❑ Is more aware of different smells

❑ Smiles for the first time, or more often than before

❑ Gurgles with pleasure more often

❑ Expresses likes or dislikes more often

❑ Expresses anticipation more often
❑ Stays awake longer, and is more alert

HIS PHYSICAL CHANGES

❑ Breathes more regularly

❑ Startles and trembles less often

❑ Cries real tears for the first time, or more often than before

❑ Chokes less

❑ Vomits less
❑ Burps less

OTHER CHANGES YOU NOTICE

_____

_____

almost robot-like, into social smiles around this age. Mothers and fathers become very excited when they see a smile at an earlier age, but once they have seen the "social smile," they will admit noticing a difference.

Your Baby's Choices: A Key to His Personality

The senses of all babies develop rapidly at this time, and they will all become clearly more interested in their surroundings. It may or may not seem obvious at first, but every baby will have his own preferences. Some bright-eyed infants really enjoy looking at and watching everything and everyone around them. Others will listen keenly to music and sounds around them and will find sound-producing objects such as rattles more appealing than anything else. Another group of babies will love to be touched, and they would like nothing better than to play games that involve being touched and caressed by someone. Some babies don't have any clear preference. Even at this very young age, you will find that every baby is different.

As you go through the "My Diary" list on page 47, you may want to mark or highlight the items that apply now to your baby. He may display only a few of the behaviors, and others may not appear for several weeks. An infant who is more interested in certain sensory experiences in his world than others is showing you that he is already an individual.

"I take my daughter along to my singing classes every day. During the first few weeks, she hardly reacted to sounds at all, and I felt quite concerned, to be honest. Now suddenly, she's totally preoccupied by noises of any kind when she is awake. If she wakes up in a bad mood and I sing to her, she stops crying immediately. She doesn't stop when my friends sing, though!"

Hannah's mom, 6th week

Rocky Times for Everyone

Going through a big change can be a stressful event for your baby and for you, and you may both find the strain unbearable at times. You may become exhausted from lack of sleep or because anxieties prevent you from sleeping well. Here's an example of how this vicious cycle can work.

• The baby is confused and cries.

• Constant crying makes her mother feel insecure and anxious.

• Tension builds, and mother finds herself unable to cope.

• The baby senses the extra tension, becomes even more fussy, and cries even louder than before.

• The cycle repeats, again and again.

When the strain gets to be too much, remember that it is normal to feel this way. Try to take time out to relax. Your baby will benefit from it as much as you will.

Use physical contact and attention to comfort your baby. This will make it easier for her to adapt to all the changes at her own pace, and it will also give her self-confidence. She will know that someone is there for her whenever she needs comfort.

As her mother, you need support, too, not criticism, from family and friends. While criticism will only undermine your already battered self-confidence, support will make you better able to cope with the difficult periods.

The very best way to help your baby is to give her tender loving care and support. It is impossible to spoil her at this age, so never feel guilty about comforting her, especially when she cries.

Help your baby on her voyage of discovery. You'll find that she is usually more interested in the world around her now. She is more perceptive, and she is often awake for a longer time to enjoy her surroundings. Try to find out what activities she likes best by watching her reactions carefully. As small as she is, she is still able to let you know what pleases or displeases her. Once you know what your baby likes, you'll be able to introduce new activities, games, and toys gently.

How Can You Tell What She Likes Best?

Your baby will smile when given the things that she enjoys most. It can be something she sees, hears, smells, tastes, or feels. Because her senses have developed and she is now able to perceive a little more of her world, she will also smile more often. It will be very rewarding to experiment and discover which activities produce these wonderful smiles.

"I dance around with my baby, and when I stop, he smiles."

John's mom, 6th week

"When I put my face close to my daughter's and smile and talk to her, she makes eye contact and grins. It's wonderful."

Laura's mom, 5th week

"My daughter smiles at her dolls and teddy bears."

Jenny's mom, 6th week

That's Just How Babies Are

Babies love anything new, and it is important that you acknowledge your baby's new skills and interests. He will enjoy it if you share these new discoveries, and his learning will progress more quickly with your encouragement.

Help Your Baby Explore the New World through Sight

Your baby looks longer at objects that interest her now. The brighter the colors, the more fascinating she will find them. She also likes striped and angular objects. And your face, of course.

If you walk around with your baby, you'll automatically discover what she likes looking at best. Give her enough time to have a good look at things—and don't forget that her range of focus is not much more than a foot. Some babies like looking at the same objects time and time again, while others get bored if they are not shown something different each time. If you notice that your baby is getting bored, show her objects that are similar to the ones she likes but slightly different.

"My baby is much more aware of everything she sees now. Her favorites are the bars of her crib, which contrast with the white walls; books on the bookshelf; our ceiling, which has long wooden slats with a dark stripe in between; and a black-and-white ink drawing on the wall. At night, lights seem to interest her the most."

Emily's mom, 5th week

"My son stares right into my face and gazes at me for quite some time. He thinks it's funny when I eat. He looks at my mouth and watches me chew. He seems to think it's fascinating."

Kevin's mom, 6th week

"When I move a green and yellow ball slowly from left to right, my daughter turns her head to follow it. She seems to think it's great fun, although this proud mom probably enjoys it more than she does."

Ashley's mom, 5th week

Help Your Baby Explore the New World through Sound

Sounds usually fascinate babies. Buzzing, squeaking, ringing, rustling, or whizzing sounds are all interesting. Babies find human voices very intriguing, too. High-pitched voices are extremely interesting, although nothing can beat the sound of mother's voice, even if she's not a natural soprano.

Even at 5 weeks old, you can have cozy little chats with your baby. Pick a comfortable place to sit and put your face close to hers. Chat to her about how beautiful she is, everyday events, or whatever comes to mind. Stop talking once in a while to give her a chance to "reply."

"I really think my son is listening to me now. It's remarkable."

> Matt's mom, 5th week

"Sometimes my baby chats back to me when I'm talking to her. She talks longer now, and sometimes it seems as if she's really trying to tell me something. It's adorable. Yesterday, she chatted to her rabbit in her crib."

> Hannah's mom, 5th week

Help Your Baby Explore the New World through Touch

All babies become more aware of being touched at this age. Too many cuddling visitors may suddenly become "too much" for one baby, whereas another one may enjoy the attention tremendously. Every baby is different! You may hear your baby laughing out loud for the very first time now, perhaps when she is being tickled. But for most babies of this age, tickling is something that they will not yet particularly appreciate.

"My daughter laughed out loud, really roared, when her brother started tickling her. Everyone was startled, and it went dead quiet."

> Emily's mom, 5th week

Baby Care

Don't Overdo It

Let your baby's responses guide you. Your baby has become more sensitive, so you need to be careful not to overstimuate him. Bear this in mind when you play with him, cuddle him, show him things, or let him listen to things. You have to adapt to him. Stop as soon as you notice something is getting to be too much for him.

Your baby is still unable to concentrate for a long period of time, so he'll need short rest breaks. You may think he's lost interest, but he hasn't. Be patient. Usually he'll be raring to go again if you let him rest for a short while.

Let Her Know You Understand Her

Your baby may use a greater range of crying and gurgling sounds than before, and she may produce these sounds more frequently at this age. She may have different sounds for different situations. Babies will often make a whimpering sound before falling asleep. If a baby is really upset, you'll be able to tell by the way she cries, because it's a totally different sound. It's telling you that something is wrong. Your baby may also make other noises, such as gurgling sounds to show she is happy, especially when she is looking at or listening to something. These sounds will help you to understand her better. If you understand what your baby is trying to tell you, let her know. Babies adore interaction.

"I know exactly when my baby is gurgling with pleasure or grumbling because she's angry. Sometimes she gurgles with pleasure when she sees her mobile, and she loves it when I imitate the sounds she makes."

Hannah's mom, 6th week

At around 6 weeks, the leap has ended, and a period of comparative peace dawns. Babies are more cheerful, more alert, and more preoccupied with looking and listening at this time. Many mothers claim that their eyes seem brighter. Babies are also capable of expressing their likes and dislikes at this age. In short, life seems a little less complicated than before.

"We communicate more now. Suddenly, the hours that my son is awake seem more interesting."

Frankie's mom, 6th week

"I feel closer to my baby. Our bond is stronger."

Bob's mom, 6th week

chapter 4

Wonder Week 8:
The World of Patterns

Sometime around 8 weeks, your baby will begin to experience the world in a new way. He will become able to recognize simple patterns in the world around him and in his own body. Although it may be hard for us to imagine at first, this happens in all the senses, not just vision. For example, he may discover his hands and feet and spend hours practicing his skill at controlling a certain posture of his arm or leg. He'll be endlessly fascinated with the way light displays shadows on the wall of his bedroom. You might notice him studying the detail of cans on the grocery store shelf or listening to himself making short bursts of sounds, such as *ah, uh, ehh*.

Any of these things—and a whole lot more—signal a big change in your baby's mental development. This change will enable him to learn a new set of skills that he would have been incapable of learning at an earlier age, no matter how much help and encouragement you gave him. But just as in his previous developmental leap, adjusting to this new world will not come easily at first.

The change in the way your baby perceives the world around him will initially make him feel puzzled, confused, and bewildered as his familiar world is turned upside down. He suddenly sees, hears, smells, tastes, and feels in a completely new way, and he will need time to adjust. To come to terms with what is happening to him, he needs to be somewhere safe and familiar. Until he begins to feel more comfortable in this new world, he will want to cling to his mommy for comfort. This time, the fussy phase could last anywhere from a few days to 2 weeks.

Note: This leap into the perceptual world of "patterns" is age-linked and predictable. It sets in motion the development of a whole range of skills and activities. However, the age at which these skills and activities appear for the first time varies greatly and depends on your baby's preferences, experimentation and physical development. For example, the ability to perceive patterns emerges at about 8 weeks, and is a necessary precondition for "sitting with minimal support," but this skill normally appears anywhere from 2 to 6 months. Skills and activities are mentioned in this chapter at the earliest possible age they might appear so you can watch for and recognize them. (They may be rudimentary at first.) This way you can respond to and facilitate your baby's development.

If you notice your baby is more cranky than usual, watch him closely. It's likely he's attempting to master new skills.

Once you're over the hump, however, you will probably experience this second leap as a real milestone in your child's development. As he begins to learn to control his body and use his senses to explore what interests him, he will start to express his own preferences. You'll learn what he likes and doesn't like, whether he listens more keenly to particular kinds of sounds, which colors he prefers, what kinds of toys or activities he enjoys, and whose face makes him light up most—beside yours, of course. These are the first signs of your baby's newly emerging personality.

Sometime between 7 and 9 weeks of age, your baby may become more demanding. She may cry more often, as this is her way of expressing how stressful these changes are to her. At this age, crying is the most effective way to show she feels lost and needs attention. More sensitive babies will sob and scream even more now than they did before and drive their mothers and fathers to distraction. Even when everything possible is done to console these tiny screamers, they may still continue to wail.

Most babies will calm down, however, when they experience close physical contact, although for some babies it can never be close enough. If such a tiny cuddler had her way, she would crawl right back into her mommy. She would like to be totally enveloped in her mother's arms, legs, and body. She may demand her mother's undivided attention and will protest as soon as it wanders.

How You Know It's Time to Grow

It's time to change again! Here are some clues that this leap is approaching.

She May Demand More Attention

Your baby may want you to spend more time amusing her. She may even want you to be totally absorbed in her, and only her. At this time, many babies no longer want to lie in their cribs or on blankets on the floor, even if they had always been happy to do so until now. They may not object to lying in baby chairs, just as long as their mothers are close by. But their ultimate goal is to be with their mommies. They want their mothers to look at them, talk to them, and play with them.

> "Suddenly, my baby doesn't like going to bed at night. She becomes restless and starts screaming and crying and refuses to settle down. But we need some peace and quiet, too. So we keep her with us on the couch, or hold and cuddle her, and then she's no trouble at all."
>
> Eve's mom, 8th week

She May Become Shy with Strangers

You may notice that your friendly bundle may not smile so easily at people she does not see often, or she may need more time to warm up to them. Occasionally, some babies will even start crying if other people try to get near them when they are lying contentedly snuggled up to their moms. Some mothers think this is a pity: "She always used to be so cheerful." Others are secretly pleased: "After all, I'm the one who's there for her all the time."

> "My daughter seems to smile more for me than anyone else. It takes her a little longer to loosen up with other people now."
>
> Ashley's mom, 9th week

She May Lose Her Appetite

At this time, it may seem that if your baby had her way, she'd be on the breast or bottle all day long. But although she is latched onto the nipple, you may notice that she hardly takes any milk at all. Many babies will do this now. As long as they feel a nipple in or against their mouths, they are content. But as soon as they are taken off the breast or the bottle, they start protesting and continue to cry until they feel the nipple again.

This generally occurs only in babies who are allowed to decide for themselves when they want to nurse. Some mothers who breastfeed may begin to think that there is something wrong with their milk supplies, while other mothers question whether the decision to breastfeed was the right one after all. It is not necessary to stop breastfeeding at this point; on the contrary, this would not be a very good time to choose to wean your baby. During this stormy period, the breast is serving as less of a nutritional purpose and more of a comfort to the baby. This explains why some babies will suck their thumbs or fingers more often during this period.

> "Sometimes I feel like a walking milk bottle, on standby 24 hours a day. It really irritates me. I wonder if other mothers who breastfeed go through the same thing."
>
> Matt's mom, 9th week

She May Cling to You More Tightly

Your baby may now hold on to you even tighter the moment she senses that she is about to be set down. Not only will she cling to you with her fingers, she may even cling to you with her toes! This show of devotion often makes it difficult for a mother to put her baby down, both literally and figuratively. You may find it touching and heart-wrenching at the same time.

> "When I bend over to put my infant down, she clutches at my hair and clothes as if she's terrified to lose contact. It's really sweet, but I wish she wouldn't do it, because it makes me feel so guilty about setting her down."
>
> Laura's mom, 9th week

She May Sleep Poorly

At a difficult time like this, your baby may not sleep as well as she did before. She may start crying the moment you carry her into her bedroom, which explains why parents sometimes think that their babies are afraid of their cribs. Various sleeping problems may affect your little one. Some babies have difficulty falling asleep, while others are easily disturbed and do not sleep for long periods. Whatever sleeping problems your baby may have, they all have the same result: lack of sleep for everybody in the house. Unfortunately, this also means that your baby is awake for longer periods, giving her more opportunities to cry.

She May Just Cry and Cry

At approximately 8 weeks, it's normal for your baby to have an urgent desire to go "back to mommy." Some infants, of course, will demonstrate this need more than others. Crying and clinging may become part of your everyday life around this age. It is a sign that your baby is making healthy progress, that she is reacting to the changes within her, and that she is taking a leap forward in her development.

Your little one is upset simply because she hasn't yet had time to adjust to these changes and is still confused. This is why she needs to have you around. She wants to return "home," to her safe haven, where she can feel secure in familiar surroundings. With you, she will gain enough confidence to explore her new world.

Imagine what it must be like to feel upset with no one around to comfort you. You'd feel the tension mounting and not know what to do. You'd need all your energy just to cope with the stress, and you'd have little strength left to solve your problems. Your baby is no different. To her, every time a big change in her mental development occurs, she feels as if she has woken up in a brand-new world. She will be confronted with more new impressions than she can handle. She cries, and she will continue to cry until she becomes accustomed enough to her new world

My Diary

Signs My Baby Is Growing Again

Between 7 and 9 weeks, you may notice your baby starting to show some of the following behaviors. They are probably signs that he is ready to make the next leap, when the world of patterns will open up to him. Check off the boxes next to the behaviors your baby shows.

❑ Cries more often

❑ Wants you to keep him busy

❑ Loses appetite

❑ Is more shy with strangers

❑ Clings more

❑ Sleeps poorly

❑ Sucks his thumb, or more often than before

OTHER CHANGES YOU NOTICE:

_____

_____

to feel at ease. If she is not comforted, all her energy will be used just for crying, and she will be wasting valuable time that she could put to much better use discovering her new and puzzling world.

How the Leap May Affect You

These major changes in your baby will have a tremendous impact on you as well. Here are some of the ways they may affect you.

You May Feel Worried

When a baby goes through an inexplicable crying fit, life can unravel for everyone around her. Babies who cry a lot more than they used to can wear down even the most confident of moms. If this is your situation, you may begin to wonder whether you're really fit for the job. But don't despair: Your experience is very normal. The average baby will cry notice-ably more than usual and will also be a lot more difficult to comfort. Only a small number of mothers are lucky enough to not have any particular worries about their babies at this age. These mothers have infants who are unusually easygoing or quiet, who won't cry much more than usual, and who are generally easier to comfort.

Temperamental, irritable babies are the most difficult ones to deal with. They will seem to cry 10 times louder and more frequently, and they will thrash around as if they were in boxing rings. Their mothers often worry that the whole family will fall apart.

"It's a nightmare, the way my baby goes on and on. She cries all of the time and hardly sleeps at all at the moment. Our marriage is going to pieces. My husband comes home in the evening, dragging his feet, because he can't face another night of torment. We're having constant arguments about how to stop her awful crying."

Jenny's mom, 7th week

"When my son won't stop crying, I always go to him, although I've reached the stage where I could agree with statements such as 'Children just need to cry sometimes.' I feel so drained. But then I start thinking about how thin these apartments walls are, and so I end up going to him again, hoping I'll be able to get him to settle down this time."

Steven's mom, 9th week

"Sometimes, when my daughter cries and won't stop no matter what I do, I get so upset that I take it out on my poor husband. I often have a good cry myself, which does help to relieve the tension a bit."

Emily's mom, 10th week

"Some days when I'm at a low ebb, I wonder if I'm doing the right thing, if I'm giving my son enough attention or too much. It's so typical that it was on one of those difficult days that I read that babies smile at their mothers when they're 6 weeks old. Mine never did. He only smiled to himself, and that really undermined my confidence. Then suddenly, this evening, he grinned at me. Tears welled up in my eyes, it was so touching. I know this sounds ridiculous, but for a moment I felt like he was trying to tell me it was okay, that he was with me all the way."

Bob's mom, 9th week

At this time, when your baby cries more than usual, you may be desperate to figure out why. You may wonder, "Is my milk supply drying up? Is she ill? Am I doing something wrong? Does she have a wet diaper? When she's on my lap, she's fine—does this mean I'm spoiling her?"

When every other avenue has been explored, some mothers finally decide it has to be colic that's upsetting their babies. Their tiny screamers do seem to be writhing around a lot, after all. Some mothers even have a good cry themselves. It is a particularly hard time for first-time moms, who tend to blame themselves. Occasionally, a mother will go to see her doctor, or she will bring the problem up with the pediatrician.

"Normally my baby never cries. He's so easygoing, as easy as they come. But this week he had terrible problems: stomach cramps, I presume."

John's mom, 9th week

Whatever you do, don't despair—tell yourself it is not your fault! Try to remember that this is your young baby's way of telling you that she is now capable of learning new skills, which means that her mind is developing well. At this age, her crying is normal and only temporary.

You May Be Irritated and Defensive

As soon as you are convinced that your noisy little infant has no valid reason to keep crying and clinging to you, you may feel irritated. You may think that she's ungrateful and spoiled. You still have so much house-work to do, and her crying is driving you mad. Plus, you're exhausted. Well, you're not alone. Most mothers have these feelings. Many mothers worry that their babies' fathers, family, friends, or neighbors may regard "mommy's little sweetheart" as a "complete nuisance." They may become defensive when other people tell them to be more stern with their babies.

> "Is this what I gave my job up for—8 weeks of crying? I'm at my wit's end. I really don't know what more I can do."
>
> Jenny's mom, 8th week

> "It really drives me up the wall when I finally get my baby to sleep after comforting her for an hour, and she starts whimpering again the moment that I set her down. She's only happy when I'm holding her. This irritates me to no end. I don't get a chance to do anything else."
>
> Laura's mom, 8th week

> "I had to keep my son occupied all day long. Nothing really helped. I tried walking around, stroking him, and singing. At first I felt completely helpless and depressed, and then suddenly, I felt really frustrated. I sat down and just started sobbing. So I asked the day care center if they would have him for two afternoons a week, just to give me a few hours to recharge my batteries. His crying sometimes drains me completely. I'm so tired. I'd just like to know how much both of us can take."
>
> Bob's mom, 9th week

Baby Care

Shaking Can Be Harmful

Having violent feelings about a demanding little screamer is not dangerous, but acting on those feelings is. Whatever you do, don't ever let yourself get into such a state that you might harm him. Never shake a baby. Shaking a young child is one of the worst things that you can do. It could easily cause internal bleeding just below the skull, which can result in brain damage that may lead to learning difficulties later on or even death.

You May Really Lose It

Only rarely will a mother admit to having been a bit rougher than necessary when putting her baby down because she was so irritated by the baby's screaming and crying. If this does happen, it is always a disturbing experience, especially because it seemed to be a gut reaction at the time.

> "My daughter cried even more this week than she did last week. It drove me crazy. I had more than enough to do as it was. I had her in my arms, and on the spur of the moment, I threw her onto her changing mat on the dresser. Afterward, I was shocked by what I'd done, and at the same time I realized it hadn't helped the situation at all. She screamed even louder. After it happened, I understood what drives some parents to abuse their children during these 'colic fits,' but I never thought I'd do something like that myself."
>
> Juliette's mom, 9th week

How Your Baby's New Skills Emerge

Because you are concerned about your baby's clinginess, you will automatically keep an extra close eye on her. At the back of your mind, you may have these nagging doubts: "What is the matter with her?

Cuddle Care: The Best Way to Comfort

A baby of this age loves to be picked up, caressed, and cuddled.
You can never give him too much of a good thing.

Why is she being so troublesome? What can I do? Am I spoiling her? Should she be doing more at this age? Is she bored? Why is she unable to amuse herself?" Soon you'll realize what's really going on—your infant is attempting to master new skills.

At approximately 8 weeks, you will notice that your baby is opening up to her new world: a world of observing and experimenting with simple patterns. She will be ready to acquire several pattern skills at this time, but your baby, with her unique inclinations, preferences, and temperament, will choose which discoveries she wants to make. You can help her do what she is ready to do.

Don't try to push her. While you may think she should be practicing holding a ball (for her future softball career), she may prefer to make her first attempts at talking by babbling to her toys. Let her go at her own pace and respect her preferences. It may be hard on you if you're tone deaf and your baby is keen on sounds. Don't worry. She doesn't need symphonies just yet—talking and humming will do very well.

About this age, your baby no longer experiences the world and himself as one universe. He will start to recognize recurring shapes, patterns, and structures. For instance, your baby may now discover that his hands belong to him. At this age, your son will look at them in wonder and wave them around. Once he realizes that they are his, your baby may also try to use his hands by closing them around a toy, for instance. Not only does he begin to see patterns in the world around him, at this time your baby may begin to distinguish patterns in sounds, smells, tastes, and textures, too. In other words, your little tyke now perceives patterns with all of his senses. This new awareness is not just confined to what is going on outside his body—it also includes an enhanced perception of what is happening inside his body. For instance, now your baby may realize that holding his arm in the air feels different than letting it hang down. At the same time, he may also gain more control from within. Your son may be able to maintain certain positions, not only with his head, body, arms and legs, but also with smaller areas of his body. For example, he may start to make all kinds of faces, now that he has more control over his facial muscles. He might make explosive sounds because he can keep his vocal cords in a certain position. He may focus more sharply on an object because he has more control over his eye muscles.

Many of the reflexes that your baby had at birth will start to disappear at this age. They will be replaced by something similar to a voluntary movement. He no longer needs the gripping reflex, for example, because your baby is now able to learn how to close his hand around a toy or other object. Your baby doesn't use the sucking reflex anymore because he is able to latch onto a nipple in one single movement, instead of finding it by what appears to be sheer coincidence after nuzzling for a while. By now, your infant is no longer completely dependent on reflexes. In general, babies will only resort to their old reflexes if they are hungry or upset.

Brain Changes

At approximately 7 to 8 weeks, a baby's head circumference dramatically increases. Researchers have recorded changes in the brain waves of babies 6 to 8 weeks old.

(continued on page 71)

My Diary

How My Baby Explores the New World of Patterns

Check off the boxes below as you notice your baby changing. Stop filling this out once the next stormy period begins, heralding the coming of the next leap.

A new world of possibilities opens up to your baby when he's 8 weeks old. Your baby cannot possibly discover at once everything there is to explore in this new world—although some babies will try to sample everything. Exactly when your baby starts to do what will depend on his preferences and the opportunities offered to him.

Each chapter from now on will list behaviors that your baby may be doing that signal that he has entered his new world. Look for the sections like this one called "How My Baby Explores the New World." Each list is divided up into activity areas, such as "body control" and "looking and seeing." As you move through the book, you may notice a pattern emerging. Each baby has a completely distinctive profile and you should be aware that your baby will not demonstrate at this time many of the skills listed —some will appear later and some will be skipped altogether. Don't forget: All babies have different talents.

BODY CONTROL

❑ Holds his head upright when he is very alert

❑ Consciously turns his head toward something interesting

❑ Consciously rolls from his side onto his stomach

❑ Consciously rolls from his side onto his back

❑ Kicks his legs and waves his arms

❑ Kicks at plaything, with jerking movements

❑ Allows himself to be pulled into a sitting position

❑ Allows himself to be pulled into a standing position

❑ Tries to lift his head and body when lying facedown

❑ Shows an increased desire to sit

❑ Is able to look left and right when lying on his stomach

❑ Makes faces

HAND CONTROL

❑ Swipes at toys

❑ Attempts to grab objects within reach but does not succeed

❑ Closes his hand around objects within easy reach

❑ Holds plaything and moves it jerkily up and down

❑ Touches and feels objects without holding them

LOOKING AND SEEING

❑ Discovers hands

❑ Discovers feet

❑ Discovers knees

❑ Watches people moving or working

❑ Is fascinated by children playing close by

❑ Enjoys watching fast-moving images on TV

❑ Watches pets eating or moving

❑ Is fascinated by waving curtains

❑ Discovers luminous object, such as a flickering candle

(continued)

 My Diary (cont.)

❑ Watches treetops outdoors and is particularly fascinated by movements such as rustling leaves

❑ Looks at items on grocery store shelves

❑ Looks at complex shapes and colors, such as abstract art, especially while being rocked

❑ Is fascinated by shiny clothing or jewelry

❑ Enjoys watching people chewing food

❑ Enjoys watching and listening to people talk

❑ Watches facial gestures

LISTENING AND CHATTING

❑ Enjoys listening to voices, singing, and high-pitched sounds

❑ Makes short bursts of sounds, such as *ah, uh, eh, mmm*, and listens to himself

❑ Makes a series of sounds, mumbles, and gurgles, as if he is telling a story

❑ Repeats these sounds if you encourage him

❑ Sings along when you dance and sing with him

❑ "Chats" to and smiles at cuddly toys

❑ Consciously makes *eh* sounds to attract attention

❑ Interrupts while others are talking

OTHER CHANGES YOU NOTICE

_____

_____

Even so, your baby's first intentional movements are very different from those of an adult. His movements will be quite jerky, rigid, and stiff, like those of a puppet, and they will remain like this until the next big change occurs.

Your Baby's Choices: A Key to His Personality

Why are all babies unique? They have all undergone the same changes and entered the same new world with new discoveries to make and new skills to learn. But every baby decides for himself what he wants to learn, and when, and how. He will choose what he considers the most appealing. Some babies will try to learn a variety of new skills, using one or more of their senses. Some will seem particularly interested in exploring this new world with their eyes. Some will prefer to try out their talking and listening skills. Others will try to become more adept with their bodies. This explains why a friend's baby may be doing something that your baby can't, or doesn't enjoy, and vice versa. A baby's likes and dislikes are determined by his unique makeup—his build, weight, temperament, inclination, and interests.

Babies love anything new. It is so very important that you respond when you notice any new skills or interests. Your baby will enjoy it if you share these new discoveries with him, and his learning will progress more quickly.

The best way to help your baby make this leap is to encourage her to develop the skills that she finds most interesting. When you notice her working on a new skill, show her that you're enthusiastic about every attempt she makes to learn something new. If you praise her, you'll make her feel good, and this will encourage her to continue. Try to find a balance between providing enough challenges and demanding too much of her. Try to discover what she enjoys doing most. Most importantly, stop as soon as you feel she has had enough of a game or toy.

Your baby may want or need to practice some games or activities on her own. As long as you show some enthusiasm, this will be sufficient to reassure her that she is doing well.

Help Her Explore the New World through Sight

If your baby loves to explore her world with her eyes, you can help her by offering her all sorts of visual "patterns," for instance by showing her brightly colored objects. Make sure you move the object slowly across her line of vision, since this will draw her attention quicker and hold her interest longer. You can also try moving the object slowly backward and then forward, but make sure she is still able to see it move, otherwise she will lose interest.

When your baby is in a playful mood, she may become bored if she always sees, hears, or feels the same objects in the same old surroundings. It's very normal for babies of this age to show boredom, as their

How to Tell When He's Had Enough

Practicing a new skill is fun, but it can also be tiring for a baby. When he's had enough for a while, he will usually let you know with some very clear body signals. For example, he may look away, or if he is physically strong enough, he may turn his body away from you.

Stop the game or activity as soon as you notice that your baby has had enough. Sometimes he will only want a short break before resuming a game or activity with renewed enthusiasm, but don't push him. He needs time to let it all sink in. Always let your baby's responses guide you.

new awareness of patterns also means that they understand when things are repetitious. For the first time in her life, your baby may get fed up with the same plaything, the same view, the same sound, the same feel of an object, and the same taste. She will crave variety and learn from it. If she seems bored, keep her stimulated. Carry her around in your arms or provide her with some different objects to look at.

At this time, toys may not be as interesting to your baby as the myriad interesting "real things" in her world. Your home is full of items that may fascinate your baby, such as books, photographs, pets, cooking utensils, and even your eyeglasses. If your baby suddenly prefers the "real thing" to her toys, she will need your help. At this age, she cannot get close enough to objects on her own. She needs you to either take her to the object or pick it up and show it to her. If you notice that she likes looking at "real things," help her do this.

> "My baby likes looking at everything: paintings, books on shelves, items in the kitchen cupboard. I have to take her everywhere. I even carry her in my arms when I go outside or when I go shopping."
>
> Hannah's mom, 11th week

At this age, your baby may notice that familiar objects keep waving across her line of vision. If she investigates, she'll discover her hands or feet. She may gaze at them in wonder and begin to study them in detail. Every baby has her own way of investigating this new phenomenon. Some babies will need a lot of time to complete their investigations, while other babies won't. Most babies have a particular fondness for hands. Perhaps this happens because their tiny hands pass by more often.

Help Your Baby Explore the New World through Touch

Hands and arms can be in a myriad of different postures. Each posture is another pattern to be seen and felt. Allow your baby to study her hands as long and as often as she wants. A baby has to learn what her hands are for

before she can learn to use them properly. Therefore, it is very important for her to get to know all about these "touching devices."

"My little darling studies every detail of how his hands move. He plays quite delicately with his fingers. When he's lying down, he holds his hand in the air then spreads his fingers. Sometimes he opens and closes his fingers, one at a time. Or he clasps his hands together or lets them touch. It's one continuous flowing movement."

Bob's mom, 9th week

Have you noticed your baby attempting to use her hands by trying to clasp a rattle, for instance? Also, in holding a plaything, a feeling pattern is involved of that hand position plus the object touching the palm of the hand. A baby's first attempts at grasping an object are generally far from successful. Show her that you are enthusiastic about the effort she is making and encourage each serious attempt. Praise from you will encourage her to continue.

"My son is trying to grab things! His little hand gropes in the direction of his rattle, or he tries to hit it. A moment later he tries to grab the rattle, using a proper clasping motion. He puts a lot of effort into it. When he thinks he's got it, he clenches his fist, but the rattle is still a few inches away. The poor darling realizes his mistake, gets frustrated, and starts to cry."

Paul's mom, 11th week

Try to bear in mind that at this age your baby is definitely not yet able to reach out and touch the things that she wants to grab. She is only capable of closing her hands around an object. Make sure that you always place easy-to-grab toys near her waving hands. Your baby will then be able to touch the object and practice closing and opening her hands whenever she wants.

Help Your Baby Explore the New World through Sound

A baby's greatest passion is the latest sounds that she makes herself. This is why you should try to respond to every sound your young infant makes. Your baby's greatest passion might be to make explosive sounds, because from this leap onward she can keep her vocal cords in a certain position. Just like a hand position, a vocal cord position is a feeling pattern. Try to imitate your baby's sounds so that she can hear them from someone else. Respond when she uses sounds to attract your attention. These "conversations" are essential for her learning process, and they will teach her to take turns, listen, and imitate—skills which form the basis of communication. These chats will also teach her that her voice is an important tool, just like her hands are.

> "My baby chats away, trying to attract my attention all day long. She listens to my voice as well. It's wonderful."
>
> Hannah's mom, 11th week

Every mother tries to encourage her baby to "chat." Some mothers talk to their babies throughout their waking hours as a matter of course, whereas other mothers do this only at certain times, such as when their babies are on their laps. The disadvantage of planned chat times is that the baby may not always be in the right mood to listen and respond. It appears that babies whose mothers "plan" chat times do not always understand what is expected of them, and their mothers become easily discouraged because they think their babies are not responding properly yet.

Help Your Baby Explore the New World through Body Postures

Your baby may be ready for pull-up games. A little bruiser who is able to lift his head on his own may love being pulled up by his arms from a half-sitting position to an upright position or being pulled from a sitting position to standing. Be careful to support his heavy head. If he is very strong, he may even actively participate. This game teaches the baby how different postures feel and how to maintain them. Each of those postures is another "pattern" that your baby can perceive inside his body. If he cooperates in the pull-up game, he will jerk rather unsteadily from one position to the next. Once he has jerked into a certain position, he will want to retain it for a moment. Although his movements are still far from supple, he will love being in a certain position for a short while. He may even become very upset when you decide it's time to end the game.

"Suddenly, my son is jerking all over the place when I pull him onto his feet. He also makes jerky, spastic movements when he's lying naked on his changing mat. I don't know if this is normal. It worries me a bit."

— Kevin's mom, 11th week

"If my baby had her way, she'd be on her feet all day, listening to me telling her how strong she is. If I don't rush in with compliments, she starts complaining."

— Ashley's mom, 10th week

Fathers are usually the first to discover that babies enjoy these pull-up games, then mothers will follow, although they tend to be slightly more enthusiastic with baby boys than with baby girls.

(continued on page 80)

Some Things to Keep in Mind

Your baby will be more eager to learn when he is discovering a new world. He will learn faster, easier, and it will be more fun, if you give him the things that suit his personality.

Very demanding babies will automatically get more attention, as their mothers strive to keep them amused and satisfied. These high-interest babies may become the best students of tomorrow if they are given the right help and encouragement in their early years.

Quiet babies are easily forgotten, because they don't demand as much attention from their mothers. Try to give a quiet baby just that little bit more encouragement and stimulation to get the best out of him.

You may think that your infant should be able to be a little bit more independent now, because you notice the great pleasure he takes in his surroundings, his playthings, his own hands and feet, and because he enjoys lying flat on his back on the floor. You may start using the playpen for the first time at this stage. It's a good place to hang toys within easy reach of your baby's hands, allowing him to swipe at them or watch them swinging backward and forward. You may also try to let your baby amuse himself for as long as possible, presenting him with new playthings when he gets bored. With your help, your baby may be able to amuse himself for about 15 minutes at this age.

Top Games for This Wonder Week

These games and activities can be used when your baby enters the world of patterns. Before you start working your way down the list, look back at "How My Baby Explores the New World of Patterns" on page 68 to remind yourself of what your baby likes to do. And remember that the games that don't work for your baby right now may do later on when he's ready.

HANDS OR FEET, A FAVORITE TOY

Give your baby ample opportunity and room to watch his hands and feet. He will need freedom of movement to take in every detail. The best thing to do is to put him on a large towel or blanket. If it is warm enough, let him play without his clothes on, since he will really enjoy the freedom of his naked body. If you want, you can tie a colorful ribbon around his hand or foot as an added attraction. If you do this, however, be sure it is securely attached and watch the baby closely so that he does not accidentally choke on the ribbon should it come loose.

COZY CHATS

When your baby is in a talking mood, sit down and make yourself comfortable. Making sure that you have enough support in your back, draw your knees up, and lie your baby on his back on your thighs. From this position he can see you properly, and you'll be able to follow all of his reactions. Chat to him about anything: his beauty, his soft skin, his eyes, the events of the day, or your plans for later. The most important thing is the rhythm of your voice and your facial expression. Be sure you give him enough time to respond. This means being patient, waiting, smiling, nodding at him so that he realizes it takes two to have a conversation. Watch your baby's reactions to discover what he finds interesting. Remember that a talking mouth, together with a face that shifts from one expression to another, is usually a smash hit!

THE GREAT INDOORS

At this age, an inquisitive baby is still unable to grab objects that catch his eye to take a closer look. Until he is able to do this himself, he will have to rely on you to bring interesting objects to him. Remember, there are many interesting things in the house that will arouse his curiosity. Explain to him what he sees. He will enjoy listening to the intonation in your voice. Let him touch and feel whatever he seems to like.

THE PULL-UP GAME

You can only play this game if your baby is able to lift his head on his own. Sit down and make yourself comfortable. Make sure that you have enough support in your back. Draw your knees up and put your baby on your legs and tummy so that he is virtually in a half-sitting position. He will feel more comfortable like this. Now, hold his arms and pull him up slowly, until he is sitting up-right, giving him words of encouragement at the same time, such as telling him what a clever little boy he is. Watch his reactions carefully, and only continue if you're sure he is cooperating and enjoying himself.

TAKING A BATH TOGETHER

Water is a wonderful toy on its own. At this age, "water babies" in particular will enjoy watching water move. Place the baby on your stomach and show him drops and little streams of water running off your body onto his. Babies will also enjoy having small waves washed over their bodies. Lay him on his back on your stomach, and play "row, row, row your boat" together. Move back and forth slowly to the rhythm of the song, and make small waves. He will enjoy the feel of the waves running over his skin. After the freedom of the bath, he is likely to love being wrapped up snugly and securely in a warm towel and given a good cuddle!

A Word of Consolation: A Demanding Baby Could be Gifted

Some babies catch on to new games and toys quickly, soon growing tired of doing the same things, day in and day out. They want new challenges, continual action, complicated games, and lots of variety. It can be extremely exhausting for mothers of these "bubbly" babies, because they run out of imagination, and their infants scream if they are not presented with one new challenge after another.

It is a proven fact that many highly gifted children were demanding, discontented babies. They were usually happy only as long as they were offered new and exciting challenges.

A new awareness or new world will offer new opportunities to learn additional skills. Some babies will explore their new world and make discoveries with great enthusiasm, but they demand constant attention and help in doing this. They have an endless thirst for knowledge. Unfortunately, they discover their new world with tremendous speed. They try out and acquire almost every skill the new world has to offer, then experiment a little before growing bored again. For mothers of babies like this, there is little more they can do than to wait for the next big change to occur.

Top Toys for This Wonder Week

Here are some toys and things that babies like as they explore the world of patterns.

- Playthings that dangle overhead
- A moving or musical mobile
- A musical box with moving figures
- Playthings to swipe at or to touch
- Cuddly toys to talk to or laugh at
- Mommy—you still top the chart as his favorite toy!

"After every feeding, I put my son in the playpen for a while. I sometimes put him under a musical mobile that he likes to watch, and sometimes I put him under a trapeze with toys dangling from it, which he takes a swipe at every now and then. I must say, he's getting rather good at hitting them now."

Frankie's mom, 11th week

Around 10 weeks, another period of comparative ease sets in. Most mothers seem to put the concerns and anxieties of recent weeks quickly behind them. They sing their babies' praises and talk about them as if they had always been easygoing and cheerful babies.

What changes can you see in your baby at this stage? At approximately 10 weeks, your baby may no longer require as much attention as he did in the past. He is more independent. He is interested in his surroundings, in people, animals, and objects. It seems as if he suddenly understands and clearly recognizes a whole range of new things. His need to be with you constantly may also diminish at this time. If you pick him up, he may squirm and wriggle in discomfort and attempt to sit up in your arms as much as possible. The only time he may seem to need you now is when you are willing to show him things of interest. Your baby may have become so cheerful and busy amusing himself that life is much easier for you. You may feel a surge of energy. Lots of mothers regularly put babies of this age in their playpens, as they feel their children are ready for it now.

"My daughter suddenly seems much brighter. She's lost that newborn dependency. I'm not the only who's noticed. Everyone talks properly to her now, instead of making funny cooing noises."

Emily's mom, 10th week

"My baby seems wiser. She's become more friendly, happier, and even roars with laughter once in a while. Thank goodness she's stopped that incessant crying! Life has changed drastically from thinking 'How can I cope with her screaming?' to enjoying having her around now. Even her father looks forward to seeing her in the evening nowadays. He used to come home dragging his feet, dreading the probable torment of her non-stop crying. Now he loves being around her. He feeds and bathes her every evening."

Jenny's mom, 10th week

"My son no longer seems so vulnerable. I see a definite change in him now. He has progressed from just sitting on my lap to gaining a bit of independence and playing."

Steven's mom, 10th week

"I think my baby is really starting to develop into a real little person with a life of her own. At first, all she did was eat and sleep. Now she has a good stretch when I take her out of bed, just like grown-ups do."

Nina's mom, 10th week

"I don't know if there's any connection, but I certainly have noticed that I had a lot more energy this past week, and this coincided with my little boy's newfound independence. I must say I really enjoy watching the progress he's making. It's fascinating the way he laughs, enjoys himself, and plays. We seem to communicate better now. I can let my imagination run wild with his stuffed toys, sing him songs, and invent different games. Now that I'm getting some feedback from him, he's turning into a little friend. I find this age much easier than when he just nursed, cried, and slept."

Bob's mom, 10th week

chapter 5

Wonder Week 12:
The World of Smooth
Transitions

At around 11 or 12 weeks, your baby will enter yet another new world as he undergoes the third major developmental leap since his birth. You may recall that one of the significant physical developments that occurred at 8 weeks was your baby's ability to swipe and kick at objects with his arms and legs. These early flailing movements often looked comically puppetlike. At 12 weeks, this jerky action is about to change. Like Pinocchio, your baby is ready to change from a puppet into a real boy.

Of course, this transformation will not happen overnight, and when it does it will entail more than just physical movement, although that's usually what parents notice most. It will also affect your baby's ability to perceive with his other senses the way things change around him—such as a voice shifting from one register to another, the cat slinking across the floor, and the light in a room becoming dimmer as the sun dips behind the clouds. Your baby's world is becoming a more organized place as he discovers the constant, flowing changes around him.

The realization of these subtleties will enable your baby to enjoy life in new ways. But it's not easy entering a world that's shifting beneath your feet. Overnight, your baby's world has changed. Nothing seems to stand still anymore.

Keep in mind that if your baby is suddenly more fussy, he's probably getting ready to master new skills. Watch him closely during this exciting time.

In this changing world, the one constant is you, his boat on the rolling seas. Is it any wonder he wants to hang on to you for dear life as he enters this next major developmental leap in his life? Fortunately, this fussy period

Note: This leap into the perceptual world of "smooth transitions" is age-linked and predictable. It sets in motion the development of a whole range of skills and activities. However, the age at which these skills and activities appear for the first time varies greatly and depends on your baby's preferences, experimentation and physical development. For example, the ability to perceive smooth transitions emerges at about 12 weeks, and is a necessary precondition for "trying to sit up while helped by an adult," but this skill normally appears anywhere from 3 to 8 months. Skills and activities are mentioned in this chapter at the earliest possible age they might appear so you can watch for and recognize them. (They may be rudimentary at first.) This way you can respond to and facilitate your baby's development.

will not last quite as long as the previous one. Some babies will behave normally again after just a day, while others may need a whole week before they feel themselves again.

When a change happens, all babies will cry more often and for longer periods, although some will cry more than others. Some babies will be inconsolable, while others may be fretful, cranky, moody, or listless. One baby may be especially difficult at night, while another may tend to get upset during the day. All babies will usually be a little less tearful if they are carried around or if they are just given extra attention or cuddles. But even under these circumstances, anybody who knows the baby well will suspect that he will cry or fret again at the least opportunity.

How You Know It's Time to Grow

Here are the major signs that your baby is about to make this developmental leap.

He May Demand More Attention

Just when you thought that your baby had learned to amuse himself, he doesn't seem to do so well anymore. He may seem to want you to play with him more and keep him entertained all the time. Just sitting with him may not be enough; he may want you to look at him and talk to him, too. This change in his behavior will be all the more obvious if he had already shown you that he could be independent after the last leap forward. If anything, you may think that he's suffered a setback. You may feel that if your baby previously took three steps forward, here come the two steps back.

"My son is so terribly dependent on me right now. He is happy only if I hold him close. If he had his way, I think I'd be dancing around with him, too."

Bob's mom, 12th week

He May Become Shy with Strangers

Some babies will be shy with everyone except their moms at this time. If your baby is shy, you will notice that he clings to you whenever you have company. He may start to cry when a stranger talks to him or even looks at him. Sometimes, he may refuse to sit on anyone's lap but yours. If he is safely snuggled up to you, he may give someone else a reluctant smile, but if he is particularly shy, he will quickly bury his head in your shoulder afterward.

He May Cling to You More Tightly

Your baby may cling to you so tightly when you carry him that it seems as if he is afraid of being dropped. Babies who do this may sometimes even pinch their mothers very hard in the process.

He May Lose His Appetite

At this time, your baby may drag out each feeding session. Breastfed babies who are allowed to decide for themselves when they want to nurse behave as if they want to eat all day long. Bottle-fed babies take longer to finish their bottles, if they manage to get that far. These fractious drinkers spend their time chewing and gnawing at the nipples without actually drinking. They do this as a form of comfort and so they hang on for dear life, afraid to let go. Often, they will drift off to sleep with the nipples still in their mouths. Your baby may try to hold on to you or grab your breast during nursing, even if he is being bottle-fed, as if he is afraid of relinquishing his only source of comfort.

"When I'm bottle-feeding my daughter, she sticks her tiny hand inside my blouse. We call it 'bosoming.'"

Emily's mom, 12th week

He May Sleep Poorly

Your baby will probably sleep less well now. Many babies wake several times a night demanding to be fed. Other babies wake up very early in the morning. Still other babies refuse to take naps during the day. For many families, the normal routine has turned into absolute chaos because the baby's regular feeding and sleeping patterns have changed so drastically.

He May Suck His Thumb More Often

Your infant may now discover his thumb for the first time, or he may suck his thumb longer and more regularly than before. Like sucking at the breast or bottle, this is a comfort and can avert another crying session. Some mothers introduce a pacifier to help soothe the baby at this time.

He May Be Listless

Your baby may be quieter or seem less lively than usual. He may also lie still for quite some time, gazing around or just staring in front of him. This is only a temporary event. His previous sounds and movements will soon be replaced by new ones.

"The only thing my baby likes doing right now is cuddling up close to me in her sling. She's very quiet and no trouble at all—she doesn't do much except sleep. To be honest, though, I'd much rather see her full of life."

Nina's mom, 12th week

How This Leap May Affect You

Obviously, your baby will not be the only one affected by the changes occurring within him. His whole family suffers too, especially his mother. Here are some of the feelings you may experience during this turbulent time.

My Diary

Signs My Baby Is Growing Again

Between 11 and 12 weeks, you may notice your baby showing any of the following behaviors. They are probably signs that she is ready to make the next leap, into the world of smooth transitions. Check off the signs your baby shows.

- ❑ Cries more often
- ❑ Wants you to keep him busy
- ❑ Loses appetite
- ❑ Is more shy with strangers
- ❑ Clings more
- ❑ Wants more physical contact during nursing
- ❑ Sleeps poorly
- ❑ Sucks his thumb, or does so more often than before
- ❑ Is less lively
- ❑ Is quieter, less vocal

OTHER CHANGES YOU NOTICE

_____

_____

_____

You May Feel Worried

It's normal to feel anxious when you notice that your once-lively infant has become more fussy, is crying more often, is sleeping poorly, or is not nursing well. You may be worried because it seems that your baby has suffered a setback in producing sounds and movements or seems to have lost the independence that he had so recently acquired. Mothers usually expect to see progress, and if this doesn't seem to be happening, even for just a short while, they get concerned. They feel insecure, and they wonder what's the matter. "Is something wrong with the baby? Can he be ill? Could he be abnormal after all?" are the most common worries. Most often, none of these is the case. (When in doubt, always consult your family doctor.) On the contrary, your baby is showing signs of progress. A whole new world is there for him to discover, but when this world reveals itself, the baby will first have to deal with the upheaval it brings. It is not easy for him, and he will need your support. You can do this by showing that you understand that he is going through a difficult time.

> "When my baby is crying incessantly and wants to be carried around all the time, I feel pressured. I can't seem to accomplish even the simplest things. It makes me feel insecure, and it saps all my energy."
>
> Juliette's mom, 12th week

> "I'm trying to find out why my baby cries so much. I want to know what's troubling her so that I can fix it. Then I'll have some peace of mind again."
>
> Laura's mom, 12th week

> "There's no way I can cope with my son's crying. I just can't take it any more. I'd even prefer getting out of bed four times a night to deal with a baby who is not crying than twice a night to deal with a tiny screamer."
>
> Paul's mom, 11th week

You May Become Irritated

During this period, many mothers grow annoyed with their babies' irregular eating and sleeping routines. They find it impossible to plan ahead. Their entire schedule is thrown off balance. They often feel under pressure from

family or friends, too. The mothers' instincts tell them to focus all their attention on their unhappy infants, but other people often seem to disapprove of too much babying. Mother may feel trapped in the middle.

> "I get irritated every time my son starts fretting, because he can't seem to amuse himself for even just a short while. He wants me to keep him occupied all day long. Of course, everybody loves giving me advice on how to deal with him, especially my husband."
>
> Kevin's mom, 12th week

> "I seem to cope better with my baby's erratic behavior if I don't make plans in advance. In the past, when my plans went completely haywire, I felt irritated. So I've changed my attitude. And would you believe it —I sometimes find I even have a few hours to spare!"
>
> Laura's mom, 12th week

You May Reach Your Wit's End

Sometimes mothers are unable, or unwilling, to suppress their anger any longer, and they let their demanding little creatures know they're fed up.

> "My boy was so fretful. I kept worrying about what the neighbors would think of the noise. Sunday afternoon was the last straw. I'd tried everything to make him settle, but nothing helped. At first I felt helpless, but then I became furious because I just couldn't cope, so I left him in his room. I had a good cry myself, which calmed me down a bit."
>
> Bob's mom, 12th week

> "We had company, and my son was being terribly trying. Everyone gave me their 2 cents' worth of advice, which always makes me really upset. When I went upstairs to put him to bed, I lost my self-control, grabbed him, and gave him a good shake."
>
> Matt's mom, 11th week

Baby Care

Shaking Can Be Harmful

While it is normal to feel frustrated and angry with your baby at times, never shake a baby. Shaking a young child can easily cause internal bleeding just below the skull, which can result in brain damage that may lead to learning difficulties later on —or even death.

You May Feel Tremendous Pressure

If a mother worries too much about her noisy little grump, and if she is not given enough support from family and friends, she may become exhausted. If she is suffering from lack of sleep as well, she may easily lose control of the situation, both mentally and physically.

Unwelcome advice, on top of panic and exhaustion, could make any mother feel even more irritable and snappish—and her partner often becomes the target. At times, however, her distressed infant will bear the brunt of a mother's pent-up frustration, and she may be a little rougher with him than necessary. When a mother admits to having slapped her baby, this nearly always occurs during one of these fussy periods. It's certainly not because she dislikes the poor infant, but simply because she longs to see him happy, and she feels threatened by other people's criticism. She feels that she has no one to turn to with her problems; she feels alone. However understandable these feeling of frustration may be, one should never act on them. Slapping, and any other form of hurting, is not acceptable.

"Every time my baby stopped crying, I felt as if a load had been lifted from my shoulders. I hadn't noticed how tense I was until then."

Emily's mom, 11th week

"After my husband's coworkers told him that he and our son look like two peas in a pod, he stopped criticizing the amount of attention I give his grumpy mirror image. In fact, my husband wouldn't have it any other way now, whereas he used to feel that I was overreacting and spoiling the baby. Things are running a lot smoother now, and I'm not as tense as I used to be when the baby gets upset, and he seems to sense that, too. I feel a lot more comfortable now."

Matt's mom, 12th week

When it all gets to be too much, just remember: It can only get better. At this stage, some mothers fear that these dreadful crying fits may never stop. This is a logical assumption because until now the fussy periods followed each other in rapid succession with only 2 to 3 weeks in between. This barely left enough time for mothers to catch their breath. But don't despair—from now on, the intervals between the fussy periods will be longer. The fussy periods themselves will also seem less intense.

How Your Baby's New Skills Emerge

When your baby is upset, you will usually want to keep an extra close watch on him because you want to know what's wrong. In doing so, you may suddenly notice that your baby has actually mastered new skills or is trying to do so. In fact, you'll discover that your baby is making his next big leap—into the world of smooth transitions.

At approximately 12 weeks, your baby will be able to perceive the many subtle ways that things change around him, not abruptly but smoothly and gradually. He will be ready to experiment with making such smooth transitions himself.

Your baby will make many new discoveries in this new world. He will select the things that appeal to him and that he is ready physically and mentally to attempt. You should, as always, be careful not to push him but help him do what he shows he is ready for. In many ways, however, he will still rely on your help. He will need you to show him things in his world, to put his toys where he can see and reach for them, and to respond to his increasing attempts at communication.

Brain Changes

At approximately 10 to 11 weeks, the head circumference of babies dramatically increases.

the Magical Leap Forward

As she enters the world of smooth transitions, for the first time your baby is able to recognize continuous changes in sights, sounds, tastes, smells, and touch. For example, she may now notice how a voice shifts from one tone to the next or how a body shifts from one position to another. Not only can she register these smooth transitions in the outside world, your infant is now able to learn to make them herself. This will enable your baby to work on several important skills.

You will see that now your baby's movements become much smoother, more flowing, and more like an adult's. This new control applies to her whole body as well as to the parts that she can move consciously—her hands, feet, head, eyes, and even her vocal cords. You will probably notice that when she stretches out toward a toy, the movement is smoother than it was just a few weeks ago. When she bends her knees to sit or pulls herself to stand, the whole exercise looks more deliberate and mature.

Her head movements also become smoother, and she can now vary their speed. She can look around the room in the way that older children do and follow a continuous movement. Her eyes are able to focus more sharply on what they see, and her vision will soon be as good as an adult's.

When your baby was first born, she came ready equipped with a reflex that moved her gaze in the direction of any new sound. This disappeared somewhere between 4 and 8 weeks after birth, but now she can do the same thing consciously, and the response will be quicker. She will be able to follow

(continued on page 96)

 My Diary ---

How My Baby Explores the New World of Smooth Transitions

Check off the boxes below as you notice your baby changing.

BODY CONTROL

❑ Barely needs support to keep his head upright

❑ Smooth head movement when turning to one side

❑ Smooth eye movement when following a moving object

❑ Is generally more lively and energetic

❑ Playfully lifts his bottom when his diaper is being changed

❑ Rolls independently from back to stomach or vice versa while holding on to your fingers

❑ Sticks his toes in his mouth and twists around

❑ Sits up straight when leaning against you

❑ Pulls himself into sitting position while holding on to your fingers

❑ Is able to move into a standing position when seated on your lap, by holding on to two of your fingers

❑ Uses both feet to push off when seated in a bouncing chair or lying in a playpen

HAND CONTROL

❑ Grabs and clutches at objects with both hands

❑ Shakes a rattle once or twice

❑ Studies and plays with your hands

❑ Studies and touches your face, eyes, mouth, and hair

❑ Studies and plays with your clothes

❑ Puts everything into his mouth

❑ Strokes his head, from neck to eyes

❑ Rubs a toy along his head or cheek

LISTENING AND TALKING

❑ Discovers shrieking and gurgling; can easily shift between loud and soft tones, low notes and high ones

❑ Produces new sounds that resemble the vowels of real speech: *ee, ooh, ehh, oh, aah, ay*

❑ Uses these sounds to "chat"

❑ Is able to blow saliva bubbles, and laughs as if he finds this very amusing

LOOKING AND SEEING

❑ Turns hands over, studies both sides

❑ Studies his own moving feet

❑ Studies a face, eyes, mouth, and hair

❑ Studies someone's clothing

OTHER SKILLS

❑ Expresses enjoyment by watching, looking, listening, grabbing, or by "talking," then waiting for your response

❑ Uses different behavior with different people

❑ Expresses boredom if he sees, hears, tastes, feels, or does the same things too often; variety suddenly becomes important

OTHER CHANGES YOU NOTICE

_____

_____

something or somebody with her eyes in a controlled, well-coordinated manner. She may even begin to do this without turning her head. She will be able to follow people or objects approaching her or moving away. In fact, she will become capable of surveying the whole room. You may feel for the first time that she is really a part of the family as she notices everybody's comings and goings.

This new responsiveness is enhanced by new vocal possibilities as she begins to recognize changes in pitch and in volume of sounds and to experiment with these by gurgling and shrieking. Her improved coordination even helps her to swallow more smoothly.

Although some remarkable developments have occurred in your baby's mind and body, what she cannot do is cope with quick changes in succession. Don't expect her to be able to follow an object that is moving up and down as well as from left to right or a toy that rapidly reverses its direction of movement. And when she moves her own hand, there will be a noticeable pause before any change of direction, almost like a tiny conductor waving a baton.

Parents are generally less concerned if their babies show a reluctance to amuse themselves at this stage. They are too proud of their babies' achievements and efforts in so many directions. There are so many new discoveries to be made and so many new things to be learned and practiced, and for the moment that is what matters the most.

Your Baby's Choices: A Key to Her Personality

If you watch your baby closely, you will be able to determine where her interests lie. As you mark off the things that she is showing you that she can do in this world, be aware of the uniqueness of your child.

Some babies are very aware of the world around them, and they prefer looking, listening, and experiencing sensations to being physically active themselves. Most of the time, professionals, as well as friends and family, assess a baby's development by looking at the physical milestones, such as grasping, rolling over, crawling, sitting, standing, and walking. This can give a one-sided view of progress as it makes the "watch-listen-feel" baby seem slower. These babies usually take longer to begin grasping objects, but once they start, they will examine them very closely. Given a new item, a watch-listen-feel baby will turn it around, look at it, listen to it, rub it, and even smell it. These babies actually are doing something very complicated that will give them a broad base for their later learning skills.

In contrast, babies who are more physically active often become engrossed in the action of grabbing itself, and once they have attained possession of the object, they quickly lose interest and drop it in favor of looking for another challenge. Babies love anything new, and it is important that you respond when you notice any new skills or interests. Your baby will enjoy it if you share these new discoveries, and her learning will progress more quickly.

what You Can Do to Help

The more your baby plays or experiments with a new skill, the more adept he will become. Practice makes perfect as far as babies are concerned, too. Your baby may want to try out a new skill over and over again. Although he will play and practice on his own, your participation and encouragement are vital. As well as cheering him on when he does well, you can help when the going gets tough and he feels like giving up. At this point, you can make the task easier for him—usually by rearranging the world so that it is a bit more accommodating. This might mean turning a toy around so that it's easier to grab, propping him up so that he can see the cat through the window, or maybe imitating the sounds he is trying to make.

You can also help to make an activity more complex or vary it a bit so that he stays with it longer and is challenged just a little more. Be careful to watch for signs that your baby has had enough. Remember that he will go at his own pace.

Just as babies are all different, so are their mothers. Some mothers have more imagination than others in certain areas. It may be a particular challenge for you if your baby is the physical type but you prefer talking, singing, and storytelling. Gather new ideas from books, your friends, and family members. The baby's father and older siblings can help—most children will be able to go on long after the baby's desire for repetition has exhausted you. But whatever type of baby you have and whatever type of mother you are, your child will always benefit from some help from you.

Help Your Baby Explore the New World through Sound

If your baby has a special love for sound, encourage him to use his voice. He may now begin to shriek, gurgle, or make vowel-like sounds himself. These may range from high- to low-pitched sounds and from soft to loud ones. If he also starts to blow saliva bubbles, don't discourage him. By doing these things, he is playing with "smooth transitions" and in the process he is exercising the muscles of his vocal cords, lips, tongue, and palate as well. Your baby may often practice when he is alone, sounding like somebody who is chattering away just for fun. He does this because the range of notes with all the high and low vowel sounds and little shrieks in between sound a lot like talking. Sometimes a baby will even chuckle at his own sounds.

The Gender Gap

Baby boys seem to take up more of their mothers' time than baby girls do during the first months. This probably happens because boys cry more and don't sleep as well as girls.

Also, mothers of baby girls are much quicker to respond to the sounds produced by their daughters than are mothers of baby boys. Mothers also tend to "chat" more to their babies if they are girls.

Most babies love to have cozy chats with their mommies. Of course, a baby has to be in the mood to do this. The best time to chat is when he attracts your attention with his voice. You will probably find yourself speaking in a slightly higher-pitched tone than usual, which is just right for your baby's ear. It is very important that you stick to the rules of conversation—your baby says something, then you say something back. Make sure you let him finish. Because if you don't give him time to reply, he will feel that you aren't listening to him, and he won't learn the rhythm of conversation. If that happens—if you do not give him enough time to reply—he may become despondent or confused that you are not listening to him. The subjects of your conversation don't matter very much at this age, but it is better to stick to familiar territory and shared experiences. Occasionally, try imitating the sounds he is making. Some babies find this so funny that they will break into laughter. This is all-important groundwork for later language skills.

It is very important to talk to your baby frequently. Voices on the radio or television, or people talking in the same room, are no substitute for a one-on-one conversation. Your baby is prompted to talk because there is someone who listens and responds to him. Your enthusiasm will play an important role here.

"I always talk back whenever my son makes sounds. Then he waits a little, realizes it's his turn, and replies with a smile or by wriggling around. If he's in the right mood, he'll gurgle back at me again. If I reply once more, he gets so excited that he waves his arms and legs all over the place and sometimes shrieks with laughter as well. When he's had enough, he turns away and looks at something else."

John's mom, 13th week

Your baby may use one of his latest sounds when he wants something. This is often a special "attention!" shriek. If he does this, always answer him. This is important since it will give him the sense that you understand what he is trying to communicate, even if you don't have time to stop and play with him at that moment. He will begin to use his voice to attract your attention. That's a significant step toward language.

When he's happy, a baby will often use a special "cry for joy" sound. He will use it when he notices something he finds amusing. It's natural to respond to these cries for joy with a kiss, a cuddle, or words of encouragement. The more you are able to do this, the better. It shows your baby that you share his pleasure and that you understand him.

"When my son saw that I was about to feed him, he shrieked with excitement and grabbed my breast, while my blouse was still only half undone."

Matt's mom, 13th week

Help Your Baby Explore the New World through Touch

As your baby now lives in the world of smooth transitions, you may notice that he stretches out toward a toy more smoothly. Help him. He just entered

When Your Baby Laughs, She's on Top of the World

When you make your baby laugh, you have struck the right chord with her. You have stimulated her in exactly the right way. Don't overdo it because you may intimidate her. On the other hand, half-hearted attempts on your part could lead to boredom on hers. You must find the comfortable middle ground for your baby.

this new world and reaching is still very difficult. Hold a toy within easy reach of your baby's hands and watch him to see if he is able to reach out for it. Hold the object right in front of him, keeping in mind that at this age he is only able to make a controlled movement with his arm in one direction at a time. Now pay close attention to what he does. If he is only just starting to master this skill, he will probably react something like this baby.

"My son is really starting to reach out to grab things! He reached for a toy dangling in front of him with both hands. He put out his right hand on one side of the toy and his left hand on the other side of the toy. Then, when both hands were just in front of the toy, he clasped them together . . . and missed! He'd tried really hard, so it wasn't at all surprising that he got very upset when he found himself empty-handed."

Paul's mom, 12th week

If your child reaches for objects and misses, encourage him to try again, or make the game a little easier for him so that he gets a taste of success. At this age, he is not yet able to make an accurate estimate of the distance between his hands and the plaything he is trying to grab. He will not be able to learn this properly until he is between 23 and 26 weeks old.

As your baby becomes more adept at grabbing objects, he will want to play the "grabbing game" more often. Because he can turn his head smoothly and look around the room, he can choose what he wants from the entire world of things that is now waiting for him to grab, feel, and touch. After the last developmental leap, most babies spent about one-third of their waking hours playing and experimenting with their hands. After about 12 weeks, this suddenly doubles to two-thirds of their waking hours.

If you notice that your baby enjoys stroking things with his hands, encourage this activity as much as you can. Not only the stroking movement involves a "smooth transition," but also the feeling in his hand caused by the moving contact with the object. Carry your baby around the house and

(continued on page 104)

Top Games for This Wonder Week

Here are some games and activities that work for babies at this point in their development. At this age, your baby will particularly enjoy games where you move her whole body around. Try to do this gently, with slow and even movements, remembering that these are the only kind that your baby can properly understand. It is better to play several different games in a row, rather than continue the same game for too long.

THE AIRPLANE

Lift your baby up slowly, while making a sound that increases in volume or changes from a low-pitched to a high-pitched sound. She will stretch out her body automatically as you raise her above your head. Then start the descent, making the appropriate airplane sounds. When she is in line with your face, welcome her by burying your face in her neck and giving her a nibble with your lips. You will soon notice that your baby expects you to do this and will open her mouth and nibble back. You will also see your baby opening her mouth again, as if anticipating the nibble, when she wants you to repeat this flying game.

THE SLIDE

Sit down on the floor or a sofa, lean back, and make your body as straight as possible. Place your baby as high up on your chest as you can and let her slide gently down to the floor, while you make the appropriate sliding sound.

THE PENDULUM

Place the baby on your knees so that she is facing you and slowly sway her from side to side. Try to make all kinds of clock sounds, such as a high-pitched, fast tick-tock, or a low-pitched, slow bong-bong. Try to make sounds that range from high to low and from fast to slow, or whatever clock sound you notice that your baby enjoys the most. Make sure that you hold her firmly and that her head and neck muscles are strong enough to move with the rhythm.

THE ROCKING HORSE

Place the baby on your knees so that she is facing you and make stepping movements with your legs, so your baby sways up and down as if she were sitting on a horse. You can also make the accompanying clip-clop noises or "schlupping" sounds that babies love at this age.

THE NIBBLING GAME

Sit in front of your baby and make sure that she is looking at you. Move your face slowly toward her tummy or nose. Meanwhile, make a drawn-out sound, increasing in volume, or changing in tone, for instance "chooooomp" or "aaaaaah-boom" or sounds similar to those the baby makes herself.

FEELING FABRICS

Here's a way to play and get chores done! Fold your laundry with your baby nearby, and let her feel different types of fabrics, such as wool, cotton, terry cloth, or nylon. Run her hand over the fabrics to allow her to feel the different textures, too. Babies like touching materials with their fingers and mouths. Try something unusual such as chamois, leather, or felt.

JUMPING AND BOUNCING

A physically active baby loves repeating the same flowing movements over and over again when she is on your lap. Let her stand up and sit down again at her own pace. She will want to repeat this "stand up, sit down, stand up, sit down" game endlessly. It will probably make her laugh, too, but, again, hold her tightly and watch her head.

garden, letting him feel all kinds of objects and experience their properties —hard, soft, rough, smooth, sticky, firm, flexible, prickly, cold, wet, and warm. Tell him what the items are, and describe the sensations. Help to get your meaning across by using your tone of voice to express the feeling an object or surface arouses. He really will be able to understand more than he is able to tell you.

> "I washed my baby's hands under running water, which made her laugh out loud. She couldn't seem to get enough of it."
>
> Jenny's mom, 15th week

Many babies like to examine their mothers' faces. As your little one runs his hands over your face, he may linger slightly longer by your eyes, nose, and mouth. He might tug on your hair or pull at your nose, simply because they are easy to grasp. Items of clothing are interesting as well. Babies like to stroke and feel fabrics. Watch out for your earrings, too!

Some babies are interested in their mothers' hands. They will study, touch, and stroke them. If your baby enjoys playing with your hands, help him to do this. Slowly turn your hand over, and show him the palm and back of your hand. Let him watch while you move your hand or pick up a toy. Try not to make your movements too fast or to change direction too quickly, or you will lose his attention. Simple movements are all he can cope with in this world. Your baby won't be able to deal with more complicated movements until after another big change in his nervous system, which is the start of the next developmental leap.

Help Your Baby Explore the New World through Body Movement

At this age, all babies are getting livelier. They are playing with smooth transitions felt inside their bodies, while they kick and wave their arms about. Some babies perform acrobatics; for example, they might stuff their toes in their mouths and almost spin around on their backs in the process. Obviously, some babies are much livelier and stronger than others. Some babies are not really interested in gymnastic feats, while others will be frustrated if their physical strengths are not yet up to the task.

> "My son moves his body, arms, and legs around like mad, grunting and groaning in the process. He's obviously trying to do something, but whatever it is he's not succeeding because he usually ends up having an angry screaming fit."
>
> Frankie's mom, 14th week

Whatever your baby's temperament, he will benefit from a little time spent without his clothes in a warm environment. You may already have noticed that he is lively when you are changing him, enjoying the opportunity to move freely without being hampered by diaper and clothes. It's easier to bend the little limbs, to wave, kick, and roll over naked. Success comes more easily, and the baby will get to know his body better and control it more precisely.

Some babies attempt to roll over at this age, but nearly all of them will need a bit of help in doing so. If your little squirmer tries to roll over, let him hold on to one of your fingers as he practices. A very persistent baby who is also physically strong may manage to roll from tummy to back. Some can do it the other way around and go from back to tummy. However persistent the infant, he won't manage it unless his physical development is far enough along. So give help and support, but also be ready to help your baby deal with his frustration if he just can't manage something that he would clearly like to do.

Top Toys for This Wonder Week

Here are some toys and things that babies like best as they explore the world of smooth transitions:

- Wobbly toys that bounce back when the baby swipes them

- The clapper inside a bell

- A rocking chair

- Toys that emit a slow squeak, chime, or other simple sound

- Rattles

- Dolls with realistic faces

Many babies love pushing themselves up with their legs. If your baby enjoys doing this, he will practice pushing off in his playpen, in his bouncing chair, on his changing table (watch out for this one!), or while sitting on your lap. You need to hold on tight to an active squirmer. If your baby is able to do these push-ups unaided, give him lots of opportunities to practice.

If your baby is physically strong, he may also try to pull himself up into a sitting position when he is on your lap. If he likes to do this, you can help him by making a game out of it.

After the Leap

Between 12 and 13 weeks, another period of comparative calm settles in. Parents, family, and friends will notice what a cheerful little person your baby has become and admire the wonderful progress she has made. You may find your baby much smarter now. When she is carried around or sits on your lap, she acts like a little person. She turns her head immediately in the direction of something she wants to see or hear. She laughs at everyone, and answers them when she is talked to. She shifts her position to get a better look at something she wants to see, and she keeps an eye on everything going on around her. She is cheerful and active. It may strike you that other family members show a lot more interest in her as a person now. It appears that she has gained her own place in the family. She belongs!

"My daughter is developing an interest in a whole variety of things now. She talks or shrieks at different objects, and when we watch her more closely, we think, 'My goodness, can you do that already?' Or 'Aren't you clever noticing all of those things?'"

Jenny's mom, 13th week

"My little one is definitely wiser. She's all eyes these days. She responds to everything and immediately turns her little head in response to sounds. She's suddenly gained her own little place in the family."

Hannah's mom, 14th week

"It's wonderful watching my baby enjoying herself so much and chatting affectionately to her cuddly toys and to people."

Juliette's mom, 14th week

"We have a lot more interaction with my child now because she responds to everything. After I've played a game with her, I can tell when she's waiting for me to play again. She also 'replies' a lot more now."

Ashley's mom, 13th week

"My daughter used to be so easygoing and quiet, but she's turned into a real little chatterbox now. She laughs and gurgles a lot more often. I really enjoy getting her out of bed to see what she'll do next."

Eve's mom, 14th week

"My son is much more interesting to watch now because the progress he's made is so obvious. He responds immediately with a smile or a gurgle, and he can turn his head in the right direction, too. I love giving him a good cuddle because he's so soft and chubby now."

Frankie's mom, 14th week

chapter 6

Wonder Week 19:
The World of Events

The realization that our experience is split up into familiar events is something that we as adults take for granted. For example, if we see someone drop a rubber ball, we know that it will bounce back up and will probably continue to bounce several times. If someone jumps up into the air, we know that she is bound to come down. We recognize the initial movements of a golf swing and a tennis serve, and we know what follows. But to your baby, everything is new, and nothing is predictable.

After the last leap forward, your baby was able to perceive smooth transitions in sound, movement, light, taste, smell, and texture. But all of these transitions had to be simple. As soon as they became more complicated, he was no longer able to follow them.

At around 19 weeks (or between 18 and 20 weeks), his ability to understand the world around him becomes far more developed and a little more like our own. He will begin to experiment with events. The word "event" has a special meaning here and has nothing to do with special occasions. In fact, here it means a short, familiar sequence of smooth transitions from one pattern to the next. Sound like a mouthful? Let's try to explain what it means.

While at 12 weeks it may have taken all your baby's cross-eyed concentration simply to grasp an object with both hands that you held in front of him, he'll now begin to understand that he can reach out to a toy, grab it with one hand, shake it, turn it around to inspect it, and put it in his mouth. This kind of physical activity is much more complicated than it

Note: The first phase (fussy period) of this leap into the perceptual world of "events" is age-linked and predictable, and starts between 14 and 17 weeks. Most babies start the second phase (see box "Quality Time: An Unnatural Whim" on page 17) of this leap 19 weeks after full-term birth. The first perception of the world of events sets in motion the development of a whole range of skills and activities. However, the age at which these skills and activities appear for the first time varies greatly and depends on your baby's preferences, experimentation and physical development. For example, the ability to perceive events is a necessary precondition for "grasping a cube with partial opposition of the thumb," but this skill normally appears anywhere from 4 to 8 months. Skills and activities are mentioned in this chapter at the earliest possible age they might appear so you can watch for and recognize them. (They may be rudimentary at first.) This way you can respond to and facilitate your baby's development.

seems and far more than just the physical mastery of his arms and hands. It actually depends upon a high degree of neurological development. This change will enable your baby to develop a whole new set of skills.

Although the subtleties of these skills may escape you at first, they will gradually become more obvious. The sounds your infant emits may still just seem like baby babble to you for a while, but they are actually becoming much more complicated. No doubt you'll notice when he strings his consonants and vowels together to say "mommy" and "dada." You also will be very aware of his attempts to roll over and his first attempts to crawl. In all of these activities, he is now capable of learning how single patterns and transitions string together like beads to become what we as adults recognize as events.

This process is also vital for your baby to understand something that adults take completely for granted—that the world is made up of objects that continue to exist, whether or not we can completely see them at the time. You can see just how hard your baby is working in this first year of life to make sense of his world.

Your baby's awareness of the new changes that accompany this leap in his development actually begins at approximately 15 weeks (or between 14 and 17 weeks). These changes affect the way he sees, hears, smells, tastes, and feels. He needs time to come to terms with all of these new impressions, preferably in a place where he feels safe and secure. He will once again show a pronounced need to be with his mommy, cling to her for comfort, and grow into his new world at his own pace. From this age on, the fussy periods will last longer than before. This particular one will often last 5 weeks, although it may be as short as 1 week or as long as 6. If your baby is fussy, watch him closely to see if he is attempting to master new skills.

this Week's Fussy Signs

Because your baby is upset by what is happening to her, she will be much quicker to cry at this time. A very demanding little one, in particular, will

cry, whine, and grumble noticeably more often than she did in the past. She will make no bones about the fact that she wants to be with her mommy.

Your baby will generally cry less when she is with you, although she may insist that you give her your undivided attention. She may not only want to be carried around constantly but also expect to be amused all through her waking hours. If she is not kept busy, she may continue to be extra cranky even when sitting on your lap.

How You Know It's Time to Grow

Watch for these sometimes subtle, sometimes not so, clues that your baby is changing and about to leap into the world of events.

She May Have Trouble Sleeping

Your baby may not settle down well at night now. It may be more difficult to get her to go to bed in the evenings, or she may lie awake at night. She may want a night feeding again, or she may even demand to be fed several times a night. She may also wake up much earlier in the morning.

She May Become Shy with Strangers

Your baby may refuse to sit on anyone else's lap but yours, or she may get upset if a stranger looks at or talks to her. She may even seem frightened of her own father if he is not around her for much of the day. Generally, her shyness will be more apparent with people who look very different from you.

"When my daughter sees my sister, she gets extremely upset and starts screaming at the top of her lungs and buries her face in my clothes, as if she's afraid to even look at my sister. My sister has dark eyes and wears black eye makeup, which tends to give her a rather hard look. I'm blonde and wear hardly any makeup at all. Perhaps that has something to do with it."

Nina's mom, 16th week

"My son won't smile at people who wear glasses anymore. He just stares at them with a stern look on his face and refuses to smile until they have taken their glasses off."

John's mom, 16th week

She May Demand More Attention

Your baby may want you to amuse her by doing things together, or at the very least, she may want you to look at her all the time. She may even start to cry the moment you walk away.

"I have to give my son extra attention between feedings. In the past, he'd lie quietly on his own. Now he wants to be entertained."

John's mom, 17th week

Her Head May Need More Support

When you carry your fussy baby around, you may notice you have to support her head and body more often. She may slump down a little in your arms when you hold her, particularly during crying fits. When you carry her, it may strike you that she feels more like the tiny newborn she used to be.

She May Always Want to Be with You

Your baby may refuse to be set down, although she may agree to sit in her bouncing chair as long as you stay near by and touch her frequently.

"My little one wants to be closer to me, which is unusual for her. If I let go of her for even a second, she starts to cry, but as soon as either my husband or I pick her up, everything's fine again."

Eve's mom, 17th week

She May Lose Her Appetite

Both breastfed and bottle-fed babies can temporarily have smaller appetites as they approach this leap. Don't worry if your little one is more easily distracted by the things she sees or hears around her than she used to be, or if she is quick to start playing with the nipple. Occasionally, babies may even turn away from the bottle or breast and refuse to drink completely. Sometimes, a fussy eater may eat her fruit but refuse her milk, for example. Nearly all mothers who breastfeed see this refusal as a sign that they should switch to other nourishments. Some mothers feel as if their babies are rejecting them personally. This is not at all the case. Your baby is simply upset. It is not necessary to stop breastfeeding at this point; on the contrary, it would be a bad time to choose to wean your baby.

> "Around 15 weeks, my daughter suddenly started nursing less. After 5 minutes, she would start playing around with my nipple. After that had gone on for 2 weeks, I decided to start supplementing my milk with formula, but she wouldn't have any of that either. This phase lasted 4 weeks. During that time, I worried she would suffer from some kind of nutrition deficiency, especially when I saw my milk supply starting to diminish. But now she is drinking like she used to again, and my milk supply is as plentiful as ever. In fact, I seem to have more."
>
> Hannah's mom, 19th week

She May Be Moody

Some babies' moods swing wildly at this time. One day they are all smiles, but the next they do nothing but cry. These mood swings may even occur from one moment to the next. One minute they're shrieking with laughter, and the next they burst into tears. Sometimes, they even start to cry in the middle of laughing. Some mothers say that both the laughter and the tears seem to be dramatic and exaggerated, almost unreal.

 My Diary

Signs My Baby Is Growing Again

Between 14 and 17 weeks, you may notice your baby starting to show any of the following behaviors, signs that he is ready to make the next leap into the world of events. Cross off the signs your baby shows on the list below.

❑ Cries more often; is often bad-tempered, cranky, or fretful

❑ Wants you to keep him busy

❑ Needs more support for his head

❑ Wants more physical contact

❑ Sleeps poorly

❑ Loses his appetite

❑ Is shier with strangers than he was before

❑ Is quieter, less vocal

❑ Is less lively

❑ Has pronounced mood swings

❑ Wants more physical contact during nursing

❑ Sucks his thumb, or sucks more often than before

OTHER CHANGES YOU NOTICE

_____

_____

She May Be Listless

Your baby may stop making his familiar sounds for a brief period or may occasionally lie motionless, staring into thin air or fidgeting with her ears, for example. It's very common for babies at this age to seem listless

and preoccupied. Many mothers find their infants' behavior peculiar and alarming. But actually, this apathy is just a lull before the storm. This interlude is a sign that your baby is on the brink of making many discoveries in a new world where she will learn to acquire many new skills.

How This Leap May Affect You

On one hand, you may find it hard to believe your baby is 19 weeks old, but on the other, you may have felt every hour of those 19 weeks, having been up for so many of them, comforting a wailing baby. Here are some ways this latest leap may be affecting you.

You May (Still) Be Exhausted

During a fussy period, most mothers complain increasingly of fatigue, headaches, nausea, backaches, or emotional problems. Some less fortunate mothers contend with more than one of these problems at the same time. They blame their symptoms on lack of sleep, having to constantly carry their little screamers, or worrying about their unhappy infants. The real cause of these symptoms, though, is the stress of constantly coping with a cranky baby. Some mothers visit their family doctor and are prescribed an iron supplement, or go to a physiotherapist for their back troubles, but the real problem is that they are nearing the end of their tether. Especially now, make time for yourself, and give yourself a treat now and then. But remember that your baby will eventually come to your aid by learning the skills that she needs to deal with her new world, and then the sun will shine again.

> "If my daughter won't settle down for a few nights in a row and wants to be walked around all the time, I get a terrible backache. At times like these, I wish she was gone for just one night. I'm a total wreck."
>
> Emily's mom, 17th week

You May Feel Trapped

Toward the end of a fussy period, a mother sometimes feels so confined by her baby's demands that she almost feels she's in prison. It seems as if the baby is calling all the shots, and the mother feels irritated by her "selfishness." It's no wonder that mothers sometimes wish their babies would just disappear for a while. Some even daydream about how wonderful it would be if they could put them out of their minds for just one night.

> "This week, there were moments when I would have liked to forget that I had a son altogether. Aren't human beings weird creatures? At times, I felt so closed in. I just had to get away from it all, and so that's what I did."
>
> Bob's mom, 18th week

> "When I'm at the store with my baby and he wakes up and starts crying, everybody stares at me. I get all hot and bothered. Sometimes I think, 'Why don't you shut up, you stupid kid!'"
>
> Steven's mom, 18th week

You May Feel Resentful

After a few weeks of living with a fussy baby, you may be shocked to find that you are beginning to resent this demanding little person who disrupts your life so much. Don't blame yourself. This is an understandable and surprisingly common reaction. Many mothers grow more irritated toward the end of a fussy period. They are convinced their baby has no valid reason for making such a fuss, and they are inclined to let their babies cry a little longer than they used to. Some begin to wonder what "spoiling" actually means, and think they may be giving in to his whims too much. They may also begin to wonder if they should be teaching their little ones to consider that mothers have feelings, too.

Now and then, a mother may feel a surge of aggression toward her persistent little screamer, especially when the baby won't stop crying, and

the mother is at her wit's end. Having these feelings is not abnormal or dangerous, but acting on them is. Get help long before you lose control. Shaking, especially, can be harmful. Remember, while it is normal to feel frustrated and angry with your baby at times, never shake a baby. Shaking a young child can easily cause internal bleeding of the spine just below the skull which can result in brain damage that may lead to learning difficulties later on or even death.

"My son refused to continue with his feeding and started having an incredible crying tantrum, while I just kept trying to get his milk down his throat. When the same thing happened with the next bottle, I felt myself becoming terribly angry because none of my little distraction tricks were working. I felt as if I were going around in circles. So I put him on the floor where he would be safe and let him scream his lungs out. When he finally stopped, I went back into the room, and he finished his bottle."

Bob's mom, 19th week

"I started to feel my temper rise every time my daughter launched into one of her crying fits because I'd left her on her own for just a second. So I let her get on with it and ignored her."

Ashley's mom, 17th week

"The last four evenings, my son started screaming at 8:00 P.M. After consoling him for 2 nights in a row, I'd had enough. So I let him cry until 10:30 P.M. He's certainly persistent, I'll give him that!"

Kevin's mom, 16th week

How Your Baby's New Skills Emerge

Because this fussy phase lasts longer than the previous ones, most mothers immediately sense that this period is different. They are concerned about their babies' seemingly slower progress and the fact that the babies seem to have a sudden aversion to the things they liked in the past. But don't worry. From this age on, the new skills are much more complicated to learn. Your little one needs more time.

"My baby seems to be making such slow progress. Before he was 15 weeks old, he developed much faster. It's almost as if he's come to a standstill these past few weeks. At times, I find this to be very upsetting."

Matt's mom, 17th week

"It's almost as if my son is on the verge of making new discoveries, but something seems to be holding him back. When I play with him, I can sense there's something missing, but I don't know what it is. So I'm playing the waiting game, too."

Steven's mom, 17th week

"My daughter has been trying to do lots of new things this week. All of a sudden, it hit me how much she can do at just 4 months, and to tell you the truth, I feel very proud of her."

Jenny's mom, 18th week

At approximately 19 weeks, you will notice that your baby is trying again to learn new skills, because this is the age when babies will generally begin to explore the world of events. This world offers her a huge repertoire of event-skills. Your baby will choose the skills best suited to her—the ones that she wants to explore. You can help her do what she really is ready to do, rather than trying to push her in any and every direction.

the Magical Leap Forward

After the last leap forward, your baby was able to see, hear, smell, taste, and feel smooth and continuous transitions. But all these transitions had to be relatively simple, such as a toy moved steadily across the floor in front of him. As soon as they became more complicated, he was no longer able to follow them. In the new world that babies begin to explore at approximately 19 weeks, most babies will start to perceive and experiment with short, familiar sequences. This new ability will affect a baby's entire behavior.

As soon as a baby is able to make several flowing movements in sequence, this will give him more opportunities with objects within his grasp. He may, for instance, be able to repeat the same flowing movement several times in succession. You may now see him trying to shake playthings from side to side or up and down. He may also attempt to press, push, bang, or beat a toy repeatedly. Besides repeating the same movement, he may now learn to perform a short sequence of different movements smoothly. For instance, he may grab an object with one hand, then try to pass it to the other hand. Or he may grab a plaything and immediately attempt to put it in his mouth. He is capable of turning a plaything around and looking at it from every possible angle. From now on, he is able to carry out a thorough examination of any object within reach.

In addition, your baby may now learn how to adjust the movements of his body, especially his upper arm, lower arm, hand, and fingers, to reach the exact spot where the plaything lies, and he can learn to correct his movements as he goes along. For instance, if a toy is farther to the left, his arm will move to the left in one flowing movement. If it is more to the right, his arm will immediately move to the correct spot. The same applies to an object near at hand, one that is farther away, or a toy hanging higher or lower. He will see it, reach for it, grab it, and pull it toward him, all in one smooth movement. As long as an object is within arm's length, your little one will now actually be able to reach out and grasp the object of his choice.

When your baby is toying with these movements, you may see him twist and turn. He may now learn to roll over or spin on his back more

Brain Changes

Recordings of babies' brain waves show that dramatic changes occur at approximately 4 months. Also, babies' head circumferences suddenly increase between 15 and 18 weeks.

easily. He may also make his first crawling attempts, because he is now capable of pulling his knees up, pushing off, and stretching.

He may also learn to make a short series of sounds now. If he does, he will develop his chatter, which started after the previous leap, to include alternating vowel and consonant sounds. He will gradually use all of these sounds to speak in "sentences." This *abba baba tata* is what adults fondly call "baby talk." You could say he is now able to become just as flexible with his voice as he is with the rest of his body.

All over the world, babies start making these short sentences when they reach this age. For example, Russian, Chinese, and American babies all babble the same language initially. Eventually, the babies will start to develop their babble-sounds into proper words of their native language, and they will stop using the universal babble sounds. Each baby will become more proficient at imitating the language he hears being spoken around him because he will get the most response and praise when he produces something close to home.

Apparently, everyone's ancestors must have felt as if they were being addressed personally when they heard their offspring say "dada" or "mommom," because the words for mommy and daddy are very similar in many different languages. The truth, though, is that the little babbler is carrying out a number of technical experiments with short, familiar sequences of the same sound element: "da" or "mom."

Your baby may now begin to recognize a short series of flowing sounds. He may be fascinated by a series of notes running smoothly up and down a musical scale. He may now respond to all voices that express approval,

(continued on page 126)

 My Diary

How My Baby Explores the New World of Events

Check off the boxes below as you notice your baby changing. Stop filling this out once the next stormy period begins, heralding the coming of the next leap.

The big change that allows your baby eventually to make sense of the world of events begins at around 15 weeks. The leap into this world is a pretty big one, and the skills that come with it only start to take wing around 19 weeks. Even then, it may be a while before you see any of the skills listed here. It's most likely he will not acquire many of these skills until months later.

BODY CONTROL

❑ Starts moving virtually every part of his body as soon as he is put on the floor

❑ Rolls over from his back onto his tummy

❑ Rolls over from his tummy onto his back

❑ Is able to fully stretch his arms when lying on his tummy

❑ Lifts his bottom and attempts to push off; does not succeed

❑ Raises himself onto his hands and feet when lying on his tummy, then tries to move forward; does not succeed

❑ Attempts to crawl; manages to slide forward or backward

❑ Supports himself with forearms, and raises upper half of his body

❑ Sits up straight (all by himself) when leaning against you

❑ Attempts to sit up straight when he's by himself and briefly succeeds by leaning on his forearms and bringing his head forward

❑ Remains upright in high chair with cushions for support

❑ Enjoys moving his mouth—puckers his lips in a variety of ways, sticks his tongue out

GRABBING, TOUCHING, AND FEELING

❑ Succeeds in grabbing objects

❑ Grabs things with either hand

❑ Is able to grab an object with either hand if it comes into contact with the object, even if he is not looking at it

❑ Is able to pass objects between hands

❑ Sticks your hand in his mouth

❑ Touches or sticks his hands in your mouth as you talk

❑ Sticks objects in his mouth to feel and bite them

❑ Is able to pull a cloth from his face by himself, slowly at first

❑ Recognizes a toy or other familiar object, even if it is partially covered by something; will soon give up unsuccessful attempts to retrieve the toy

❑ Tries shaking a plaything

❑ Tries banging a plaything on a tabletop

❑ Deliberately throws a plaything on the floor

❑ Tries grabbing things just out of reach

❑ Tries to play with an activity center

❑ Understands the purpose of a particular toy; for example, he will dial his toy telephone

❑ Studies objects closely; he is especially interested in minute details of toys, hands, and mouths

(continued)

My Diary (cont.)

WATCHING

❑ Stares in fascination at repetitive activities, such as jumping up and down, slicing bread, or brushing hair

❑ Stares in fascination at the movements of your lips and tongue when you are talking

❑ Searches for you and is able to turn around to do this

❑ Looks for a plaything that is partially hidden

❑ Reacts to his own reflection in mirror; he is either scared or laughs

❑ Holds a book in his hands and stares at pictures

LISTENING

❑ Listens intently to sounds coming from your lips

❑ Responds to his own name

❑ Is now able to distinguish one particular sound in a medley of different sounds, so responds to his own name even if there are background noises

❑ Genuinely understands one or more words; for example, he looks at his teddy bear if asked "Where's your teddy bear?" (Won't respond correctly if the toy is not in its usual place.)

❑ Will respond appropriately to an approving or scolding voice

❑ Recognizes the opening bars of a song

TALKING

❑ Makes new sounds, using his lips and tongue: *ffft-ffft-ffft, vvvvvv, zzz, sss, brrr, arrr, rrr, grrr, prrr.* This *rrr* is known as the "lip r." Your baby may particularly like to do this with food in his mouth!

❑ Uses consonants: d, b, l, m

❑ Babbles. Utters first "words": *mommom, dada, abba, hadahada, baba, tata*

❑ Makes noises when yawning and is aware of these noises

BODY LANGUAGE

❑ Stretches his arms out to be picked up

❑ Smacks his lips when hungry; waves arms and legs

❑ Opens his mouth and moves his face toward food and drink

❑ "Spits" when he's had enough to eat

❑ Pushes the bottle or breast away when he has had enough

❑ Turns away from the feeding of his own accord when full

OTHER SKILLS

❑ May exaggerate his actions; for example, when you re-spond to his coughing, he will cough again, then laugh

❑ Gets grumpy when becoming impatient

❑ Screams if he fails to do what he seems to be trying to do

❑ Has one special cuddly toy, such as a blanket

OTHER CHANGES YOU NOTICE

_____

_____

and he may be startled by voices that scold. It doesn't matter what language is used to express these feelings, since he will be able to perceive the differences in tones of voice. For the first time, he is now able to pick out one specific voice in the middle of a commotion.

Your baby may also start to recognize short, familiar tunes. At 19 weeks, babies are even capable of hearing whether interruptions in a piece of music being played are genuine or do not belong to that particular piece of music, even if they have never heard the music before. In an unusual experiment, researchers found that if a part of a minuet by Mozart was played to babies, they showed a definite response if the music was interrupted by random pauses. Babies may also start recognizing words for the very first time.

Your baby may now learn to see a short, familiar sequence of images. For instance, he may be fascinated by the up-and-down motion of a bouncing ball. There are endless examples to be seen, all disguised as normal, everyday activities or events, such as someone shaking his bottle up and down, stirring a saucepan, hammering a nail, opening and closing a door, slicing bread, filing nails, brushing hair, the dog scratching itself, somebody pacing back and forth in the room, and a whole range of other events and activities.

Two more basic characteristics of the world of events should be mentioned here. First, as adults, we usually experience an event as an inseparable whole. We do not see a falling-rising-falling ball—we see a bouncing ball. Even when the event has only just begun, we already know it is a bouncing ball. As long as it continues, this remains one and the same event—an event for which we have a name. Second, most events are defined by the observer. For instance, when we speak, we don't separate the words clearly, but run one into the next without a pause. The listener creates the boundaries between words, giving the impression that they are heard one at a time. It is exactly this special power of perception that will begin to be available to your baby between 14 and 17 weeks.

Your Baby's Choices: A Key to His Personality

The world of events offers a wide range of new skills to your baby. From the opportunities available to him, your little one will make his own selections, based on his own inclinations, interests, and physical characteristics. Some babies may want to concentrate on feeling skills, while others may choose the watching skills, and yet another group will specialize in physical activities. Obviously, there are also babies who like to learn a variety of different skills without specializing in any one of them. Every baby makes his own choice, because every baby is unique.

Watch your baby closely to determine his particular interests. If you respect his choices, you will discover the special pattern that makes your baby unique. All babies love anything new. It's important that you respond when you notice any new skills or interests. Your baby will enjoy it if you share these new discoveries, and his learning will progress more quickly.

The more your baby comes in contact with events and the more she plays with them, the greater her understanding of them will be and the more proficient she will become. It doesn't matter which discoveries she chooses to make in this new world. She may pay close attention to music, sounds, and words. Or she may choose looking and observing, or physical activities. Later on, it will be easy for her to put the knowledge and experience she has gained learning one skill to good use when learning another.

Besides wanting to experiment with the discoveries she makes in this world of events, your baby will also become tremendously interested in everything going on around her. This may now occupy most of her waking hours, because she will want to look at and listen to everything she possibly can. Even better (or worse!), every toy, household item, and

gardening or kitchen utensil within a small arm's length is hers for the taking. You are no longer her only toy. She may try to become involved in the world around her by pushing herself forward with her hands and feet, toward something new, and away from her mom. She may now have less time to spare for her old cuddling games. Some parents feel a little rejected by this.

Even so, she still needs your help just as much as ever. Your baby's fascination with the whole world around her is typical at this age. You probably have begun to sense these new needs, and your main contribution can be supplying your baby with enough playthings and waiting to see how she responds. Only if you notice that she has real difficulties in fully understanding a toy should you give her a hand. You'll also want to keep an eye on your baby to make sure she uses her hands, feet, limbs, and body properly when reaching out to grab objects. If you see that she has a particular problem, you can help her to practice activities like rolling over, turning, and sometimes even crawling, sitting, or standing up.

Help Your Baby Explore the New World through Body Movement

Perhaps you have seen your baby spin on her back and squirm in an attempt to roll over from her tummy onto her back. If you did, you saw your little one toying with a short series of flowing movements of several body parts. She can now make these because she is living in the world of events. However, being able to make several flowing movements in succession does not automatically mean that she is successful in rolling over or crawling, for that matter. It usually takes quite some trial and error to get there.

> *"My little one is trying to roll over from her back onto her tummy. She's not having much success yet, and it's making her awfully upset. She really gets exasperated."*
>
> Ashley's mom, 20th week

"My son is practicing like crazy to learn to roll over properly. But when he's lying facedown, he pulls both arms and legs up at the same time, straining and moaning like mad, and that's as far as he gets."

John's mom, 21st week

"My daughter manages to roll over only when she gets really angry. To her own surprise, I might add."

Laura's mom, 20th week

Here's a playful way to help your baby practice rolling from her back onto her tummy. Lay your baby on her back, and hold a colorful plaything next to her. To reach it, she will be forced to stretch her body and turn so that she can't help but roll over. Of course, you have to encourage her in her efforts and praise her for trying.

You can also make a game out of helping her to roll from her tummy onto her back. One way is to lay your baby on her stomach and hold a colorful toy behind her, either to her left or to her right. When she turns to reach for it, move the plaything farther behind her back. At a certain point, she will roll over, simply from turning a little too much when reaching for the toy. Her heavy head will automatically help her in the process.

At about this age, babies often try to crawl. The problem with crawling is the moving forward part. Most babies would love to move forward, and they do try. Some babies get into the right starting position—they tuck their knees under their bodies, stick their bottoms in the air, and push off—but they're not successful. Other babies get into the crawling position but bounce up and down without moving forward. There are also little squirmers who slide backward, because they push off with their hands. Others push off with one foot, thus going around in circles. Some lucky babies fumble around for a while and hit on forward motion seemingly by accident. This is the exception rather than the rule at this age.

"I think my baby may want to crawl, but I have the feeling he doesn't know how yet. He squirms and wriggles, but he doesn't move an inch. He gets really upset then."

Frankie's mom, 20th week

Many mothers try to help their babies crawl. They carefully push their wriggling infants' bottoms forward, or they put all kinds of attractive objects just out of their reach in an attempt to coax them forward. Sometimes these maneuvers will do the trick, and the baby somehow manages to move a little. Some babies do this by throwing themselves forward with a thud. Others lie on their tummies and push themselves forward with their legs, while using their arms to steer themselves in the right direction.

If you imitate your baby's attempts, she may find it absolutely hilarious. She may also really enjoy watching you show her how to crawl properly. Nearly every child who is having crawling problems will be fascinated by your attempts. Just try it and see!

Let Him Wriggle Around Naked

Your baby has to practice if he wants to learn how to roll over, turn, and crawl properly. It will be a lot more fun, and much easier for him, if he is not wearing his clothes and diaper. Lots of physical exercise will give him the opportunity to get to know his body and help him to increase his control over it.

Help Your Baby Explore the New World through Manipulation and Examination

In the world of events, your baby's arms, hands, and fingers are just like the rest of her body—able to make several flowing movements in succession. As a result, she is able to practice reaching for, grabbing, and pulling a toy toward herself in one smooth movement and manipulate it in all sorts of ways such as shaking, banging, or poking. Thus she can examine the objects she can lay her hands on. And that is just what she wants to do at this age, though again she needs a lot of practice to become perfect.

Let her explore as many objects as she wants. She may turn them around, shake them, bang them, slide them up and down, and stick an interesting part in her mouth to feel and taste it. An activity center offers a variety of these hand and finger exercises all on one board. It usually has an element that one can turn. It may have a knob that also makes a noise when pressed. There could be animals to slide up and down and revolving cylinders and balls to turn, and so on. Each separate activity will emit a different sound when your baby handles it. Lots of babies love their activity centers. But don't expect your little one to understand and use all these features properly at first. She's just a beginner!

When you see that your baby is trying to do something without much success, you can help her by holding her hand to show her how to do it properly. Or if your baby has a preference for observing how things are done, let her watch how your hand does it. Either way, you will encourage her to be playful and clever with her little hands.

"We had an activity center hanging in the playpen for weeks. My son looked at it from time to time, but he wouldn't do anything with it. But this week, he suddenly started grabbing it. Now he just loves touching and turning all those knobs. You can tell he's really exploring the whole board. He does get tired quickly, though, because he has to push himself up with one hand all the time."

Paul's mom, 18th week

If your baby gets tired because she has to push herself up with one hand all the time, support her so she can use her hands freely. For instance, put her on your lap and examine a toy together. She will love being able to play while sitting comfortably. Besides, when she is sitting, she will be able to look at playthings from a completely different angle. Just watch her to see if she does different things with toys when she is sitting comfortably. Perhaps you may even see new activities.

"I put my baby in his high chair for the first time and propped him up with a cushion. He immediately discovered that you can do certain things with toys while sitting up that you can't do on the floor. When I gave him his plastic key ring, he first started banging it on the tabletop, and then he kept throwing it on the floor. He did that about 20 times in a row. He thought it was great fun and couldn't stop laughing."

Paul's mom, 19th week

If your baby is a keen explorer, you can enrich her environment by offering her playthings and other objects of different shapes, such as round or square things, or made of different materials, such as wood and plastic. Give her fabrics with different textures or soft, rough, and smooth paper to play with. Many babies love empty, crisp bags, because they slowly change shape and make wonderful crackling sounds when crumpled. Give your baby objects with rough edges or dents. Most babies have a weakness for weird shapes. The shape of a plastic key, for instance, will challenge her to make a closer inspection. Many babies find the jagged edge particularly intriguing and will want to touch it, look at it, and taste it.

Some babies are drawn to the smallest details. If you have such a tiny researcher, she will probably look at an object from all sides, examining it very carefully. She will really take her time and carry out a close inspection of the object. She will fuss with the smallest of protrusions. It may take ages before she's finished stroking, feeling, and rubbing textures and examining shapes and colors. Nothing seems to escape her inquisitive eyes and probing mind. If she decides to examine you, she will do this meticulously, too. If she studies your hand, she will usually begin with

 Baby Care

Make Your Home Baby-Proof

You probably began this process a long time ago, but since your baby is now becoming increasingly mobile, it's time to do a quick safety check to make sure he is safe.

- Never leave small objects, such as buttons, pins, or coins, near your baby.

- When your baby is on your lap during feeding, make sure he can't suddenly grab a cup or mug containing a hot drink.

- Never leave hot drinks on a table within your baby's reach. Don't even leave them on a high table. If the baby tries to reach it by pulling at the leg of the table—or, even worse, the tablecloth—he could spill the drink over himself.

- Use a guard or fence around stoves and fireplaces.

- Keep poisonous substances such as turpentine, bleach, and medicine out of your baby's reach and in childproof containers when possible.

- Make sure electrical outlets are secured with socket covers and that there are no trailing wires anywhere.

one finger, stroke the nail, and then look and feel how it moves, before she proceeds to the next finger. If she's examining your mouth, she will usually inspect every single tooth. Stimulate her eye for detail by giving her toys and objects that will interest her.

"My daughter is definitely going to be a dentist. I almost choke every time she inspects my mouth. She probes around and practically shoves her whole fist inside my mouth. She makes it very clear she doesn't appreciate being interrupted while she's working when I try to close my mouth to give her a kiss on the hand."

Emily's mom, 21st week

Does your baby want to grab everything you are eating or drinking? Most babies do. So, take care not to drink hot tea or coffee with a wriggly baby on your lap. In an unguarded moment, she may suddenly decide to grab your cup and tip the hot contents all over her hands and face.

"My son will try to grab my sandwich with his mouth already open in anticipation. Whatever he manages to grab, he swallows immediately. The funny thing is, he seems to enjoy everything."

Kevin's mom, 19th week

Help Your Baby Explore the New World through Sight

Is your baby a real observer? The daily routine in every household is full of events that your baby may enjoy watching. Many babies love to watch their mothers preparing food, setting the table, getting dressed, or working in the garden. They are now capable of understanding the different actions or events involved in various activities, such as putting plates on the table, slicing bread, making sandwiches, brushing hair, filing nails, and mowing the lawn. If your baby enjoys observing things, let her watch your daily activities. All you have to do is to make sure she is in a perfect position to observe them. It really is no extra trouble for you, but it will be an enjoyable learning experience for her.

> "My little one smacks her lips, kicks her legs, and reaches out with her hands as soon as she sees me making sandwiches. She's obviously aware of what I'm doing, and she's asking to be fed."
>
> Hannah's mom, 20th week

Some babies at this age already enjoy looking at picture books in which events are shown. If your baby enjoys this, she may want to hold the book herself, using both hands, and gaze at the illustration in wonder. She may make a real effort to hold the book and concentrate on the pictures, but after a while the book will usually end up in her mouth.

You can start to play the first peek-a-boo and hide-and-seek games at this age. As soon as your baby becomes familiar with the world of events, she may recognize a plaything, even when she can see only part of it. If you see her looking quizzically at a partially hidden toy, or if you want to turn her attempts to retrieve a toy into a game of hide-and-seek, move the object about a little to make it easier for her to recognize. At this age, she is still quick to give up. The idea that an object continues to exist all the time, wherever it is, is not yet within her mental grasp.

(continued on page 138)

Top Games for This Wonder Week

Here are games and activities that most babies like best now. Remember, all babies are different. See what your baby responds to best.

HAPPY TALK

Talk as often as possible to your baby about the things he sees, hears, tastes, and feels. Talk about the things he does. Keep your sentences short and simple. Emphasize the important words. For instance: "feel this—*grass*," "*daddy*'s coming," "listen—the *doorbell*," or "open your *mouth*."

WHAT HAPPENS NEXT?

First you say, "I'm going to (dramatic pause) pinch your *nose*." Then grab his nose and gently wiggle it about. You can do the same with his ears, hands, and feet. Find out what he enjoys most. If you play this game regularly, he will know exactly what you are going to do next. Then he will watch your hands with increasing excitement and shriek with laughter when you grab his nose. This game will familiarize him with both his body and the words for its parts as you play together.

LOOKING AT PICTURES

Show your baby a brightly colored picture in a book. He may even want to look at several pictures. Make sure the pictures are bright, clear, and include things he recognizes. Talk about the pictures together, and point out the real object if it's in the room.

SING SONGS

Many babies really love songs, particularly when they are accompanied by movements, such as "*Pat a cake, pat a cake, baker's man.*" But they also enjoy being rocked to the rhythm of a song or nursery rhyme. Babies recognize songs by their melody, rhythm, and intonation.

TICKLING GAME

This familiar song encourages tickling, which your baby may love.

This little piggy went to market . . .
And this little piggy stayed at home . . .
This little piggy ate roast beef . . .
And this little piggy had none . . .
This little piggy went . . .
Weeweeweewee all the way home.

While saying this, wiggle each of your baby's toes in turn, before finally running your fingers up his body and tickling him in the neck.

PEEK-A-BOO

Cover your baby's face with a blanket, and ask: "Where's. . . . ?" Watch him to see if he can remove the blanket from his face on his own. If he can't do this yet, help him by holding his hand and slowly pulling the flannel away with him. When he can see you again each time, say "boo"—this helps to mark the event for him. Keep the game simple at this age; otherwise, it will be too difficult for him.

MIRROR GAME

Look in a mirror together. Usually a baby will prefer looking and smiling at his own reflection first. But then, he will look at your reflection, and then back to the real you. This normally bewilders him, and he will usually look back and forth at you and your reflection, as if he can't make up his mind which one is his real mother. If you start talking to him, he will be even more amazed, because no one but his real mother talks like that. This may reassure him that he's with the right person, so he may start laughing before he snuggles up to you.

Help Your Baby Explore the New World through Language and Music

Does your baby make "babbling sentences"? Sometimes it may sound as if your little one is really telling you a story. This is because in the world of events your baby becomes just as flexible with her voice as with the rest of her body. She starts to repeat whatever syllables she already knows and string them together to form a "sentence," such as *dadadada* and *bababababa*. She may also experiment with intonation and volume. When she hears herself making a new sound, she may stop for a while and laugh before resuming the conversation.

It's still important to talk to your baby as often as possible. Try to respond to what she says, imitate her new sounds, and reply when she "asks" or "tells" you something. Your reactions encourage her to practice using her voice.

You may notice that your baby understands a word or short sentence, although she cannot say the word or words herself. Try asking in familiar surroundings "Where's your teddy?" and you may see her actually look at her teddy bear.

In the world of events, babies are able to understand a short, familiar series of sounds such as "Want to go for a ride?" This doesn't mean that they understand a sentence in the same way that an older child or an adult does. Your baby is hearing a familiar pattern of syllables along with the intonation of your voice as a single sound event. This is just the kind of simple string of patterns and changes that makes up an event for her in this world.

Being able to recognize the teddy-bear-sentence event doesn't mean that your baby can recognize sound events under all circumstances. If you were looking in a toy store window with your baby and saw a teddy identical to her own, for example, you might try "Where's your teddy?" with absolutely no success, since she really won't be able to understand meaning in a context so far removed from her own familiar surroundings.

Top Toys for This Wonder Week

Here are toys and other objects that most babies like best as they explore the world of events. Nearly all everyday household items will appeal to your baby. Try to find out what your baby likes best. Be careful, though, to screen out any that may be harmful to him.

- Bath toys. Your baby will enjoy playing with a variety of household items in the bath, such as a measuring cup, plastic colander, plant spray bottle, watering can, soap dish, and plastic shampoo bottles.

- Activity center

- Ball with gripping notches, preferably with a bell inside

- Plastic or inflatable rattle

- A screw-top container with some rice in it

- Crackly paper

- Mirror

- Photographs or pictures of other babies

- Photographs or pictures of objects or animals he recognizes by name

- CD with children's songs

- Wheels that really turn, such as those on a toy car

Because mothers naturally repeat the same or similar sentences over and over again as they go through their daily routines, babies gradually come to recognize them. This is the only way they can begin to learn about speech, and all babies understand words and phrases long before they can say them.

"In our living room, there's a painting of flowers on one wall and a photo of my son on another. When I ask him 'Where are the flowers?' or 'Where's Paul?' he always looks at the correct picture. I'm not imagining it, because the pictures are on opposite sides of the room."

Paul's mom, 23rd week

You will be really enthusiastic and proud when you discover that your baby understands her first short sentence. Initially, you may not believe what happened. You may keep repeating the sentence until you are convinced it wasn't just a coincidence. Next, you may create a new situation to practice the little sentence your baby already recognizes. For instance, you may put the teddy bear in every conceivable spot in a room to test if your baby knows where it is. You may even show her photographs of her teddy bear to see if she recognizes it. Many mothers change the way they talk to their babies at this age. They will say sentences more slowly to their babies, and often they will use just single words instead of whole sentences.

Is your baby a budding music lover? In the world of events she may be fascinated by a series of notes running smoothly up and down the musical scale, and she is able to recognize a short, familiar sequence such as the opening tune of a commercial on TV. Help her with her musical talents. Let her hear the music she likes best. Your music lover may also appreciate all kinds of sounds. If so, it is worth stimulating and encouraging this interest. Some babies grab toys and objects primarily to find out if they will make a noise of any kind. They turn around sound-producing objects, not for inspection, but to see if the sound changes when the object is turned quickly or slowly. These babies will squeeze a toy in a variety of ways to see if it produces different sounds. Give her sound-producing objects to play with and help her to use them properly.

The Virtue of Patience

When your baby is learning new skills, she may sometimes try your patience. Both you and your baby have to adjust to her progress and re-negotiate the rules to restore peace and harmony. Remember, from now on your baby will no longer be completely dependent on you for her enjoyment, since she is now in touch with the world around her. She can do and understand a lot more than she did in the past, and, of course, she thinks she knows it all. You may think *she* is a handful. She thinks *you* are! If you recognize this behavior, you could say you are having the first independence struggle with your infant.

> "Every time my daughter sits with me on my favorite chair, she tries to grab the tassels on the lamp shade. I don't like her doing that, so I pull her away and say 'no.'"
>
> Jenny's mom, 20th week

What irritates many mothers more than anything else is a baby's obsession for grabbing everything within reach or anything she sees in passing—especially when she seems to prefer doing this over playing with her mother. Some see it as antisocial—sometimes even slightly selfish—on

the part of their little ones. Others feel that the baby is still too young to be touching everything in sight—plants, coffee cups, books, stereo equipment, eyeglasses—nothing is safe from her exploring hands. Most mothers try to curb this urge for independence by stopping their babies in every way possible when they again push away from them and toward the things that take their fancy now. A mother may often try to distract her infant with cuddling games or a tight embrace as she wriggles and squirms in her arms to get at something. But both methods will nearly always have the opposite effect. The baby will squirm and wriggle with even more determination as she struggles to free herself from her long-suffering mother. Other mothers try to discourage this grabbing mania by firmly saying "no." Sometimes this works.

Impatience can be a nuisance. Most mothers think their babies should learn a little patience at this age. They don't always respond to their babies as quickly as they used to. When the baby wants something, or wants to do something, a mother may now make her wait for a few brief moments. She may insist on sitting up straight, on being where the action is, and staying somewhere as long as she likes. The same goes for eating and sleeping. Grabbing food impatiently is particularly irritating to most mothers. Some put an immediate stop to it.

 Baby Care

Don't Lose Control

Now and again, a mother may feel a surge of aggression toward her little troublemaker. Remember that having these feelings is not abnormal or dangerous, but acting on them is. Try to calm yourself, and if you can't, be sure to get help long before you lose control.

"My daughter went berserk as soon as she saw her bowl of food. She couldn't seem to gobble it up fast enough. I found it terribly annoying, so I taught her to wait until we all sat down at the table. Now she's no longer impatient. She really waits and watches us serve dinner."

Nina's mom, 22nd week

Hurting someone is not funny. Now that the baby is stronger and understands the world of events, she is also capable of causing physical pain. She may bite, chew, and pull at your face, arms, ears, and hair. She may pinch and twist your skin. Sometimes she will do this hard enough that it really hurts. Most mothers feel that their babies could easily show a little more consideration and respect for others. They are no longer amused by biting, pulling, and pinching.

Some mothers rebuke their babies if they get too excited. They do this by letting them know immediately that they have gone too far. Usually they do this verbally by saying "ouch," loudly and sternly. If they notice that a baby is preparing to launch a new attack, they warn her with "careful." At this age, babies are perfectly capable of understanding a cautioning voice. Occasionally, a mother will really lose her temper.

"When my baby bites my nipple really hard, I really have to work to keep my cool. My immediate reaction is a furious desire to slap him. Before I had a baby, I couldn't understand how people could hit their children. Now I can."

Matt's mom, 20th week

Matt's mom is very honest about her feelings. Fortunately, she does not act on them. Although your baby may inflict physical pain on you during this difficult period, he is not doing this "on purpose." Giving your baby "an eye for an eye" is not acceptable and it certainly does not teach him not to hurt his mother.

After the Leap

Between 20 and 22 weeks, another period of comparative calm begins. Many mothers praise their babies' initiative and love of enterprise. Babies seem to have boundless energy now.

You are no longer your baby's only toy. He explores his surroundings with great determination and enjoyment. He grows increasingly impatient with only mother to play with. He wants action. He may try to wriggle off of your lap at the least opportunity if he spots anything of interest. He is obviously a lot more independent now.

"I put away my son's first baby clothes today and felt a pang of regret. Doesn't time fly? Letting go isn't easy. It's a very painful experience. He suddenly seems so grown up. I have a different kind of relationship with him now. He has become more of his own little person."

Bob's mom, 23rd week

"My baby drinks her bottle with her back toward me now, sitting up straight, not wanting to miss any of the world around her. She even wants to hold the bottle herself."

Laura's mom, 22nd week

"When my son is on my lap, he tries to lie almost flat so he doesn't miss anything going on behind him."

Frankie's mom, 23rd week

"I hardly ever put my baby in the playpen now. I think that he's too restricted in such a small space."

Bob's mom, 22nd week

"My son is starting to resent being carried around in the sling. At first, I thought he wanted more room because he's so active. But then I put him facing forward, and he's happy now that he's able to see everything."

Steven's mom, 21st week

Babies who like to be physically active no longer need to be handed the objects they want, because they will twist and turn in every direction to get them themselves.

"My daughter rolls from her tummy onto her back and wriggles and squirms all over the place to get to a plaything, or she'll crawl over to it. She's as busy as a bee all day long. She doesn't even have time to cry. I must say she seems happier than ever, and so are we."

Jenny's mom, 21st week

"My baby crawls and rolls in every direction. I can't stop her. She tries getting out of her bouncing chair, and she wants to crawl up onto the sofa. The other day we found her halfway into the dog basket. She's also very busy in the bath. There's hardly any water left in it once she's practically kicked it all out."

Emily's mom, 22nd week

During this time, the calm before the next storm, most babies are more cheerful. Even demanding, trying babies are happier at this stage. Perhaps this is because they are able to do more now and are less bored. Parents delight in this less-troubled, well-deserved time.

"My little one is in such a cheerful mood now. She laughs and 'tells stories.' It's wonderful to watch her."

Juliette's mom, 23rd week

"I'm enjoying every minute I spend with my daughter again. She's such a cutie, really easygoing."

Ashley's mom, 22nd week

"My son is suddenly easier. He's back in a regular routine, and he's sleeping better."

Frankie's mom, 23rd week

"My son is surprisingly sweet and cheerful. He goes to sleep without any complaining, which is an achievement in itself. He sleeps much longer now in the afternoons, compared to these past weeks. He's so different from how he was several months ago when he cried all day. Apart from a few ups and downs now and again, things are steadily improving."

Paul's mom, 22nd week

chapter 7

Wonder Week 26:
The World of Relationships

At about 26 weeks, your baby will start to show the signs of yet another significant leap in his development. If you watch closely, you will see him doing or attempting to do many new things. Whether or not he is crawling at this stage, he will have become significantly more mobile as he learns to coordinate the action of his arms and legs and the rest of his body. Building on his knowledge of events, he his now able to begin to understand the many kinds of relationships among the things that make up his world.

One of the most significant relationships that your baby can now perceive is the distance between one thing and another. We take this for granted as adults, but for a baby it is an alarming discovery, a very radical change in his world. The world is suddenly a very big place in which he is but a tiny, if very vocal, speck. Something he wants can be on a high shelf or outside the range of his crib, and he has no way of getting to it. His mother can walk away, even if only into the next room, and she might as well have gone to China if he can't get to her because he's stuck in his crib or hasn't yet mastered crawling. Even if he is adept at crawling, he realizes that she moves much faster than he does and can get away from him.

This discovery can be very frightening for a baby, and it may make these few weeks quite taxing for his parents. But when you understand the source of this fear and uneasiness, there are many things you will be able to do to help. Naturally, once your baby learns to negotiate the space around him and control the distance between himself and the things he

Note: The first phase (fussy period) of this leap into the perceptual world of "relationships" is age-linked and predictable, emerging about 23 weeks. Most babies start the second phase (see box "Quality Time: An Unnatural Whim" on page 17) of this leap 26 weeks after full-term birth. It sets in motion the development of a whole range of skills and activities. However, the age at which these skills and activities appear for the first time varies greatly and depends on your baby's preferences, experimentation and physical development. For example, the ability to perceive spatial relationships is a necessary precondition for "crawling inside or under things," but this skill normally appears anywhere from 6 to 11 months. Skills and activities are mentioned in this chapter at the earliest possible age they might appear so you can watch for and recognize them. (They may be rudimentary at first.) This way you can respond to and facilitate your baby's development.

wants, he will be able to do much more on his own than he used to. But there will be a period during which he will need a lot of support.

Entering the world of relationships will affect everything your baby perceives and does. He senses these changes taking place at around 23 weeks, and that's when the disturbances begin. Caught up in a tangle of new impressions, he needs to touch base, return to his mommy, and cling to her for comfort. The familiar feeling of security and warmth she provides will help him to relax, let the newness sink in, and grow into the new world at his own pace. This fussy period often lasts about 4 weeks, although it may be as short as 1 week or as long as 5. Since one of the important skills he has to learn during this leap is how to handle the distance between his mom and himself, your baby may actually become fussy again for a while around 29 weeks, after his new skills have started to take wing. Do remember that if your baby is fussy, watch him closely to see if he is attempting to master new skills.

When your baby becomes aware that her world is changing, she will usually cry more easily. Many mothers may now call their babies cranky, bad-tempered, whiny, or discontented. If your baby is already strong willed, she may come across as being even more restless, impatient, or troublesome. Almost all babies will cry less when they are picked up and cuddled, nestled up against mommy, or at least kept company while they're playing.

> "My baby is starting to stand up for herself more and more. She makes demands, angrily ordering me to come to her or stay with her. In this way, she makes sure I am there to help reach her toys."
>
> Hannah's mom, 25th week

How You Know It's Time to Grow

Here are some of the signals that your baby may give you to let you know he's approaching this leap into the world of relationships.

She May Sleep Poorly

Your baby may sleep less than you are used to. Most babies have difficulty falling asleep or wake up sooner. Some don't want to nap during the day, and others don't want to go to bed at night. There are even those who refuse to do either.

"Bedtime and naptime are accompanied by terrible screaming fits. My son yells furiously and practically climbs the walls. He'll shout at the top of his voice and practically wind himself. I just can't handle it. It seems as if I never see him lying peacefully in his crib anymore. I just pray it doesn't last forever."

                                    Bob's mom, 26th week

"My baby's rhythm is totally off because he keeps waking up a little earlier each day. But apart from that, his sleep is normal."

                                    Frankie's mom, 25th week

She May Have "Nightmares"

Your baby may sleep uneasily at this time. Sometimes, babies can toss and turn and thrash about so much during their sleep that it looks as if they're having nightmares.

"My daughter is a very restless sleeper. Sometimes, she'll let out a scream with her eyes closed, as if she's having a nightmare. So I'll lift her up for a minute to comfort her. These days, I usually let her play in the bathtub in the evening. I'm hoping it will calm her down and make her sleepier."

                                    Emily's mom, 23rd week

She May Become Shyer

Your baby may not want other people to look at him, talk to him, or touch him, and he certainly won't want to sit on their laps. He may even start to want you in plain sight more often from this age on, even when there aren't any strangers around. Almost every mother will notice this now. At this age, shyness is especially obvious, for a very good reason—your baby is now able to understand that you can walk away and leave him behind.

> "My baby gets shyer every day now. I need to be where he can see me at all times, and it has to be close to him. If I walk away, he'll try to crawl right after me."
>
> Matt's mom, 26th week

> "Even when I sit, I can hardly move without my daughter crying out in fear."
>
> Ashley's mom, 23rd week

She May Demand More Attention

Your baby may want you to stay with her longer, play with her more, or just look at her and her alone.

> "My daughter is easily discontented and has to be kept busy. When she wakes up in her crib, for instance, she's really eager to see one of us right away. Also, she's quick to react. She doesn't just cry; she gets really mad. She's developing a will of her own."
>
> Hannah's mom, 26th week

> "All my baby wants is to get out of his playpen. I really have to keep him occupied on my lap or walk around with him."
>
> Frankie's mom, 27th week

"My daughter was up to mischief all the time, behaving badly and act-ing cranky when she wanted attention. I had to play with her or find some way to occupy her all day long. As long as I did that, everything was okay."

Jenny's mom, 25th week

She May Always Want to Be with You

Your baby may insist on remaining in your arms. Many babies don't want to be put down very much. But some are not completely satisfied with the peaceful rest on mommy's lap that they cried for. As soon as they reach their goal, they start to push off and reach out for interesting things in the world around them.

"My son keeps on bothering me to sit on my lap. But as soon as I take him, there's almost no controlling him. He crawls all over me and gropes around like a monkey for anything he can get his hands on. It bothers me. I try playing games, but it's a waste of time. So he doesn't feel like playing with me, okay, but at least he could stop being so difficult. To be honest, I feel rejected when he refuses to play my game, so I put him back in his playpen. But as soon as I do, he'll immediately start wailing for me again."

Matt's mom, 27th week

The Gender Gap

Girls who want physical contact usually agree to play with their mothers, but boys who want physical contact insist on exploring the world around them at the same time.

She May Lose Her Appetite

Both babies who are breastfed and those who are bottle-fed sometimes drink less milk or refuse to drink at all. Other food and drink may be rejected, too. Often, babies also take longer to finish their meals. Somehow they seem to prefer the comfort of sucking or playing with the nipple over the contents of the bottle or breast.

> "My baby always refuses to nurse in the morning and at night. He just pushes my breast away, and it really hurts. Then, when he's in bed and can't get to sleep, he does want to nurse. He'll drink a little and doze off in the middle of it."
>
> Matt's mom, 26th week

She May Be Listless

Your baby may stop making her familiar sounds. Or she may lie motionless, gazing around or staring in front of her. Mothers always find this behavior odd and alarming.

> "Sometimes, all of a sudden, my little one will stare or gaze around silently. On days when she does it more than once, it makes me feel insecure. I start to wonder whether perhaps there's something wrong. I'm not accustomed to seeing her that way. So lifeless. As if she's sick or mentally challenged."
>
> Juliette's mom, 24th week

She May Refuse to Have Her Diaper Changed

Your baby may cry, kick, toss, and turn when she is set down to be changed or dressed. Many babies do. They just don't want their mothers to fiddle with their clothes.

My Diary

Signs My Baby Is Growing Again

Between 22 and 26 weeks, you may notice your baby starting to show any of these behaviors. They are probably signs that he is ready to make the next leap into the world of relationships. Check off the signs you see on the list below.

- ❏ Cries more and is bad-tempered, cranky, or whiny more often
- ❏ Wants you to keep him busy
- ❏ Wants more physical contact
- ❏ Sleeps poorly
- ❏ Loses appetite
- ❏ Doesn't want to be changed
- ❏ Is shier with strangers than he used to be
- ❏ Is quieter, less vocal
- ❏ Is less lively
- ❏ Sucks his thumb, or sucks more often than before
- ❏ Reaches for a cuddly toy, or does so more often than before

OTHER CHANGES YOU NOTICE

_____

_____

"When I put my baby on her back for a clean diaper, she'll cry every time. Usually not for very long, but it's always the same old story. Sometimes I wonder if there could be something wrong with her back."

Juliette's mom, 23rd week

"Almost every time I dress or change my baby, he'll scream bloody murder. When I have to pull a sweater over his head, we really have a field day. It drives me crazy."

Bob's mom, 24th week

She May Reach for a Cuddly Object More Often

Some babies reach for a teddy, slipper, blanket, or towel more often. For most babies, anything soft will do, but some babies will accept only that one special thing. Sometimes, they'll cuddle it while sucking a thumb or twiddling an ear. It seems that a cuddly object spells safety, especially when mommy is busy.

"When my daughter realizes whining and complaining aren't going to get her out of her playpen, she gives up. She sits and sucks her thumb with her blanket in her hand. It's adorable."

Ashley's mom, 24th week

"Thumb sucking is the big thing now. A lot of the time when my son starts to grow tired, he'll stick his thumb in his mouth, put his head on his teddy bear, and fall asleep. It's so touching."

Steven's mom, 23rd week

How This Leap May Affect You

Your baby certainly lets you know how these changes make her feel. This is bound to affect you. Here are some emotions you may feel this time around.

You May Be (Even More) Exhausted

Fussy periods can be nerve-racking. Mothers of especially demanding babies may feel like complete wrecks toward the end. They complain of stomachaches, backaches, headaches, and tension.

Being Fussy Doesn't Necessarily Mean Teething

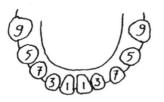

The illustration at left shows the order in which teeth emerge most often. Just remember that babies are not machines. Your baby will cut his first tooth whenever he is ready. How quickly teeth are cut in succession also has nothing to do with the state of health or mental or physical development of the baby. All babies can cut their teeth early or late, fast or slow.

Generally speaking, the lower front teeth are cut when the baby reaches 6 months. By his first birthday, a baby generally has six teeth. At about age 2½, the last molars come through, completing the full set of baby teeth. The toddler then has 20 teeth.

Despite the old wives' tale, a high temperature or diarrhea has nothing to do with teething. If your baby shows one of these symptoms, call his pediatrician.

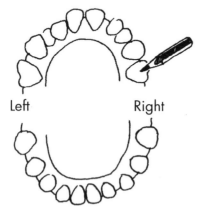

Left   Right

Date

L1	R1 ....
L2	R2 ....
L3	R3 ....
L4	R4 ....
L5	R5 ....
L6	R6 ....
L7	R7 ....
L8	R8 ....
L9	R9 ....
L10	R10 ....

"My son's crying gets on my nerves so much that I'm totally obsessed with keeping myself from crying. The tension it creates swallows up all of my energy."

Steven's mom, 25th week

"One night, I had to keep walking back and forth to put the pacifier in my daughter's mouth. Suddenly, at 12:30 A.M., she was wide awake. She stayed awake until 2:30 A.M. I'd already had a busy day, with a lot of head-aches and backaches from walking her up and down. I just collapsed."

Emily's mom, 27th week

You May Be Concerned

It's natural that you may feel troubled or nervous every time something seems to be the matter, and you can't figure out what it is. When very young babies are involved, mothers generally rationalize that they must be suffering from colic because nothing else seems to be wrong. At this age, however, mothers are quick to put two and two together and embrace the thought that their babies are fussy because they're teething. After all, most babies start cutting their teeth around this age. Still, there is no connection between clinginess due to a big change in the baby's mental development and teething. Just as many babies start teething during a fussy period as in between them. Of course, if your baby starts teething at the same time as she undergoes a big change in her mental development, she can become super-troublesome.

"My daughter right now is extremely bad-tempered, only wanting to sit on my lap. Perhaps it's her teeth. They've been bothering her for 3 weeks now. She seems pretty uncomfortable, but they still haven't come through."

Jenny's mom, 25th week

"My little guy became very weepy. According to the doctor, he has a whole bunch of teeth waiting to come through."

Paul's mom, 27th week
(His first tooth was not cut until 7 weeks later.)

You May Become Annoyed

Many mothers get angry as soon as they feel sure their babies have no good reason for being so troublesome and fussy. This feeling tends to get stronger toward the end of the fussy period. Some mothers, especially those with very demanding babies, just can't take it anymore.

> "It was a terribly trying week. My son would cry over anything. He demanded attention constantly. He was up until 10:00 P.M., and agitated. I carried him around an awful lot in the infant carrier. This he liked. But I felt tired, tired, tired from all that schlepping and the continuous crying. Whenever he'd start to throw one of his temper tantrums in bed at night, it was as if I'd crossed a line. I could feel myself getting really angry. This happened often this past week."
>
> Bob's mom, 25th week

Don't lose control. Remember that having feelings of anger and frustration at times is not abnormal or dangerous, but acting on them is. Try to get help long before you lose control.

You May Start to Argue

Arguments may develop around mealtimes. Most mothers hate it when their babies won't eat and continue to feed them. They try doing it playfully, or they try to pressure them into eating. Whatever the approach, it's usually to no avail.

At this age, strong-willed babies can be extremely stubborn about their refusal. This sometimes makes mothers, who are also being stubborn (but out of concern!) very angry. And so mealtimes can mean war.

When it happens to you, try to stay calm. Don't fight about it. You can't force her to eat, anyway. During this fussy phase, many babies are poor eaters. It's a temporary thing. If you make an issue out of it, chances are your baby will continue to refuse food even after the fussy period is over. She will have made a habit of it.

At the end of the fussy phase, you may correctly sense that your baby is capable of a lot more than you thought possible. Many mothers do. That is why an increasing number of mothers now get fed up with the annoying clinginess and decide that it's time to put a stop to it.

> "My little girl keeps whining for attention or to be picked up. It's really aggravating and, what's worse, she has no excuse whatsoever! I have enough to do as it is. So when I'm fed up now, it's off to bed with her."
>
> Juliette's mom, 26th week

How Your Baby's New Skills Emerge

At about 26 weeks, you'll discover that your baby is again trying to learn one or more new skills. This is the age at which babies will generally begin to explore the world of relationships. This world offers her many opportunities to develop skills that depend upon understanding the relationships among objects, people, sounds, and feelings. Your baby, depending on her own temperament, inclinations, preferences, and physical makeup, will focus on the sorts of relationships that appeal to her the most. She will use this understanding to develop the skills best suited to her personally. You can help her best by encouraging her to do what she is ready to do, rather than trying to push her in directions that don't interest her. This will be increasingly hard to do, anyway, as her personality begins to emerge and her own ideas start to dominate.

> "I keep seeing this pattern of a difficult, sometimes extremely trying period that peaks at the end, and is then followed by a peaceful stage. Every time I think I can't take it anymore, my little boy changes course and suddenly does all these new things."
>
> Bob's mom, 26th week

(continued on page 164)

 My Diary ------

How My Baby Explores the New World of Relationships

The world of relationships opens up so many possibilities that your baby could not explore them all, even if she wanted to. What aspects of this world she will explore depend entirely on what sort of child she is growing up to be and what her talents are. A very physical baby will use the distance perception to improve balance and to crawl after you if she is able. The watching-listening baby will find plenty to occupy her as she tries to figure out just how this world works. As you read the following list of possibilities, check off the ones that apply to your baby just now. You might want to do this two or three times before the next leap happens, since not all of the skills your baby will develop are going to appear at once. In fact, some won't appear at all until much later.

BALANCE

❑ Sits up by herself from lying down

❑ Stands up by herself; pulls herself up

❑ Sits down again by herself after standing

❑ Stands without support

❑ Walks with support

❑ Makes a jumping movement without leaving the ground

❑ Grabs a toy from an overhead shelf or table

BODY CONTROL

❑ Walks around the edge of the crib, table, or playpen while holding on

❑ Walks around, pushing a box in front of her

❑ Lunges from one piece of furniture to another

- ❏ Crawls inside or under things, such as chairs and boxes
- ❏ Crawls back and forth over small steps
- ❏ Crawls in and out of rooms
- ❏ Crawls around the table
- ❏ Bends over or lies flat on her stomach to get something from under the couch or chair

GRABBING, TOUCHING, AND FEELING

- ❏ Opposes her thumb and index finger to grasp small objects
- ❏ Can play with something using both hands
- ❏ Lifts a rug to look under it
- ❏ Holds a toy upside down to hear sound inside
- ❏ Rolls a ball across the floor
- ❏ Invariably grabs a ball rolled toward her
- ❏ Knocks over wastepaper basket to empty out its contents
- ❏ Throws things away
- ❏ Puts toys in and next to a basket, in and out of a box, or under and on a chair, or pushes them out of the playpen
- ❏ Tries to fit one toy inside another
- ❏ Tries prying something out of a toy, like a bell's clapper
- ❏ Pulls own socks off
- ❏ Pries your shoelaces loose
- ❏ Empties cupboards and shelves
- ❏ Drops objects from high chair to test how something falls
- ❏ Puts food in the mouth of the dog, mommy, or daddy
- ❏ Pushes doors closed

(continued)

 My Diary (cont.)

WATCHING

- ❑ Observes adult activities, such as putting things into, on, or through something
- ❑ Looks from one animal to another in different picture books
- ❑ Looks from one person to another in different photographs
- ❑ Looks from one toy, object, or food to another in her hands
- ❑ Observes the movements of an animal, particularly when it's unusual, such as a dog pattering across a wooden floor
- ❑ Observes the movements of a person behaving unusually, such as daddy standing on his head
- ❑ Explores own body—particularly the penis or vagina
- ❑ Pays a lot of attention to smaller details or parts of toys and other objects, such as labels on towels
- ❑ Selects a book to look at
- ❑ Selects a toy to play with

LISTENING

- ❑ Makes connections between actions and words; comprehends short commands, such as "no, don't do that" and "come on, let's go"
- ❑ Listens to explanations intently and seems to understand
- ❑ Likes to hear animal sounds when looking at animal pictures
- ❑ Listens intently to voices on the telephone
- ❑ Pays attention to sounds that are related to a certain activity, such as chopping vegetables. Listens to sounds she makes herself, such as splashing bathwater

TALKING

❑ Understands the link between actions and words. Says her first words in the correct context. For instance, says oo (for "oops") when she falls and a-choo when you sneeze

❑ Puffs and blows

MOTHER-BABY DISTANCE

❑ Protests when her mommy walks away

❑ Crawls after her mommy

❑ Repeatedly makes contact with her mommy although busy playing on her own

MIMICKING GESTURES

❑ Imitates waving good-bye

❑ Claps her hands on request

❑ Mimics clicking with her tongue

❑ Mimics shaking and nodding her head, although often only nods with her eyes

MISCELLANEOUS

❑ Dances to the sound of music (sways her tummy)

OTHER CHANGES YOU NOTICE

_____

_____

the
**Magical Leap
Forward**

For the first time, your baby can perceive all kinds of relationships and act on them. He can now discover that there is always a physical distance between two objects or two people. And of course, his distance from you is one of the first things he will notice and react to. While observing this phenomenon, he discovers that you can increase the distance too much for his liking, and it dawns on him that he cannot do anything about it. Now he knows that he has lost control over that distance, and he gets frightened. So he will start to cry.

> "We have a problem. My girl doesn't want to be put in her playpen any more. Her lips start to tremble if I even hover her anywhere above it. If I put her in it, she starts screaming. It's fine, though, if I put her on the floor, just outside of the 'cage.' Immediately, she rolls, swivels, and squirms in my direction."
>
> Nina's mom, 25th week

The juxtaposition of objects comes as a real revelation to your baby when the idea first dawns. He begins to understand that something can be *inside, outside, on top, above, next to, underneath* or *in between* something else. He will love to toy with these notions.

> "All day long, my son takes toys out of his toy box and puts them back in again. Sometimes, he'll toss everything over the side of the playpen.

Another time, he'll carefully fit each item through the bars. He clears cupboards and shelves and is thrilled by pouring water from bottles and containers into the tub. But the best thing yet was while I was feeding him. He let go of my nipple, studied it with a serious look on his face, shook my breast up and down, sucked once, took another look, and continued this way for a while. He's never done this before. It's as if he was trying to figure out how anything could come from there."

Matt's mom, 30th week

Next, your baby can begin to understand that he can cause certain things to happen. For example, he can flip a switch that causes music to play or a light to come on. He becomes attracted to objects such as stereo equipment, television sets, remote controls, light switches, and toy pianos.

He can now start to comprehend that people, objects, sounds, or situations can be related to each other. Or that a sound is related to an object or a particular situation. He knows, for example, that bustling in the kitchen means that someone is preparing his dinner, the key in the front door means "daddy's home," the dog has its own food and toys, and mommy and daddy and he belong together. Your baby's understanding of "family" won't be anywhere near as sophisticated as your own, but he does have his own understanding of what it means to belong together.

Next, your baby can begin to understand that animals and people coordinate their movements. Even if two people are walking separately, he still notices that they are taking each other's movements into consideration. That is a "relationship" as well. He can also tell when something goes wrong. If you drop something, let out a yell, and bend down quickly to catch it, if two people accidentally bump into each other, or if the dog falls off the couch, he understands that it is out of the ordinary. Some babies find this highly amusing; others are scared out of their wits. And still others become curious or take it very seriously. After all, it is something that is not meant to happen. Each brand-new observation or skill can, for that matter, make your baby feel wary until these things prove themselves harmless.

"I've noticed my son is scared of the slicing machine at the bakery. As soon as the bread goes into it, he glances at me as if to ask, 'Are you sure that it's okay?' Then he looks frightened, then he looks at me, then frightened again, then at me again. After a while, he calms down."

Paul's mom, 29th week

Your baby may also begin to discover that he can coordinate the movements of his body, limbs, and hands and that they work together as one. Once he understands this, he can learn to crawl more efficiently. Or he may try to sit up by himself or pull himself up to stand and sit down again. Some babies now take their first steps with a little help. And the exceptional baby will even do it without help, just before the next leap begins. All this physical exercise can also be frightening to a baby. He fully realizes that he could be losing control over his body. He still needs to learn how to keep his balance. And keeping one's balance has a lot to do with being familiar with the idea of distances.

When your baby starts to be active in the world of relationships, he will do it in his unique way. He will use the skills and concepts that he has acquired from previous leaps in his mental development. So he will only be able to perceive and experiment with relationships that involve things he already understands—things he has learned from the worlds of patterns, smooth transitions, and events.

Your Baby's Choices: A Key to His Personality

Between 26 and 34 weeks, you can discover what your baby likes best in the world of relationships. Take a good look at what your baby is doing. Use the "My Diary" list to help you determine where his interests lie, and respect your baby's choices. It's only natural to make comparisons with other mothers' observations of their babies, but don't expect all babies to be the same. The only thing you can be certain of is that they won't be!

Keep in mind that babies love anything new. Whenever you notice your baby showing any new skills or interests, be sure to respond. Your baby will enjoy it if you share these new discoveries. Your interest will help his learning progress more quickly. That's just how babies are.

Every baby needs time, support, and lots of opportunities to practice and experiment with new skills. You can help her by encouraging her when she succeeds and comforting her when she fails (by her own baby standards). If she persists too long in trying something she's not able to master yet, you may be able to distract her by coming up with something she can do.

Most of your activities as an adult are firmly rooted in the world of relationships—loading the car, getting dressed, putting cards in envelopes, holding a conversation, following an exercise video, to name a few. Let your baby watch these and join in where she can. Let her share your experience of sights, sounds, sensations, smells, and tastes whenever she wants to. You are still her guide in this complex world.

Always keep in mind that she will almost certainly be specializing in some kinds of activities at the expense of others. It really doesn't matter whether your baby learns about relationships from the watching or listening areas only. Later on, she will quickly and easily be able to put this understanding to use in other areas.

Show Her That You Are Not Deserting Her

In the world of relationships, almost every baby begins to realize at this time that her mommy can increase the distance between them and can walk away and leave her. Previously, her eyes could see it, but she didn't grasp the full meaning of leaving. Now that she does, it poses a problem. She gets frightened when it hits her that her mommy is unpredictable and beyond her control—she can leave her behind at any time! Even if she's already crawling, Mommy can easily outdistance her. She feels she has no control over the distance between herself and her mother, and this makes her feel helpless. It's hard to accept at first that this state of affairs is progress, but it is a clear sign of a mental leap forward. Your baby has to learn how to deal with this development and make it a part of her new world so that it is no longer frightening. Your task is to help her achieve

this. It takes understanding, compassion, practice, and above all, time.

If your baby shows fear, accept that fear. She will soon realize that there is nothing to be afraid of, since her mother is not deserting him. Generally, babies panic the most around 29 weeks. Then it improves somewhat, until the next leap begins.

> "My son has his moods when he screams until he's picked up. When I do, he'll laugh, utterly pleased with himself."
>
> Frankie's mom, 31st week

> "Everything's fine as long as my daughter can see me. If not, she starts crying out in fear."
>
> Eve's mom, 29th week

> "My little girl had been with the babysitter, as is usual. She wouldn't eat, wouldn't sleep, wouldn't do anything. Just cried and cried. I've never seen anything like it with her. I feel guilty leaving her behind like that. I'm considering working shorter hours, but I don't know how to arrange it."
>
> Laura's mom, 28th week

> "If my daughter even suspects I'll be setting her down on the floor to play, she starts to whine and cling with intense passion. So now, I carry her around on my hip all day long. She has also stopped smiling the way she used to. Just last week, she had a smile for everyone. Now it's definitely less. She's been through this once before, but in the past she'd always end up with a tiny grin on her face. Now, it's out of the question."
>
> Nina's mom, 29th week

> "This was a week of torment. So many tears. Five minutes on his own was already too much for my guy. If I so much as stepped out of the room, there'd be a crying fit. I've had him in the infant carrier a lot. But at bedtime, all hell would break loose. After 3 days, I was beat. It was too much. I started feeling extremely angry. It looked like it was starting to become a

vicious circle. I was really pushing myself, feeling lonely and completely exhausted. I kept breaking things, too—they would just drop from my hands. That's when I took him to the day care center for the first time. Just so I could catch my breath. But it didn't work out, so I quickly went to get him. I felt really bad about dumping him somewhere, while at the same time, I had given it a lot of thought and felt it was the best solution. I push myself too far too often, and it only makes me feel lonely, aggressive, and confined. I also keep wondering whether it's me, whether I'm to blame for being inconsistent or for spoiling him too much."

Bob's mom, 29th week

To ease your baby's anxiety, make sure she feels you near her in case she really needs you. Give her the opportunity to grow accustomed to the new situation at her own pace. You can help her by carrying her more often or staying a bit closer to her. Give her some warning before you walk away, and keep talking to her while you walk away and when you're in the other room. This way, she will learn that you are still there, even if she can't see you anymore. You can also practice "leaving" by playing peek-a-boo games. For example, you can hide behind a newspaper while sitting next to your baby, then you can hide behind the couch close to your baby, then behind the cupboard a little farther away, and finally behind the door.

If your baby is already a little mobile, you can reassure her on the question of desertion by helping her to follow you. Try first telling her you are leaving—this way, your baby will learn that she does not have to keep an eye on you, that she can continue to play at ease. Then slowly walk away, so that she can follow you. Always adjust your pace to your baby's. Soon, your baby will learn that she can control the distance between the two of you. She will also come to trust you not to disappear when you have to get something from another room, and she won't bother you as much.

"At first, my son used to cling to my leg like a monkey and ride on my shoe when I walked. I had to drag this 'ball and chain' around every-

where. After a few days, he started keeping a slight distance. I could take a few steps to the side before he'd crawl up to me. Now, I can go into the kitchen while he's crawling around. He won't actually come looking for me unless I stay there for a while."

                                                    Bob's mom, 31st week

Often, the desire to be near you is so strong that even the inexperienced crawler is willing to put in some extra effort and ends up improving her crawling. The desire to keep up with mommy, along with the coordination she's able to utilize at this point, might provide just the extra incentive she needs.

If your baby was already a little mobile after the last leap, you will see a big difference now. Her effortful journeys used to take her farther away from you, and she would stay away longer than she does now. Suddenly, she's circling you and making short dashes backward and forward, making contact with you each time.

"My baby keeps crawling back and forth. Then he'll sit under my chair for a while. He also stays nearer to me than he used to."

                                                    John's mom, 31st week

Offer your baby the chance to experiment with coming and going, with you as the center point. If you sit on the floor, you'll notice she will interrupt her excursions to crawl over you.

Over the weeks, parents grow more and more irritated if they don't get the opportunity to continue their everyday activities. Once their baby has reached 29 weeks, most mothers call it a day. They start to gradually break the old habit ("I am always here for you to cling to") and lay down a new rule ("I need some time and space to move as well"). They do so most times by distracting the babies, sometimes by ignoring their whines for a while, or by putting the babies to bed if they are really fed up with their behavior.

The Gender Gap

Are boys different from girls after all?

Mothers of boys sometimes seem to have a harder time with their babies than mothers of girls. They often don't understand their sons. Does he or doesn't he want to play with his mom?

"My son often whines for contact and attention. I always respond. But when I pick him up to play a game, it's obviously not what he had in mind. Then he'll spot something, and all of a sudden that's what he wants, and he reaches and whines to get at it. He seems to want two things—me and exploring. But he always makes a mess of these ad ventures. He'll grab something pretty roughly and hurl it aside. He likes to go through the entire house this way. I would have liked him to be a bit more cuddly. We could talk, play games—just do nice things together and have some fun. Whereas now, I'm constantly trying to prevent accidents from happening. Sometimes I feel dissatisfied myself."

Matt's mom, 32nd week

Mothers with both boys and girls usually find that they can do more with their girls. They feel they can better sense what a girl wants. They share more of the same interests, which they call sociable and fun.

"I'm able to play mother with my daughter more. We do all kinds of things together. When I talk, she really listens. She enjoys my games and asks for more. Her brother was much more his own man."

Eve's mom, 33rd week

Whatever you decide to do, take into consideration how much your baby can handle before she gets really afraid. Knowing that you can leave her whenever you choose can be very frightening for her and very difficult to deal with.

> "It's so annoying the way he keeps clinging to my legs when I'm trying to do the cooking. It's almost as if he chooses to be extra difficult because I am busy. So I put him to bed."
>
> Kevin's mom, 30th week

Help Your Baby Explore the New World through Roaming His Surroundings

If your baby loves to crawl, allow him to roam around freely in a room where he can do no harm. Watch him to see just what he does. When he enters the world of relationships, an early crawler begins to understand that he can crawl *into, out of, under, over, in between, on top of,* and *through* something. He will love to toy with these various relationships between himself and the objects in his surroundings.

> "I like to watch my son play in the living room. He crawls up to the couch, looks under it, sits down, quickly crawls over to the closet, crawls into it, rushes off again, crawls to the rug, lifts it up, looks under it, heads toward a chair that he crawls under, whoosh, he's off to another cupboard, crawls into that one, gets stuck, cries a little, figures out how to get out and closes the door."
>
> Steven's mom, 30th week

If your baby takes pleasure in doing these things, leave some objects around that will encourage him to continue his explorations. For instance, you can make hills for him to crawl over out of blankets, quilts, or pillows. Of course, you should adjust this soft play circuit to suit what your baby can do.

You can also build a tunnel from boxes or chairs that he can crawl through. You can make a tent out of a sheet, which he can crawl into, out of, and under. Many babies enjoy opening and closing doors. If your baby likes this, too, you can include a door or two. Just watch out for his fingers. If you crawl along with him, it will double the fun. Try adding some variety with peek-a-boo and hide-and-seek games, too.

If your baby enjoys moving his toys around, make this into a game. Give him the opportunity to put playthings *inside, on top of, next to,* or *under* objects. Allow him to throw his toys—it's important in getting to understand how the world works. Let him pull toys *through* something, such as the legs of a chair or a box made into a tunnel. To the outsider, it may seem as if he is flying like a whirlwind from one object to the next, but this frenzied activity is providing exactly the input his brain needs to understand this new world of relationships.

"My baby will lay her blocks, her pacifier, and her bear in a basket. When she's standing, she'll pick up toys from the floor and toss them on the chair. She also pushes things into her playpen through the bars. If she's actually in the playpen, she'll throw everything out over the top. She likes to watch what she's done. She's a real little rascal."

Jenny's mom, 30th week

Give your baby a shelf or cupboard of his own, which he can empty *out* and you can easily tidy up again. Give him a box he can put his things *in.* Turn a box upside down, so he can put things *on top of it.* Allow him to push things *out of* the playpen *through* the bars, or throw them out over the top. This is an ideal way for babies who aren't yet interested in crawling to explore relationships like *inside, outside, underneath,* and *on top of.*

Another way your baby can toy with relationships is by throwing, dropping and overturning objects. He may do so to see and hear what happens. Maybe he wants to find out just how a particular object breaks

into several pieces. You can watch him enjoy knocking over towers of blocks, which you have to keep building up again. But he will gain just as much pleasure from tipping over the wastepaper basket, overturning the cat's water bowl, dropping a glass of milk or a bowl of cereal from his high chair, or any other activity that is bound to make a mess.

"My daughter loves experimenting with the way things fall. She's been trying it with all kinds of things—her pacifier, her blocks, and her cup. Then, I gave her a feather from Big Bird, the parakeet. This took her by surprise. She prefers things that make a lot of noise!"

Nina's mom, 28th week

"Boy, did my son laugh when I dropped a plate, and it shattered into a million pieces. I've never seen him laugh so hard."

John's mom, 30th week

In the world of relationships your baby may discover that things can be *taken apart*. Give him some things that are designed for exactly that purpose—nesting cups and bright laces tied into bows. He will tug and pull at things that are attached to objects or toys, such as labels, stickers, eyes and noses of cuddly toys, and wheels, latches, and doors of toy cars.

 Baby Care

Make Your Home Baby-Proof

Remember that your baby can be fascinated by things that are harmful to him. He can stick a finger or tongue into anything with holes or slots, including things such as electrical outlets, electronic equipment, drains, and the dog's mouth. Or he can pick up and eat little things he finds on the floor. Always stay near your baby whenever you let him explore the house freely.

But take care: Buttons on clothing, switches and wires trailing from electrical equipment, and bottle caps are equally attractive and just as liable to be taken apart whenever possible. To your baby, there is no such thing as off limits in this new and exciting world.

"My son keeps pulling his socks off."

Frankie's mom, 31st week

If your baby dearly loves watching things disappear *into* something else, invite him to watch your activities. You may think cooking is ordinary, but to him it is magic to watch all the ingredients disappear *into* the same pot. But keep an eye on him, too, because he may look for disappearing acts of his own.

"My daughter likes to watch the dog emptying his bowl. The closer she can get, the better. It seems pretty dangerous to me, because with all that attention, the dog gulps it down faster and faster. On the other hand, the dog suddenly seems to be paying more attention to my daughter as well when she's eating. She'll be sitting at the table in her high chair, with the dog right next to her. So what do you know? It turned out she was dropping little pieces of bread and watching him wolf them down."

Laura's mom, 31st week

Sometimes babies like putting one thing *inside* another. But this happens only by coincidence. He can't yet distinguish between different shapes and sizes.

"My girl tries fitting all kinds of things together. A lot of the time, the size is right, but the shape never is. Also, she isn't accurate enough. But if it doesn't work, she gets mad."

Jenny's mom, 29th week

"My son discovered his nostrils. He stuck an inquisitive finger in one. I hope he doesn't try the same with a bead!"

John's mom, 32nd week

Is your baby intrigued by a toy with a squeak in it when he pushes, or a toy piano that produces a musical tone when he hits a key? Let him explore these things. They concern relationships between an action and an effect. But beware, he can also turn over a bottle filled with nail polish or perfume or some other dangerous substance.

"I held a toy bear upside down so that it growled. Then I put the bear on the floor, and my son crawled right over and rolled it around, until it made that sound. He was so fascinated that he kept turning the bear over and over, faster and faster."

Paul's mom, 33rd week

Help Your Baby Explore the New World through Using His Body

In your baby's body, relationships abound between the various body parts. Without the efforts of all the muscles the relationships between the various parts of the skeleton would be lost and we would collapse like a sack with bones. About this time, your baby may start to try to sit up by himself, depending on his balance skills.

"My son's learned to sit up now. He started out by balancing on one buttock with both hands flat on the floor in front of him. Then he lifted one hand. Now he can sit without using his hands at all."

> Matt's mom, 25th week

"Now my baby sits alone without any fear of losing her balance. She couldn't do that last week. She sometimes takes things, holds them over her head with both hands, and then throws them away."

> Jenny's mom, 28th week

"When my little one sits up, he often rolls over. He also topples forward or backward. Whenever that happens, I'm quick to laugh. Then he'll often start laughing, too."

> Bob's mom, 26th week

If your baby is not sitting steadily enough to feel confident on his own, help him. Try to find out if you can make him more confident by playing balancing games in which he has to regain his balance every time the wobble sets in. Look for favorite balancing games under "Top Games for This Wonder Week" on page 187.

Some babies try to stand up. If your baby does, how is his balance? Help your baby when he's not standing firmly, or if he's afraid of tumbling down. Play balancing games with him—these will make him familiar with his vertical position. But never try to hurry your baby toward sitting or standing. If you try too early for his liking, he may get afraid and you may even slow his development.

"We tried to put my son on his feet by the table. He stood there, very unstable, swaying like a puppet on a string, looking as if he was about to topple over. It's too soon for him."

> Steven's mom, 31st week

"My daughter is beginning to stand up, but she doesn't know how to sit back down. It's tiring. Today, I found her standing in her crib for the

first time, wailing. That irritates me. She's supposed to go to sleep when she's in bed. I just hope it doesn't take too long and that she works out how to sit back down sometime soon."

Juliette's mom, 31st week

"My baby insists on me sitting her back down after she's stood up. Her sister isn't allowed to help her, even though there are many things she will let her do. She's obviously scared that she won't be able to do it well enough."

Ashley's mom, 32nd week

"My baby kept trying to pull herself up this week, and at a certain point she succeeded. She had pulled herself up in bed, stood up right away, and stayed standing up, too. Now she can really do it. She pulls herself up using the bed, playpen, table, chair, or someone's legs. She also stands by the playpen and takes toys from it with one hand."

Jenny's mom, 28th week

If and only if you notice that your baby has great fun walking, give him a hand. Hold on to him tightly, because his balance is usually unstable. Play games with him that will familiarize him with keeping his balance, especially when he shifts his weight from one leg to the other. Never go on hour-long walks with him. He really won't learn any faster that way. Your baby won't start walking until he is ready to.

"When I hold both of my baby's hands, she walks in perfect balance. She crosses the small gap between the chair and the television when she's standing. She walks alongside the table, around the bends. She'll walk through the room pushing a Pampers box. Yesterday, the box slid away, and she took three steps by herself."

Jenny's mom, 34th week

"I'm irritated by my son's slow coordination. He doesn't crawl, he won't pull himself up. He just sits there and fiddles with his playthings."

Frankie's mom, 29th week

Remember that your baby has no motive for learning to walk or crawl just yet. Plenty of other activities will teach him things worth knowing. For him, these things are more important right now.

Babies who have entered the world of relationships can also begin to understand the connection between what their two hands are doing, and they can get better control over them. This way, they can cope with two things at once. If you see your baby trying to use both hands at the same time, encourage him to go on. Let him hold a toy in either hand and clash them together. Or let him make this clashing movement without toys, so that he claps his hands. Let him knock toys against the floor or the wall. Encourage him to pass toys from one hand to the other. And let him put two toys down at the same time, and pick them up again.

"My daughter has the hitting syndrome. She beats anything she can lay her hands on."

Jenny's mom, 29th week

First Steps

Once your baby has acquired the knack of perceiving and experimenting with relationships, she can understand what walking is, but understanding doesn't mean she will actually do it. To really start walking, she must choose to. And even if she does, she might not succeed because her body is not ready. Your baby won't learn how to walk at this age unless the proportions between the weight of her bones, her muscles, and the length of her limbs compared to her torso meet certain specifications. If your baby is occupied with something else—for instance, speech, sounds, and music—there may simply be no time left to spend on walking. She can't do everything at once.

If your baby tries to master the concerted action between two fingers —for instance his thumb and forefinger—again he is toying with relationships between the two. In the process he is also busy inventing a new tool, the pincer grip, that he can put to use immediately. He can learn how to pluck extremely small objects, such as threads, from the carpet. He can learn to pick blades of grass, or he may take pleasure in touching and stroking all kinds of surfaces with his finger. And he may have great fun examining every detail of very small objects.

"My baby goes through the entire room and spots the smallest irregularities or crumbs on the floor, picks them up between her thumb and her index finger, and sticks them in her mouth. I really have to pay attention so she doesn't eat anything peculiar. I let her eat small pieces of bread by herself now. At first, she kept sticking her thumb in her mouth instead of the bread she was holding between her fingers. But she's starting to improve now."

Hannah's mom, 32nd week

Help Your Baby Explore the New World through Language and Music

Babies who were extra sensitive to sounds and gestures in the past may start to grasp the connection between short sentences and their meaning or particular gestures and their meaning as soon as they have entered the world of relationships. In fact, they may even make the connection between words and gestures that go with them. But you will still find that these babies can understand these things only in their own surroundings and as a part of a familiar routine. If you were to play the same sentences from a tape recorder in a strange place, they wouldn't have a clue. That skill doesn't develop until much later.

If your baby likes playing with words and gestures, use this to his advantage. There are several things you can do to help your baby to understand what you're saying. Use short sentences with clear and obvious gestures. Explain the things you are doing. Let him see, feel, smell, and taste the things you are talking about. He understands more than you think.

"Once, I told my son to watch the rabbit, and he understood what I meant. He listens very closely."

Paul's mom, 26th week

"I get the feeling that my son knows what I mean when I explain something or make a suggestion, such as, 'Shall we go for a nice little walk?' or 'I think it's bedtime!' It's so cute—he doesn't like hearing the word 'bed'!"

Bob's mom, 30th week

"When we say, 'Clap your hands,' my daughter does. And when we say, 'Jump up and down,' she bends her knees and bounces up and down, but her feet don't leave the ground."

Jenny's mom, 32nd week

"When I say 'bye, say bye, bye' while waving at daddy who is leaving, my daughter waves while keeping a steady eye on my waving hand."

Nina's mom, 32nd week

Her First Word

Once your baby has gained the ability to perceive and experiment with relationships, she may discover her first word. It doesn't mean that she will start to talk, though. The age at which babies begin to use words differs greatly. So don't worry if she puts it off for a few more months. Most babies produce their first real word during the 10th or 11th month.

If your baby is obsessed with something else, such as crawling and standing, there may simply be no time left to spend on words. She can't do everything at once.

If your baby attempts to say or ask something with a sound or ges-tures, make sure you let him know that you are thrilled with his potential. Talk and signal back to him. The best way to teach your baby to talk is by talking to him a lot yourself. Call everyday items by their names. Ask questions, such as, "Would you like a sandwich?" when you put his plate down. Let him hear nursery rhymes, and play singing games with him. In short, make speech attractive.

"Whenever my son wants to do something, he'll put his hand on it and look at me. It's as if he's trying to ask, 'May I?' He also understands, 'no.' Of course, it doesn't stop him from trying, but he knows what it means."

Bob's mom, 32nd week

"Last week, my daughter said 'oo' (oops) for the first time when she fell. We also noticed that she was starting to copy sounds from us, so we've started teaching her to talk."

Jenny's mom, 29th week

"My daughter is a real chatterbox. She's especially talkative while crawl-ing, when she recognizes someone or something. She talks to her stuffed toys and to us when she's on our laps. It's as if she's telling entire stories. She uses all kinds of vowels and consonants. The variations seem end-less."

Hannah's mom, 29th week

"My son nods his head and makes a certain sound. If I imitate him, he starts giggling uncontrollably."

Paul's mom, 28th week

If your baby loves music, make sure you do a lot of singing, dancing, and clapping songs with him. This way, your baby can practice using words and gestures. If you don't know many children's songs, you can buy a music CD. Some public libraries lend these out, too.

"When we were singing at the baby swimming class, my baby suddenly started singing along."

Nina's mom, 30th week

"Whenever my daughter hears music or I start to sing, she immediately starts wiggling her tummy."

Eve's mom, 32nd week

Promoting Progress by Raising Expectations

Whatever new things your baby comprehends, you can demand from him nothing more, but also nothing less. Breaking old habits and setting new rules are also part of developing new skills. When your baby is busy learning new skills, he can be very irritating in the process. This is because old ways of doing things and established rules of behavior may no longer suit the baby's current progress. Both mother and baby have to renegotiate new rules to restore peace and harmony.

At first parents worry when their baby enters a new fussy phase. They get annoyed when they discover that nothing is wrong with their baby and, to the contrary, he is in fact ready to be more independent. It is then that they start demanding that their baby do the things they feel he is able to do. As a consequence, they promote progress.

"I've always rocked him to sleep while breastfeeding. But now it irritates me. I feel he's old enough to just go straight to bed. My husband likes putting him to bed, too, but that's out of the question now. And you never know, someday it might have to be done by someone else. I've started getting him used to going straight to bed once a day. But he's certainly putting up a fight."

Matt's mom, 31st week

(continued on page 190)

 Top Games for This Wonder Week

Here are some games and activities that work best for babies exploring the world of relationships. Whatever kind of game you choose, language can now begin to play a big part in your games.

PEEK-A-BOO AND HIDE-AND-SEEK GAMES

These are very popular games at this age. The variations are endless.

PEEK-A-BOO WITH A HANDKERCHIEF

Put a handkerchief over your head and see if your baby will pull it away. Ask "Where's mommy?" Your baby will know you're still there, because he can hear you. If he doesn't make any attempts to pull away the handkerchief, take his hand and pull it away together. Say "peek-a-boo" when you reappear.

VARIATIONS WITH PEEK-A-BOO

Cover your face with your hands and take them away, or pop up from behind a newspaper or book held between you and the baby. Babies also like it when you appear from behind a plant or under a table. After all, they can still see parts of you.

Or hide in a conspicuous place, such as behind a curtain. This way, she can follow the movements of the curtain. Make sure your baby sees you disappear. For example, announce that you're going to hide (for non-crawlers), or that she has to come look for you (for crawlers). If she didn't watch you or was distracted for a moment by something else, call her name. Try it sometime in the door opening too. This will teach her that leaving is followed by returning. Reward her every time she manages to find you. Lift her up high or cuddle her—whatever she likes best.

WHERE'S THE BABY?

A lot of babies discover they can hide themselves behind or under something. They usually start with a cloth or an item of clothing while being changed. Take advantage of any opportunity to develop a game that the baby has started. This way, he'll learn that he can take the lead.

HIDING TOYS

Try hiding toys under a blanket. Make sure you use something your baby likes or that she's attached to. Show her how and where you hide it. Make it easy for her the first time around. Make sure she can still see a tiny part of the toy.

HIDING TOYS IN THE BATHTUB

Use bath foam in the bathtub and allow your baby to play with it. Try hiding toys under the foam some time and invite him to look for them. If he can blow, try blowing at the foam. Or give him a straw and encourage him to blow through it.

TALKING GAMES

You can make talking attractive by talking to your baby frequently, by listening to him, by reading books together, and by playing whispering, singing, and word games.

LOOK AT PICTURE BOOKS TOGETHER

Take your baby on your lap—he usually likes that best. Let him choose a book to look at together. Call by name whatever your baby looks at. If it's a book with animals in it, mimic the sounds the animals make. Babies generally love hearing and making sounds like bark, moo, and quack. Let him turn the pages by himself, if he wants to.

(continued)

Top Games for This Wonder Week (cont.)

WHISPERING GAME

Most babies love it when sounds or words are whispered in their ears. Making little puffs of air that tickle his ear is interesting, too, perhaps because a baby can now understand what blowing is.

SONG AND MOVEMENT GAMES

These games can be used to encourage both singing and talking. They also exercise the baby's sense of balance.

GIDDY-UP, GIDDY-UP, LITTLE ROCKING HORSE

Take your baby on your knee, upright and facing you. Support him under his arms and jog him up and down gently, singing:

Giddy-up, giddy-up, little rocking horse
Giddy-up, giddy-up, little rocking horse
Giddy-up, giddy-up, little rocking horse
Ride away, away to Candy Land.

THIS IS THE WAY THE LADY RIDES

Take your baby on your knee, upright and facing you. Support her under her arms, and sing the following song:

This is the way the lady rides,
The lady rides,
The lady rides,
This is the way the lady rides,
So early in the morning.

(Sing slowly and solemnly, and jog her neatly up and down on your knee.)

This is the way the gentleman rides,
The gentleman rides,
The gentleman rides,

This is the way the gentleman rides,
So early in the morning.
(Sing faster, and jog her faster.)
This is the way the farmer rides,
The farmer rides,
The farmer rides,
This is the way the farmer rides,
So early in the morning.
(Sing wearily and jog her up, down, and sideways.)
CLIP CLOP CLIP CLOP
AND DOWN INTO THE DITCH!
("DOWN" comes as a surprise. Pull your knees apart and let
her "fall" between your knees.)

BALANCING GAMES

A lot of singing games, like those above, are also balancing
games. Here are some others.

SITTING GAME

Sit down comfortably. Take your baby on your knee. Hold his
hands, and move him gently from left to right, so that he shifts his
weight from buttock to buttock. Also try letting him lean forward
or backward carefully. Babies find the latter the most exciting.
You can also move him in small or large circles, to the left, backward, to the right, and forward. Adjust yourself to your baby.
The movement has to challenge him just enough to make him
want to find his balance himself. You can also let him swing like
a pendulum of a clock while you sing: *tick tock, tick tock* in time
with the movement.

(continued)

Top Games for This Wonder Week (cont.)

STANDING GAME

Kneel comfortably on the floor and let him stand in front of you while you hold his hips or hands and move him gently from left to right, so that he transfers his weight from one leg to the other. Do the same thing in a different plane so that his body weight shifts from back to front. Adjust yourself to your baby. It has to challenge him just enough to make him want to find his balance himself.

FLYING GAME

Grasp your baby firmly, lift her, and let her "fly" through the room. Let her rise and descend. Turn left and right. Fly in small circles, in a straight line, and backward. Vary the movement and speed as much as possible. If your baby enjoys this, then try letting her land carefully upside down, head first. Naturally, you'll accompany the entire flight with different zooming, humming, or screeching sounds. The more alert you can be to her reactions, the more easily you will be able to adjust this game so it's just right for her.

STANDING HIM ON HIS HEAD

Most physically active babies love horsing around and being stood on their heads. However, others find standing on their heads frightening or over-exciting. Play this game only if your baby likes playing rough. It's a healthy exercise for him. Remember to support his body completely as you hold him upside down.

GAMES WITH TOYS

For now, the best "toys" are all the things babies can find to get into around the house. The best games are emptying cupboards and shelves, dropping things, and throwing things away.

BABY'S OWN CUPBOARD GAME

Organize a cupboard for the baby and fill it with things that she finds super attractive. Usually this will include empty boxes, empty egg cartons, empty toilet paper rolls, plastic plates, and plastic bottles with lids and filled with something rattly. But also include things she can make a lot of noise with, such as a pan, wooden spoons, and an old set of keys.

FALLING GAME

Some babies like hearing a lot of noise when they drop something. If your baby does, you could make a game of it by putting him in his high chair and placing a metal serving tray on the floor. Hand him blocks, and show him how to let them go so that they fall on the tray and make a big bang.

OUTDOOR GAMES

Babies love riding in a baby seat on a bicycle, in a baby jogger, or in a baby backpack. Stop frequently to point out things along the way and talk to your baby about what she is seeing.

SWIMMING FOR BABIES Many babies love playing in the water. Some swimming pools have specially heated pools for small children and special hours when a group of babies can play games with parents in the water.

CHILDREN'S FARMS

A visit to a children's farm or duck pond can be extremely exciting for your baby. She can see the animals from her picture book. She'll enjoy looking at their wobbly, pattering, or leaping motions. And she'll particularly like feeding the animals and watching them eat.

Just like mothers get annoyed when their babies keep insisting on being rocked to sleep, so there are at least three other situations where you may feel the urge to make demands: mealtime aggravations, having to forbid things, and impatience.

At this age, many babies get fussy over food, while before they enjoyed whatever they grabbed from your mouth. In the world of relationships many babies come to realize that certain foods taste better than others. So why not pick the tastier one? Many mothers think it's funny at first. Soon, however, almost every mother becomes irritated when her baby gets fussy. She wonders whether the baby is getting enough nutrition. She tries to distract the fussy eater so she can stick the spoon in her mouth at an unsuspected moment. Or she runs after her the whole day with food.

Don't do it. Strong-willed babies will resist something that is being forced upon them even more. And a worried mother will in turn react to that. This way, meals become a battleground. Stop arguing. You cannot force a baby to swallow, so don't even try it. If you do, you might only increase his dislike of anything that has to do with food. Resort to different tactics and make use of other new skills your baby can learn now. He can try holding something between his thumb and forefinger now, but he still needs a lot of practice, so it's good for his coordination to feed himself. A baby this age also loves to make his own decisions, and the freedom to eat by himself will make eating more enjoyable. Use these new skills to his advantage. While he finger-feeds himself, he could be in a better mood to allow you to feed him as well. It can be messy, but encourage him anyway. Keep putting two pieces of food on his plate, so that he will keep himself occupied. Usually, it will be easy to feed him in between.

You can also make eating more pleasurable for your baby by feeding him in front of a mirror. This way, he can watch as you put a spoonful of food in his mouth or in your own. Don't worry if it doesn't work the first time. Many babies go through eating problems, and they also get over them.

Finally, certain eating habits are perceived as irritating by some mothers, while others find them perfectly normal.

"What really gets to me is that she wants to stick her thumb in her mouth after every bite. I won't allow it! Minor disagreement!"

Ashley's mom, 29th week

Now that the baby is in the middle of learning new skills, many mothers constantly find themselves having to forbid things. A crawling baby especially is liable to inspect all your possessions. After all, her pleasures are by no means the same as yours. So anything you can do to make life easier for both of you will be worthwhile. Try to prevent what you cannot allow and help her with the activities she is interested in. Above all, remember that you are not the only mother with this problem.

"I constantly have to forbid things. My daughter rampages from one thing to the next. Her favorite targets are the wine rack, the video, my needlepoint kit, cupboards, and shoes. Another one of her hobbies is knocking down plants, digging up plants, and eating cat food. I can't warn her enough. So sometimes, I slap her hand when I feel it's gone far enough."

Jenny's mom, 31st week

Top Toys for This Wonder Week

These are toys and things to play with that suit the new skills your baby is developing as he explores the world of relationships.

- His very own cupboard or shelf

- Doors (watch his fingers)

- Cardboard boxes in different sizes; also empty egg cartons

- Wooden spoons

- Round nesting or stacking cups

- Wooden blocks

- Balls (light enough to roll)

- Picture books

- Photo books

- CDs with children's songs

- Bath toys: things to fill and empty out, such as plastic bottles, plastic cups, a plastic colander, a funnel, a watering can

- Toy cars with rotating wheels and doors that can be opened

- Cuddly toys that make noise when turned upside down

- Squeaky toys

- Drums

- Toy pianos

- Toy telephones

It's important to put away or take precautions with electrical outlets, plugs, wires, keys, drains, stairs, bottles (such as perfume and nail polish and remover), tubes (such as toothpaste and antiseptics), stereo equipment, remote controls, television sets, plants, wastepaper baskets, trash cans, alarm clocks, and watches.

Your baby does not learn anything from a "correcting" slap on the hand. What is more important, hitting a baby is absolutely not acceptable, even when it is "only" a correcting slap on the hand. It is better to remove your baby from things he is not allowed to touch. And to clearly say "no" when he is doing something that is against your rules. After this leap, babies can be very impatient. This may have several reasons. They don't want to wait for their food. They get mad if a toy refuses to behave as they wish it would. Or if something is not allowed. Or if mommy doesn't pay attention to them quickly enough. Unfortunately, babies do have an idea of what it is they want to have or achieve, but they don't understand why their mommies don't allow it or why they can't have it in a flash. This frustrates them, so be understanding but see what you can do to stop the "I want it now" problem.

"My daughter's becoming very impatient. She wants to have it all, and she gets furious if she can't reach something and I tell her 'no.' Then she'll really start screaming. It irritates me and makes me think she's only doing it because I work. She's much sweeter with the babysitter."

Laura's mom, 31st week

"I put my baby to bed this past week because she was carrying on something awful and screaming during supper. She feels it isn't going fast enough, so she starts yelling, twisting, and wriggling after every bite. Once I got over my anger, about 5 minutes later, we continued. Both of us had calmed down by then."

Ashley's mom, 28th week

After the Leap

Between 30 and 35 weeks, another comparatively easy period begins. For anywhere from 1 to 3 weeks, the baby is admired for her cheerfulness, independence, and progress.

"My girl is becoming less and less shy. She laughs a lot. And she's good at keeping herself occupied. She has become very agile and active again. Actually, I started to see this change last week, but it seems to be progressing."

          Nina's mom, 33rd week

"Because she was so sweet, my baby seemed like a totally different child. She used to cry and whine a lot. The way she tells stories is also delightful. She's actually already like a little toddler, the way she trots through the room."

          Jenny's mom, 35th week

"My son was extremely cheerful, so it wasn't hard to have fun with him. It also pleases me to see him a little more active and lively in the physical sense. But he's at his best when he can observe people. He's very talkative, too, a great kid."

          Frankie's mom, 30th week

"My daughter's obviously gotten bigger and older. She reacts to everything we do. She watches everything. And she wants to have whatever we have. I'd almost say that she wants to be a part of it."

          Ashley's mom, 34th week

"Finally, some rest after a long period of constant changes. A wonderful week. He's gone through another change. He cries less, sleeps

more. I can see a certain pattern starting to develop again, for the umpteenth time. I talk to him much more. I've noticed myself explaining everything I do. When I go to prepare his bottle, I tell him. When it's time for him to go to bed, I tell him. I explain why he has to take a nap. And these talks seem to do me good. The day care center is going well now, too."

Bob's mom, 30th week

"We seem to have a different kind of contact now. It's as if the umbilical cord has finally been cut. The feeling of complete dependency is also gone. I'm quicker to rely on a babysitter. I also notice that I've been giving my son a lot more freedom. I don't have to be on top of him all the time."

Bob's mom, 31st week

"This was a really nice week. My baby is cheerful, and he can occupy himself pretty well on his own with his toys. Everything's still going fine at day care. He reacts in a friendly way to other children. He is a cute little guy, and he's much more his own little person."

Bob's mom, 32nd week

chapter 8

Wonder Week 37:
The World of Categories

Wonder Week 37: The World of Categories

At about 37 (or between 36 and 40) weeks, you may notice your baby attempting to do new things. At this age, a baby's explorations can often seem very methodical. For example, you may notice your little tyke picking up specks from the floor and examining them studiously between his thumb and forefinger. Or a budding little chef may rearrange the food on his plate by testing the way a banana squashes or spinach squishes through tiny fingers. He will assume the most serious, absorbed expression while carrying out these investigations. In fact, that is just what they are—investigations that will help the little researcher begin to categorize his world.

Your baby is now able to recognize that certain objects, sensations, animals, and people belong together in groups or categories. For example, a banana looks, feels, and tastes different than spinach, but they are both food. These are important distinctions and similarities to sort out. The leap into the world of categories will affect every sense—sight, hearing, smell, taste, and touch. Your baby will learn more about other people and his own emotions, too. Language skills will be developing. Your baby may not yet use words himself, but he will understand much more.

Like all of the previous worlds, the arrival of these new perceptions begins by turning your baby's world inside out. Babies' brain waves show drastic changes again around this time. These changes will begin to alter the way your baby perceives his world, which will be disturbing to him at first. You can expect a fussy period to begin around 34 weeks, or be-

Note: The first phase (fussy period) of this leap into the perceptual world of "categories" is age-linked and predictable, emerging at about 34 weeks. Most babies start the second phase (see box "Quality Time: An Unnatural Whim" on page 17) of this leap 37 weeks after full-term birth. The initial perception of the world of categories sets in motion the development of a whole range of global concepts such as "animal," for instance. However, the first categories are acquired through real-time, feedback-corrected, trial and error experience in comparing things and learning the within-category similarities and the between-category differences. Consequently, there may be a difference of many weeks or even months between two babies in mastering a particular concept. Skills and activities are mentioned in this chapter at the earliest possible age they might appear so you can watch for and recognize them. (They may be rudimentary at first.) This way you can respond to and facilitate your baby's development.

tween 32 and 37 weeks. This fussy period will often last for 4 weeks, but it may last anywhere from 3 to 6 weeks. As your baby enters this fussy phase, play close attention to see if he is attempting to master new skills.

As they prepare to leap into the world of categories, all babies will cry more easily than they did during the past few weeks. To their mothers, they may seem cranky, whiny, fidgety, grumpy, bad-tempered, discontented, unmanageable, restless, or impatient. All of this is very understandable.

Your little one is now under extra pressure because from her last leap she knows that you can go away from her whenever you please and leave her behind. At first, most babies were temporarily distressed by this discovery, but over the past few weeks they have learned to deal with it in their own ways. It all seemed to be going much more smoothly—and then the next big change came along and ruined everything. Now the little worrier wants to stay with her mommy again, while at the same time she realizes perfectly well that her mother can walk away whenever she chooses. This makes the baby feel even more insecure and increases her tension.

"These past few days, my daughter insists on sitting on my lap constantly. For no apparent reason, I might add. When I don't carry her around, she screams. When I take her for walks in her stroller, the moment she even thinks I've stopped, she demands to be lifted out."

Ashley's mom, 34th week

"My baby acts cranky and seems to be bored. She picks up everything and just tosses it away again."

Laura's mom, 35th week

"Everything's fine, as long as my little girl can sit on someone's lap. Otherwise, she whimpers and wails. I'm not used to this behavior from

her. She seems to grow bored quickly wherever she is—in the playpen, in her high chair, or on the floor."

Eve's mom, 34th week

A fussy baby will usually cry less when she is with her mother, especially when she has her mother all to herself.

"My son kept screaming and grumping and acting horribly. Everything was fine as long as I stayed with him or took him on my lap. I put him to bed several times when I got fed up with his demands."

Frankie's mom, 36th week

How You Know It's Time to Grow

Here are some giveaways that your little one is about to make another developmental leap.

She May Cling to Your Clothes

Your baby may become anxious when you walk around. Non-crawlers can do nothing but cry. For some, every step her mommy takes is reason for genuine panic. Crawling babies are able to follow their mothers, and sometimes they cling to them so tightly that they can hardly move.

"It was another difficult week with a lot of crying. My son literally clings to my skirt. When I leave the room, he starts crying and crawling after me. When I'm cooking, he'll crawl behind me, grab hold of my legs, and hold on in such a way that I can't move. He'll only play if I play with him. A few times, it just got to be too much. Putting him to bed is a struggle all over again. He falls asleep very late."

Bob's mom, 38th week

"At the moment, my daughter is a real little mommy's girl. As long as she can see me, everything's okay. Otherwise she howls."

Jenny's mom, 38th week

"I call my baby my little leech. She persists in holding on to my trousers. Once again, she wants to be around, with, and on me constantly."

Emily's mom, 36th week

She May Be Shy

Your baby may want to keep other people at a greater distance now than she usually does. The desire to be close to you may become even more apparent in the presence of other people—sometimes even when that other person is the father or a brother or sister. Often, mother is the only one allowed to look at her and talk to her. And she is almost always the only one allowed to touch her.

"My daughter is shyer with strangers again."

Hannah's mom, 34th week

"When strangers talk to my son or pick him up, he starts yelling, immediately."

Paul's mom, 34th week

"When visitors arrive, my son will race to me, climb on my lap, tummy-to-tummy, cling to me, and only then look to see who's here."

Kevin's mom, 34th week

"My girl's shy around strangers again. She becomes very frightened when someone wants to touch her or lift her up."

Emily's mom, 36th week

She May Tightly Hold On to You

When she is sitting on your lap or being carried, your baby may hold on to you as tightly as she can. She may even react furiously if you dare to put her down unexpectedly.

"My baby gets mad if I put her down even for a second. Then, when I lift her up again, she always pinches me. When our poor old dog happens to be within the reach of her hand, she'll pinch him even before I can lift her up."

Emily's mom, 35th week

"My son wants to be carried all of the time, and he clings to my neck or hair really tightly in the process."

Matt's mom, 36th week

"It's almost as if there's something about my baby's bed. I'll take her upstairs, sound asleep, and as soon as she feels the mattress, her eyes pop open. And boy, does she start screaming!"

Laura's mom, 33rd week

She May Demand Attention

Most babies start asking for more attention, and even easy ones are not always content at being left alone. Some demanding little persons are not satisfied until their mothers' attention is completely focused on them. Some may become super troublesome as soon as their mothers dare to shift their attention to someone or something else, as if they are jealous.

"When I'm talking to other people, my son always starts screaming really loudly for attention."

Paul's mom, 36th week

"My baby is having more difficulty staying in the playpen on his own. He's clearly starting to demand attention. He likes having us close."

Frankie's mom, 34th week

She May Sleep Poorly

Your baby may start sleeping less well. Most babies do. She may refuse to go to bed, fall asleep less easily, and wake up sooner. Some are especially hard to get to sleep during the day. Others at night. And some stay up longer both during the day and at night.

> "My son keeps waking up at night. Sometimes, he'll be up playing in his crib for an hour and a half at 3:00 A.M."
>
> Matt's mom, 33rd week

> "My daughter stays up late in the evenings and doesn't want to go to bed. She doesn't sleep much."
>
> Hannah's mom, 35th week

> "My baby cries herself to sleep."
>
> Juliette's mom, 33rd week

She May Have "Nightmares"

A fussy baby can also be a very restless sleeper. Sometimes, she may yell, toss, and turn so much that you think she is having a nightmare.

> "My son wakes up often during the night. One time, he seemed to be dreaming."
>
> Paul's mom, 37th week

> "My daughter keeps waking up in the middle of the night screaming. When I lift her from her crib, she quiets down again. Then, I put her back, and she'll go back to sleep."
>
> Emily's mom, 35th week

She May Act Unusually Sweet

At this age, your baby may employ entirely new tactics to stay close to you. Instead of whining and complaining, she may opt for something entirely different and kiss and cuddle up to you. Often, she will switch back and forth between troublesome and sweet behavior, trying out what works best to get the most attention. A mother of an independent baby is often pleasantly surprised when her baby finally starts cuddling up to her!

"Sometimes, my baby didn't want anything. At other times, she became very cuddly."

Ashley's mom, 36th week

"My son is more affectionate than he's ever been. Whenever I get near him, he grabs and hugs me tightly. My neck is full of red blotches from nuzzling and snuggling. He's also not as quick to push me away any more. Sometimes, he'll sit still so I can read a book with him. I love it! He finally wants to play with me, too."

Matt's mom, 35th week

"My baby expresses his clinginess by acting sweeter and more affectionate, coming to lie down with me and snuggling up against me. I enjoy being with him."

Steven's mom, 36th week

She May Be Listless

Your baby may become altogether more quiet. You may hear her babbling less often, or you may see her moving around and playing less. At other times, she might briefly stop doing anything and just lie there, gazing into the distance. Don't worry, it is only temporary.

"My son's quieter and often lies there staring into nothingness. I wonder if something's bothering him or he's starting to get sick."

Steven's mom, 36th week

She May Refuse to Have Her Diaper Changed

When you set your baby down to be dressed, undressed, or changed, she may protest, scream, wriggle, act impatient, and be unmanageable. Most babies do now.

 My Diary

Signs My Baby Is Growing Again

Between 32 and 37 weeks, you may notice your baby starting to show any of these behaviors. They may be signs that he is ready to make the next leap. Check off the signs that your baby shows below.

❑ Cries more often and is frequently bad-tempered or cranky

❑ Is cheerful one moment and cries the next

❑ Wants you to keep him busy, or does so more often than before

❑ Clings to your clothes, or clings more often than before

❑ Acts unusually sweet

❑ Throws temper tantrums, or does so more often than before

❑ Is more shy

❑ Wants physical contact to be tighter or closer

❑ Sleeps poorly

❑ Seems to have nightmares, or does so more often than before

❑ Loses appetite

❑ Babbles less

❑ Is less lively

❑ Sometimes just sits there, quietly daydreaming

❑ Refuses to have diaper changed

❑ Sucks his thumb, or does so more often than before

❑ Reaches for a cuddly toy, or does so more often than before

❑ Is more babyish

OTHER CHANGES YOU NOTICE

_____

_____

"Dressing, undressing, and changing diapers is a nightmare. My baby screams the moment I put her down. It drives me crazy."

Juliette's mom, 35th week

"My daughter has started to hate getting dressed and undressed. She usually carries on like there's no tomorrow."

Emily's mom, 36th week

She May Seem More Babyish

For the first time, some mothers will notice the recurrence of infantile behavior that they thought had been left behind. Setbacks have probably been experienced before, but the older the baby gets, the more obvious they become. Mothers dislike seeing setbacks. It makes them feel insecure, but they really are perfectly normal. They promise you that something new is on the verge of breaking through. Try to find out what it is. Brief setbacks may happen during every fussy phase. Be happy with them; your baby is doing well.

"My baby has difficulty falling asleep. She starts crying the same sort of cries as she did when she'd just been born."

Juliette's mom, 32nd week

"I have to rock and sing my son to sleep again every night, just like I used to."

Steven's mom, 35th week

She May Lose Her Appetite

Many babies seem less interested in food and drink at this time. Some seem to have no appetite and may dig in their heels and refuse some meals altogether. Others will only eat what they put into their mouths themselves. Others still are picky, spill things, and spit things out. Because of this, mealtimes may take longer than they used to.

If you have a fussy eater, she may also be unmanageable during meals, not wanting to eat when her food is there and wanting it as soon as it has been taken away. Or she may demand a lot of food one day and refuse to eat the next. Every variety is possible.

"My son refused my breast for 3 days. It was terrible. I felt like I was going to explode. Then, just when I decided it might be time to start cutting down on breastfeeding because it was getting to be that T-shirt time of year again, he decided he wanted to nurse all day long. So then I was afraid I might not have enough because he wasn't eating anything else anymore. But it seems to be working out okay. So far, I haven't heard him complain."

Matt's mom, 34th week

How This Leap May Affect You

Like the leaps that preceded it, the changes that your baby is going through will inevitably affect you. Here are some emotions you may encounter.

You May Feel Insecure

A fussy baby usually makes a mother worry. She wants to understand what is making her behave this way, and when she believes she has found a good explanation, it puts her mind at ease. At this age, most mothers decide it must be teething pain, but this may not be the case.

"My daughter's top teeth are bothering her. She keeps wanting me to do things with her, such as go for walks or play with her."

Eve's mom, 34th week

(She did not cut her next tooth until the 42nd week.)

You May Be Exhausted

If you have a demanding little tyke who needs little sleep, you may feel extremely tired, especially toward the end of the fussy phase. Most mothers of demanding babies get very exhausted. They may think that they can't go on much longer. Some also complain of headaches, backaches, and nausea.

"It makes me feel so discouraged at times when my little one stays up until midnight, even if she keeps playing happily. When she's finally asleep, I completely collapse. I feel drained and unable to think straight. My husband gives me no support whatsoever. He's even angry that I pay so much attention to her. His philosophy is 'just let her cry.'"

> Nina's mom, 37th week

"The days seem to linger on forever when my son's cranky, cries, and sulks a lot."

> Bob's mom, 35th week

You May Become Aggravated

Almost all mothers become increasingly irritated by their babies' behavior during fussy periods. They become more and more annoyed by bad tempers, impatience, crying, whining, and constant demands for physical contact or attention. They are aggravated by constant clinging, the trouble they have to go through to change or dress their babies, and finicky eating habits.

"When my baby was having another one of her moods, not wanting anything and being terribly restless, I put her to bed. I am dog tired of it and terribly annoyed."

> Jenny's mom, 37th week

"While I was getting my daughter dressed, her whining really got to me, and I put her down very roughly. I just couldn't stand her whining and wriggling anymore. She'd been whimpering all day."

> Juliette's mom, 35th week

"When my son became so unmanageable during changing, I put him on the floor in his room and left him there. That made him stop immediately. A few moments later, he came to get me, with a howl. Then he was willing to be a bit more cooperative."

> Kevin's mom, 37th week

"This week, I got angry with my baby once. He'd been screaming so relentlessly that I suddenly shouted out angrily, 'Now shut up!' That frightened him out of his wits. First he looked at me with big, round eyes, then his head drooped, as if he was genuinely ashamed of his behavior. It was such a touching sight. After that, he became a lot calmer."

> Paul's mom, 37th week

"I've decided to let my son breastfeed only twice a day. I'm fed up with his fickleness. One day, he wants it all, the next he wants nothing. At home, I don't lull him to sleep at my breast anymore either. That seems to be working out fine. But when we're at someone else's house, I still do it."

> Matt's mom, 37th week

You May Quarrel

Toward the end of every fussy period, most mothers who breastfeed consider stopping. The baby's fickle behavior, sometimes wanting to nurse, sometimes not, irritates them. And the demanding fashion in which a little one continuously tries to get his way is another reason mothers think seriously about giving up breastfeeding.

"My son wants my breast whenever it suits him. And he wants it immediately. If it happens to be in some way inconvenient for me, he'll throw a raging temper tantrum. I'm afraid those tantrums are starting to turn into a habit and that pretty soon he'll try getting his way every single time by kicking and screaming. So I'm stopping right now, I think."

> Steven's mom, 36th week

Quarrels can also develop when mothers and babies fail to negotiate the amount of physical contact and attention the little person wants and her mommy is willing to give.

> "I keep getting more and more annoyed by my baby's clinging and whining. When we go to visit friends, he'll hardly let go of me. It makes me feel like just pushing him away from me, and sometimes I do. But that only makes him angrier at me."
>
> Kevin's mom, 37th week

It's just part of life. Having feelings of anger and frustration at times is not abnormal or dangerous, but acting on them is. It's critical that you get help long before you lose control.

How Your Baby's New Skills Emerge

When your baby is approximately 37 weeks, you will notice her becoming calmer. If you watch closely, you may see her trying or doing new things.

For example, you may see her handling her toys in a different way, enjoying new things, or behaving in a more concentrated and inquisitive way. Congratulations! Your baby is making another leap. She is beginning to explore the world of categories.

> "I noticed a big change. My son's toys are lying somewhere in a corner. They have been for some weeks now. I think that I need to supply him with more stimulating toys that will challenge him. But outside, he's very lively because there's plenty to see."
>
> Bob's mom, 36th week

After the last leap, your baby started to understand relationships between different things he came across, both in the outside world and as they relate to his own body. He became more familiar with every aspect of his world. He discovered that he is the same kind of being as his mommy and that he could move in exactly the same way she does. He learned that other things can move as well, but that they move in very different ways from human beings, and that still other things cannot move at all on their own.

Once your baby acquires the ability to perceive and experiment with categories, he begins to understand that he can classify his world into groups. It will dawn on him that certain things are very much alike, that they look similar, or they make a similar sound, or they taste, smell, or feel the same. In short, he discovers that different things can share the same traits.

For instance, he can now discover the meaning of the word "horse." He can learn that every horse falls into this category, whether it is brown, white, or spotted; whether the horse is out in a field, in a stable, in a photograph, in a painting, or in a picture book; whether it is a clay horse or a live horse. It is still a horse.

Naturally, this new understanding will not happen overnight. He must first get to know people, animals, and objects well. He has to realize that things must possess certain similarities in order to belong to a certain category. Therefore, he has to be able to spot these similarities, and this takes practice and time. When your baby acquires the ability to perceive categories, he will start experimenting with them. He will start to study people, animals, and objects in a particular way. He will observe, compare, and arrange them according to similarities, and then place them in specific categories. Your baby's comprehension of a category is the result of a lot of research that he conducts much as a real researcher would.

More Like One of Us

The use of different categories in our speech is indicative of our way of thinking. Now your baby will be able to start understanding and using this way of thinking as well. This will make it easier for you and your baby to understand one another from now on.

He observes, listens to, feels, tastes, and experiments with both similarities and differences. Your baby works hard at his investigations.

Later on, when your child starts talking, you will see that he has already discovered many of the categories we use and sometimes will have made up his own names for them. For instance: he may call a garage a "car house," an apartment building a "block house," or a fern a "feather plant." The names he uses refer directly to whatever trait he found most characteristic.

As soon as your baby acquires the ability to divide his world into categories, he can start doing just that. He not only examines what makes something a *horse, dog,* or *bear,* but also what makes something *big, small, heavy, light, round, soft,* or *sticky,* as well as what makes something *sad, happy, sweet,* or *naughty.*

Games played during research with babies clearly show that from this age on, babies' reactions take on a different quality. Some researchers believe that intelligence makes its first appearance at this age. At first look, it might seem that way, but it does not follow that babies never had any thoughts prior to this age. In fact, they have had their own way of thinking that perfectly suited each stage of their development. Unfortunately, these ways are lost to adults, and we can only imagine what they might be like. When the baby begins to classify the world in groups as we do, though, his way of thinking becomes more like an adult's. Because he starts to think in the same way we do, we are able to understand him better.

This ability to perceive and experiment with categories affects everything a baby does. His way of experiencing things has changed, and it is now time to make sense of it.

Your Baby's Choices: A Key to His Personality

A new world, full of possibilities, is open to your baby in the world of categories. Between the ages of 37 and 42 weeks, your baby will make his own selection from the wide array of things available for him to experiment with. He will choose whatever suits him best at this stage in his development and his interests. You may find him building on certain strong inclinations he showed previously, or he may launch out into new territory at this point. There's a very big world out there for him to explore, and it's important not to compare your baby too closely to other babies. Every baby is unique.

Watch your baby closely as you check off the skills he selects from the list "How My Baby Explores the New World of Categories" on page 226. You will learn where his interests lie and what makes him unique. Respect his choices, and help him explore the things that interest him.

Babies love anything new and it is important that you respond when you notice any new skills or interests. He will enjoy it if you share these new discoveries, and his learning will progress more quickly.

 Brain Changes

> Your baby's brain waves will show dramatic changes again at approximately 8 months. In addition, the baby's head circumference increases, and the glucose metabolism in the brain changes at this age.

(continued on page 216)

 My Diary

How My Baby Explores the New World of Categories

Don't be alarmed if many of these activities don't show up until much later. What your baby is really learning in this world is the concept of categories, and once she has got a grasp of this through learning one skill, it will sooner or later be carried forward into other skills. The golden rule is "help, don't push."

RECOGNIZING ANIMALS AND OBJECTS

❑ Shows that she can recognize a category, such as animals, in pictures, toys, and real life

❑ Shows that she distinguishes shapes

❑ Shows that she thinks something is dirty, for instance by wrinkling her nose

❑ Shows that she thinks something is fun or good by making a characteristic sound or movement

❑ Understands names of animals or objects, such as toothbrush, sock, bread stick, cat, lamb, or duck. When you ask, "Where's . . . ?" she will look for it. When you say, "Get your . . . " she will sometimes get it

❑ Repeats words after you now and then

❑ Compares things seen directly and through a screen, for instance through a sieve, the mesh of a screen door, or glass

RECOGNIZING PEOPLE AS PEOPLE

❑ Relates more to other people with sounds and gestures

❑ Imitates other people more often; mimics what they do

❑ Clearly wants to play games with other people more often

❑ Calls family members. Each has his or her own sound

RECOGNIZING PEOPLE IN DIFFERENT CIRCUMSTANCES

❑ Recognizes people, even in unrelated situations

❑ Makes silly faces at his mirror image and laughs

❑ Looks at a thing or person in the room and then tries to find the same thing or person in the mirror

RECOGNIZING EMOTIONS

❑ Becomes jealous for the first time when another child is receiving mother's attention

❑ Comforts a cuddly toy when dropped or thrown

❑ Acts extra sweet when she wants something

❑ Exaggerates her mood to let everyone know how she is feeling

❑ Starts to cry when another child is crying

SWITCHING ROLES

❑ Can initiate a game by himself

❑ Plays peek-a-boo with a younger baby

❑ Uses the bottle to feed mother

❑ Asks mother to sing a song, then starts clapping his hands

❑ Asks to play hide-and-seek by crawling behind something

❑ Asks you to build blocks by handing you his blocks

OTHER CHANGES YOU NOTICE

_____

_____

what You Can Do to Help

Your baby needs time and help to come to understand why something does or does not fall into a certain category. You can help her with this by giving her the opportunity and the time to experiment and play in such a way that she will learn why something belongs to a certain category. You can encourage and console her when necessary and present her with new ideas.

Give your baby the opportunity to expand her understanding of categories. It makes no difference which categories she explores first. Once she gets the idea about one or two categories, it will become easier for her to apply this understanding to other categories later on. Some little ones will prefer to start out with recognizing objects, while others will begin with recognizing people. Let your baby be your guide. After all, it is impossible for her to learn everything at once.

Help Your Baby Explore the New World through Investigation

When your baby starts experimenting with categories, you will notice that she is actually busy examining an entire range of characteristics and comparing them. She is using relationships to work out what categories are about. By doing this, she will learn the most important characteristics of whatever she is examining. She will find out whether or not something bounces back, whether it is heavy or light, how it feels to the touch, and so on. She will examine something from all sides, hold it upside down or hold her head sideways, move it around quickly and slowly. This is the only way for her to find out: "This is a ball, that isn't" or "This block is round, the other one isn't."

Some babies are particularly interested in different shapes, such as *round*, *square*, and *notched* shapes. They look at the shape and trace its perimeter with one little finger. Then they do the same with a different shape. They are comparing shapes, so to speak. With blocks, they usually pick out round ones first, which shows they are able to recognize them. If your baby seems fascinated by shapes, give her a set of blocks with all sorts of different shapes.

You may also see that your baby will find plenty of things in the house that have shapes that interest her. Have you ever noticed how your baby looks at things that are at a distance and attract her attention? She usually does this while moving her head from left to right. She does this to learn that even when she moves around, things stay the same size and shape. Find out what your baby likes to explore and how she wants to do it. Offer her the opportunities she needs.

> "My son tries to catch the running water in the tub when the tap is on. Apparently he thinks it's something he can grab. He'll close his hand around the water, and then when he opens it there's nothing in it. He finds this most peculiar. But he can keep it up for some time."
>
> Paul's mom, 43rd week

Many babies like to examine the different components of things. By exploring an object this way, she will eventually find out how that object is assembled and to what category it belongs. If your baby is such a scientist, she may suck successively on different sides of an object, for instance, or press on the top, in the middle, and on the bottom of something. But her explorations can have surprising side-effects.

> "My baby's crazy about knobs. This week, he explored every nook and cranny on the vacuum cleaner. He touched the knobs as well. Accidentally, he pushed the right button and whoosh, the vacuum switched on. It scared the living daylights out of him."
>
> Bob's mom, 38th week

Some babies love touching things with their hands to find out how they feel. This way they test for categories such as *firmness, stickiness, roughness, warmth, slipperiness*, and so on. Allow your baby to explore.

The Advantages of Demolishing

If your baby is examining the different components of things, he often ends up by taking something apart bit by bit. If your baby starts to demolish, give him playthings he can explore in this way. Stack some blocks for him so that he can remove them one by one. Show him how to do it. You can do the same with dough-nut rings of different sizes that stack on a rod. Also try giving him a pile of magazines, which he can move one by one. See what other games your baby invents by himself and support him if it is not dangerous or too costly. You may also show how you take things apart yourself. This experience is very important, because after the next leap he can use this knowledge to his advantage when he starts to assemble instead of demolish.

"My son likes to fiddle with locks on cabinets and doors. Even if the key's been turned a quarter of the way, he still manages to get it out."

John's mom, 37th week

"My son's playing is much more concentrated now. Sometimes, he'll even examine two things at the same time. For instance, he will take his time to mash a piece of banana with one hand, and crush a piece of apple with the other. Meanwhile, he'll look from one hand to the other."

Frankie's mom, 42nd week

"My baby examines sand, water, pebbles, and sugar by putting some in his fist and feeling it for a very long time. Then he'll put it in his mouth."

Bob's mom, 40th week

Sometimes, a baby loves rubbing other parts of her body against objects, or she will pick something up and run it past her body. This way, the baby will become even more familiar with whatever she is examining, so give her this opportunity.

"I put a swing up for my son in a doorway. There's a knot under the seat, and that's his favorite part. He'll sit under the swing and hold on to the doorpost, so that he can raise himself a little when the knot swings past his head and touches his hair. He'll just sit there, experiencing the feeling of it."

Bob's mom, 39th week

In the world of categories some babies like to experiment with handling people, animals, and objects *roughly* and *carefully*. If you see yours doing this, let her know that certain things hurt and objects can break. If she experiments like this, she knows perfectly well what she is doing.

"My son often bites me and sometimes handles his toys and other things very roughly. And yet, at times he can also be careful in an exaggerated way. He'll stroke flowers and ants with one little finger, only to squash them seconds later. Then, when I say 'shh, careful' he'll start touching with one little finger again."

Bob's mom, 40th week

Wonder Week 37: The World of Categories

"When we were in the bath, my son started to examine my nipple very carefully, with one little finger, only to continue pushing, pulling, and poking it around. His own penis was next. He was a bit more careful with that!"

Matt's mom, 41st week

"First, my baby examines my eyes, ears, and nose with her little index finger. Then she tickles them. Then, as she gets more and more excited, she gets rougher, pushing and poking at my eyes, pulling at my ears and nose, and sticking a finger up my nostril."

Nina's mom, 39th week

Some babies compare the weights of playthings and other objects. If yours is discovering the categories *heavy* and *light*, give her the opportunity to experiment.

"My baby lifts everything she walks past up for a moment."

Jenny's mom, 41st week

Usually, your baby studies the concepts *high* and *low, little* and *large* through crawling, climbing, standing, or walking. She will climb onto, over, and under everything. She will do this sedately, in a controlled manner, almost as if she is planning out how to do things.

"My son tries to crawl under and through everything. He looks for a while, then off he goes. Yesterday, he got stuck under the bottom step of the stairs. We all panicked!"

John's mom, 40th week

Give an Active Baby Room to Investigate

From this age on, it usually becomes more and more important to give a mobile baby enough room in order to give him ample opportunity to investigate all sorts of categories. An already physically active baby may now become more dexterous and stable while sitting, standing, crawling, and walking. As a result, he will be able to do much more with his body. He can choose to squat, crawl, or climb up onto furniture or stand on his toes when he wants to reach something. Allow him to crawl through your home, climb onto things, and hoist himself up on the most impossible ledges. Secure the safety gates by the stairs on the second or third step, and allow him to practice going up and down stairs. Place a mattress at the bottom of the stairs, so that he can not hurt himself.

> "My son clambers up everything. He even tried to scale the smooth surface of a wall."
>
> John's mom, 42nd week

> "My little girl was sitting in her high chair at the table, and before I knew it, she had climbed onto the table. I guess I need eyes in the back of my head now."
>
> Emily's mom, 42nd week

Your little crawler can learn a lot outside as well. Give him room there, too. For instance, walk with him in the woods, at the beach, at a lake, in the sandbox, and in the park. Just as long as you do not lose sight of him.

 Baby Care

Make His Surroundings Baby-Proof

Make sure that the space your baby is exploring is safe. But nevertheless, do not take your eyes off him for a single second. He will always manage to find something that can be dangerous that you might not have thought of.

(continued on page 226)

Top Games for This Wonder Week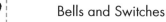

Here are games and activities that most babies like best now and that will help them practice their newly developing skills.

EXPLORING

Some things will seem absolutely fascinating to your baby, but venturing out on his own voyage of discovery may be dangerous or impossible. So help him. You can help him handle breakable picture frames or heavy figurines, for instance, so that he won't break them or hurt himself but will satisfy his curiosity.

Bells and Switches

Allow your baby to ring a doorbell. He will be able to hear right away what he is doing. You could let him press a button in the elevator as well. This way, he will feel he's doing something grown-up. Allow him to turn on the light when it is very dark, so that he can see what the effect is. Let him push the button in the bus sometimes, or at a pedestrian crossing, and explain to him what is happening that he should look for. This will teach him something about the relationship between what he is doing and what happens next.

Outdoor Exploration

At this age, most babies can not get enough of being outdoors. Taking your baby outdoors will teach him a lot as well. He will see new things. Whether you're bike riding, walking, stroller jogging, or backpacking, be sure to stop now and then to allow your baby to look closer at, listen to, and touch things.

Dressing

Many babies seem to have no time for dressing and grooming. They are far too busy with other things. But they love to look at themselves and are even more interested when something is being done to them. Use this to its advantage. Towel your baby off, dress, and undress him in front of a mirror so that he can play a sort of peek-a-boo game with himself at the same time.

WORDS

Your baby often understands a lot more than you think, and he loves being able to demonstrate this. He will now start to expand the range of words and phrases he understands with pleasure.

Naming

Name the things your baby looks at or listens to. When your baby expresses with gestures what he wants, translate his question for him by putting it into words. This will teach him that he can use words to express himself.

Let your baby choose a book and hand it to him. Take him on your lap or seat him close beside you. This way he can turn the pages by himself. Point to the picture he is looking at and name the object. You can also make the appropriate sounds for the particular animal or object you are pointing to. Encourage your baby to make that word or sound as well. Don't try to continue if your baby loses interest. Some babies need a momentary cuddle or tickle after each page to keep their attention focused.

Tasks

Ask your baby if he will give you whatever he is holding by saying, for instance, "Give it to Mommy." Ask him to give it to Daddy as well sometime. You can also ask him to get something for you—for instance, "Pass me the toothbrush," and "Get me the ball." Also try calling him sometime when you are out of sight:

(continued)

 Top Games for This Wonder Week (cont.)

"Where are you?" and have him answer. Or ask him to come to you, "Come over here." Praise him if he participates, and continue only as long as your baby still enjoys it.

COPYCAT

Many babies study other people with great interest and love imitating what they see other people do. If your baby does this as well, mimic him and encourage him to mimic you.

Do This

First, challenge your baby to imitate whatever you are doing, then imitate him again. Often he will be able to go on forever, taking turns doing the same thing over and over. Try alternating your gestures as well. Make the gestures a little faster or slower. Try making them with the other hand, or with two hands. Try making them with sound or without, and so on. Try doing this game in front of a mirror as well. Some babies love repeating gestures in front of a mirror while watching themselves to see how everything is done.

Talking to the Mirror

If your baby is interested in the positions of the mouth, try practicing them sometime in front of a mirror. Turn it into a game. Sit down in front of the mirror together and toy with vowels, consonants or words, whatever your baby likes best. Give him time to watch and copy. Many babies love watching themselves imitating gestures as well, such as movements of hand and head. Try this sometime, too. If your baby can see himself while he is imitating you, he will immediately be able to see whether he is doing it just like you.

Pat a Cake

Sing *Pat a cake, pat a cake, baker's man*, and let your baby feel every move that goes with the song. In order to do this, take his hands in yours and make the movements together. Sometimes babies will imitate the clapping of their own accord. Or they will raise their hands. They are still unable to imitate all the movements in sequence at this age, but they are able to enjoy them.

ROLE SWITCHING

Encourage your baby to take up a role he has seen you or an older child perform. Then try to switch roles.

Chase

You can consider this the first game of tag. It can be played crawling or walking. Try turning the game around sometime as well—crawl or walk away, and clearly indicate that you expect he will come after you. Try to escape if your baby makes attempts at catching you. If your baby does catch you, or you have caught him, then cuddle him or raise him up high in the air.

Hide-and-Seek

Hide yourself in such a way that your baby sees you disappear, then let him look for you. Also try pretending sometime that you have lost him and are looking for him. Sometimes babies are quick to hide and will stay behind their beds or hide in corners very quietly. Usually, they will pick the spot you were just hiding in or one that was a smash hit the day before. React with enthusiasm when you have found each other.

Help Your Baby Explore the New World through Play-acting

If your baby is very bright socially, she will be able to pretend that she is *sad, sweet,* or *distressed* from this point on. Such emotional states are categories, too. This means that she can start manipulating or taking advantage of you. Usually, mothers fall for this at first. Some simply refuse to believe that their children, still only babies, could be capable of doing anything like this deliberately. Others are secretly a little proud. If you see your little one is putting on an act, allow her to have a taste at success, if possible. But at the same time, let her know that you know what she is doing. This will teach her that the use of emotions is important, but that she can not use them to manipulate you.

"During the day, my girl is very troublesome, really pesky, but when it's time for her to go to bed in the evening, she plays like a little angel. It's as if she thinks, 'As long as I behave myself, I don't have to go to bed.' It's useless, anyway, trying to put her to bed when she isn't tired yet, because she'll refuse to stay lying down. Last Friday, she went to bed at 11:30 P.M."

$\qquad$ **Jenny's mom, 37th week**

"If I'm talking with someone, my son will suddenly need instant help, or he'll pretend that he injured himself on something."

$\qquad$ **Matt's mom, 39th week**

Sometimes a baby will take up a role she has seen her mother or an older child perform. This is possible now because she knows that she is a person, the same way other people are. In other words, both she and other people belong to the same category. As a result she is able to do the same things that other people can do. She can hide, just as her mother used to, and make her the seeker. She can go get her own toys when she feels like playing with them. Always respond to this, even if only for a short while.

This will teach her that she is making herself understood and that she is important.

Top Toys for This Wonder Week

Here are toys and things that most babies like best as they explore the world of categories.

- Anything that opens and closes like doors and drawers
- Pans with lids
- Doorbells, bus bells, elevator buttons, traffic light buttons
- Alarm clocks
- Magazines and newspapers to tear
- Plastic plates and cups with plastic silverware
- Things that are larger than he is, such as boxes or buckets
- Cushions and duvets to crawl over and under
- Containers, especially round ones, pots, and bottles
- Anything that he is able to move, such as handles or knobs
- Anything that moves by itself, such as shadows or branches
- Balls of all sizes, from ping-pong balls to large beach balls
- Dolls with realistic faces
- Blocks in all shapes and sizes, the larger the better
- Baby pools
- Sand, water, pebbles, and plastic tools
- Swings
- Picture books with one or two large, distinct pictures per page
- Posters with several distinct pictures
- Toy cars

But beware of other things they are attracted to like: electrical plugs and switches, washing machines, dishwashers, vacuum cleaners, hair dryers, other appliances and stairs.

"This week, another child a little older than my son visited our home. My son and the other little girl each had a bottle. At a certain point, the little girl stuck her bottle in my baby's mouth and started feeding him. She kept holding the bottle herself. The next day, I had him on my lap and was giving him a bottle. Suddenly, he took the bottle and stuck it in my mouth, then started laughing, drank some himself, then stuck it back in my mouth. I was amazed. He'd never done anything like that before."

Paul's mom, 41st week

The Importance of Consistency

Mothers are always proud of their babies' progress and accomplishments, and they automatically react with excitement and surprise. But some of those accomplishments can be mischievous. At first, a mischievous accomplishment may be amusing and your baby may take your delight or surprise as approval. She thinks she is being funny and will repeat the behavior time after time, even when mother tells her "no."

You will now need to be more consistent with your baby. When you disallow something once, it is better not to condone it the next time. Your baby loves putting you to the test.

"My baby's getting funnier and funnier because she's starting to become mischievous. She says *brrr* when she's got a mouth full of porridge, covering me with the stuff. She opens cupboards she's not allowed to touch and throws the cat's water all over the kitchen."

Laura's mom, 38th week

"My daughter won't listen to me. When I tell her 'no,' she laughs, even if I'm really angry with her. But when her babysitter says 'no,' she cries. I wonder if this is because I work. Perhaps I give in too much when I'm home, out of guilt."

Laura's mom, 39th week

"My daughter stood by a stroller with the neighbors' little boy in it and started playing peek-a-boo with him. Together, they thought it was the funniest thing."

> Emily's mom, 40th week

Some little ones love to play the role of giver. It doesn't matter what things they give, just as long as they can keep giving and receiving—preferably the latter. If your baby gives anything at all, it goes without saying that she expects to get it back immediately. She will often understand the words "Can I have . . . ," as well as "please." So you can combine the giving-and-receiving game with speech, helping her to understand things even better.

"My daughter likes to show everyone her biscuit with a big smile on her face. Of course, one is not expected to take the biscuit. She quickly retreats her hand when she thinks this would happen. The other day, she proudly reached out to show granddad's dog her cookie, but he wolfed it away in a flash. Flabbergasted, she looked at her empty hand and then she cried of anger."

> Hannah's mom, 41st week

Show Understanding for Irrational Fears

When your baby is learning a new skill, she may also discover a new danger and develop fear. One of these is the fear of the category *heights*. Another one is the fear of *being confined*. When your baby suddenly acts scared, sympathize with her, try to find out what is bothering her, and help her. Babies tend to be wary of new things until they are sure they are harmless.

"My baby always used to like walking when I would practice with her. Now, suddenly, she's stopped. She seems scared. If she even suspects I might let go of one hand, she'll sit down right away."

> Ashley's mom, 46th week

"My son can't stand being confined now. When he's strapped into a car seat, he becomes absolutely hysterical."

                        Paul's mom, 40th week

Between 40 and 45 weeks, another relatively easy period sets in. For the following 1 to 3 weeks, many babies are admired for their progress, independence, and cheerfulness. A wide range of things is interesting to them now, from people on horseback to flowers, leaves, ants, and mosquitoes. Many children wish to spend more time outdoors now. Other people suddenly start to play a much more important part in their lives, as well. They make contact with them much more often and are sooner prepared to play games with them. In short, baby's horizon is broader than ever.

"At the moment, my boy's a doll. He laughs all day long. Sometimes, he'll play by himself sweetly for an hour. He seems like a completely different child this past week. He doesn't look as bloated anymore, and he feels very lithe. He was always a little unwieldy, but now he seems to have loosened up a lot more. He's much livelier, energetic, and adventurous."

                        Frankie's mom, 42nd week

"My son understands much more, so he's getting to a new place, somewhere with more possibilities. I have to make it easier to talk to him. He needs to be where he can communicate with everyone, at the table for instance. It's important now. He's focusing on other people much more outside of the house as well. He makes contact with them right away by blowing bubbles, making certain calling sounds, or by tilting his head questioningly."

                        Bob's mom, 40th week

chapter 9

Wonder Week 46:
The World of Sequences

Babies are natural mess makers. During the last leap in your baby's mental development, this talent probably seemed at its peak. You may have marveled at your baby's knack for destruction as he disassembled, tossed around, and squished everything in his path. If you are alert for newly developing skills in your baby, at around 46 weeks you may suddenly notice him doing things that are quite the opposite. He will begin, for the first time, to try to *put things together*.

Your baby is now ready to discover the world of sequences. From this age on, he can begin to realize that to reach many of his goals, he has to do things in a certain order to be successful. You may now see your baby looking first to see which things go together and how they go together before trying to put them in each other, pile them on top of each other, or piece them together. For instance, he may concentrate on aiming as well as he can before trying to pile one block on top of another. He may push a peg through a hole in a peg board only after he has compared the shape of the peg to the hole.

This world offers whole new areas of exploration for your baby. You will notice that for the first time, he really seems to be able to put two and two together. He is sometimes able to put one action after another quite spontaneously. It may become apparent that the baby is more conscious of his actions than ever before—that he is aware of what he is doing now.

The onset of this new leap in his mental development begins at around 42 weeks, or between 40 and 44 weeks. While he grows into his new skills

Note: The first phase (fussy period) of this leap into the perceptual world of "sequences" is age-linked and predictable, emerging between 40 and 44 weeks. Most babies start the second phase (see box "Quality Time: An Unnatural Whim" on page 17) of this leap 46 weeks after full-term birth. The initial perception of the world of sequences sets in motion the development of a whole range of skills and activities. However, the age at which these skills and activities appear for the first time varies greatly and depends on your baby's preferences, experimentation and physical development. For example, the ability to perceive sequences is a necessary precondition for "pulling a string to get a ring toy attached to it," but this skill normally appears anywhere from approximately 46 weeks to many weeks or even months later. Skills and activities are mentioned in this chapter at the earliest possible age they might appear so you can watch for and recognize them. (They may be rudimentary at first.) This way you can respond to and facilitate your baby's development.

and learns to be comfortable in this new world, your baby will tend to be fussy and demanding once again. After all, it's a lot harder to figure out how things go together than to take them apart. The sudden alteration in his thinking can understandably be upsetting. This fussy period will often last for 5 weeks, but it may last anywhere from 3 to 7 weeks. If your baby is cranky, watch him closely to see if he is attempting to master new skills.

Your baby may cry more than he did during the past weeks. Most babies do. They may be fussy, cranky, whiny, weepy, grumpy, bad-tempered, unmanageable, and restless. They will do whatever they can to be able to be with their mothers. Some are preoccupied by this all day long. Some little clingers are more frantic at the prospect of separation than others. They will use every possible means they can think of to be able to stay with their mothers.

> "Whenever my baby's brother comes anywhere near him and touches him, he'll start to cry immediately because he knows it will get a reaction out of me."
>
> Kevin's mom, 41st week

Your baby may cry less when she is near you. Most fussy babies cry less when they are with their mothers. And they complain even less when they have their undivided attention.

> "Because I want to keep my baby's sniveling down to an absolute minimum, we do everything together. I do my housekeeping carrying her on my hip or my arm because otherwise I can't move an inch with her clinging to my leg. I explain to her what I'm doing, for example, how I'm making tea or folding towels. We also usually go to the bathroom together. When I do go on my own, I leave the door open. I do this first

so that I can see if she's doing anything dangerous, but also because then she can see me and follow me to her heart's content. And she always does. This way of going about things is the only way either of us will get any peace of mind."

Emily's mom, 43rd week

How You Know It's Time to Grow

She May Cling to Your Clothes

Your baby may go to great lengths to be able to stay as close to you as possible. She may literally wrap himself around you, even when there are no strangers present. Some babies do not necessarily cling to their mothers but do want to stay remarkably close to them so that they can keep an eye on them at all times. And there are those who keep coming back to their mothers, as if they need a "mommy refill," to be reassured when they leave her again.

"My son wants to sit on my lap, ride on my arm, crawl all over me, sit on top of me, or cling to my legs all day long, like a parasite clings to a fish. When I put him down, he bursts into tears."

Bob's mom, 41st week

"My daughter will sit on my shoe and wrap her little arms round my leg. Once she's hanging on, she won't let go if she can help it. I really need to think of some kind of diversion to get her to let go."

Emily's mom, 43rd week

"At the moment, my daughter tends to stay near, but she still does her own thing. It's almost as if she's circling around me like a satellite orbits the earth. If I'm in the living room, she'll be doing something next to me, and when I go to the kitchen, she'll be emptying a cupboard next to me there."

Jenny's mom, 47th week

"Often, my son comes to me to rub tummies, and then he runs off again. I tend to notice it particularly when I'm sitting somewhere doing something."

Matt's mom, 41st week

She May Be Shyer with Strangers

When there are strangers near her, looking at her, talking to her, or, worse still, reaching a hand out toward her, your little one may become even clingier with you than she already is. Many babies are shy now.

"My son is a little shy. When he sees new people, or if someone suddenly enters the room, he'll bury himself in my neck. It doesn't last long, though. He just needs to get used to them."

Matt's mom, 42nd week

"My son is shyer than he ever was before. Even his grandfather isn't allowed to look at him."

Kevin's mom, 43rd week

"I noticed this week that my baby was really starting to cling to me a lot. Now, whenever a stranger reaches out to embrace her, she'll grab me. But if people give her some time, she often ends up going to them by herself in the end. They just have to make sure that they don't pick her up too soon."

Ashley's mom, 47th week

She May Want Closer Physical Contact with You

Some little worriers hold on to their mothers as tightly as they can once they have a hold on them or when they are sitting on their laps, as if they do not want to give their mothers the chance to let go. Other babies react furiously when they are set down or when their mothers walk across the room.

"If we're apart for even a moment, my daughter cries with rage. When I return, she'll always hit, claw, pinch, and push me for a moment first. If the dog's around, she'll immediately go for him. Once, I came back to find her with a whisker in her hand."

Emily's mom, 43rd week

She May Want to Be Kept Busy

Most babies start asking for more attention now. Your baby may do the same. Even an easy little one usually prefers doing things with you. A demanding little person would, if she could have her way, keep you busy keeping her busy night and day. She is often not satisfied until she has her mother's undivided attention. She can have eyes only for her and only be focused on her.

"My son keeps coming up to me to read a book. He sits with me much more patiently, too. It's just what I've always wanted. He's usually busy as a bee. So when he finally does want to spend some time with me, it makes up for all the arrears."

Paul's mom, 44th week

"My son is becoming less lively in general. His motor development is starting to grind to a halt. He's paying less attention to it now. His toys aren't particularly popular now either. Even when I play along, he has a very short attention span. He'd rather have me than his toys."

Bob's mom, 41st week

"When my son is nursing, if I do anything or talk to anyone, he wails. I have to look at him, fidget with him, or stroke him. As soon as I stop for a second, he'll wriggle uncontrollably and kick furiously, as if to say: 'I am here.'"

Matt's mom, 43rd week

She May Be Jealous

Your little one can be extra cranky, naughty, or sweet when you pay attention to someone or something else. This change in behavior usually makes a mother wonder if her baby might be jealous. This discovery usually comes as a surprise.

> "I babysit a 4-month-old baby. My son always finds it very interesting when I give her a bottle. But this week, he was impossible. He kept doing things he normally never does. He was really causing trouble, being obnoxious. I think he was a bit jealous."
>
> John's mom, 44th week

She May Be Moody

Your baby might be cheerful one day and the total opposite the next. Her mood can also change suddenly. One moment, she may be busy and happy doing something, the next she could start whining and complaining. The mood swings come out of the blue for no apparent reason as far as her mother can tell. At times this can make a mother feel insecure.

> "My baby would cling and cry her eyes out one moment and seem to be having the greatest fun the next—as if she could turn it on and off at the flick of a switch. I just don't know what to do. I wonder if something could suddenly be hurting her."
>
> Nina's mom, 43rd week

She May Sleep Poorly

Your baby may sleep less well. Most babies do now. They either refuse to go to bed, have more difficulty falling asleep, or wake up earlier. Some are particularly troublesome sleepers during the day. Others are worse at night. And still others are reluctant to go to bed at any time.

"My daughter doesn't need much sleep. She stays up hours later in the evening, playing happily."

> Hannah's mom, 43rd week

"My baby wakes up 2 or 3 times a night and doesn't sleep well in the afternoon either. Sometimes it takes me 3 hours to get her to go to sleep."

> Jenny's mom, 48th week

"My son is more restless now. When it's time for bed, I have to force him to calm down. Then, he wakes up a few times during the night."

> Frankie's mom, 45th week

"My son used to sleep in wonderfully long. Unfortunately, he doesn't any more."

> Matt's mom, 41st week

She May Have "Nightmares"

Your baby may turn into a restless sleeper. She could even toss and turn so much that you suspect that she is having a nightmare.

"My baby woke up screaming at the top of her lungs, like she does when she's angry. I think she must have dreamed something she didn't like."

> Emily's mom, 45th week

She May Be Listless

Your baby may temporarily be a little apathetic. Sometimes babies are. They are less active or babble a little less. They may even stop all activity for a while and simply lie and stare. Mothers do not like to see this happen. They think that it is abnormal, and they may try to get the little tykes moving again.

"My daughter is not as active anymore. Often she just sits there, wide-eyed, looking around."

Hannah's mom, 45th week

"Occasionally, my son will just sit there, gazing into thin air. This is a change because he always used to be doing something."

Matt's mom, 43rd week

"My son is more passive, quieter. Sometimes, he'll sit there, staring off into the distance for a few moments. I don't like it one bit. It's as if he's not normal."

Bob's mom, 41st week

She May Refuse to Have Her Diaper Changed

Your little one may become more impatient and unmanageable when she is being dressed, undressed, or changed. She may whine, scream, and writhe as soon as you touch her. Sometimes mothers become aggravated with or concerned about a troublesome squirmer.

"My son won't stay still for a minute. Sometimes, getting his diaper off is like being in a wrestling match. I love the fact that he's become more active, but I don't see why he can't lie still for a few seconds."

Frankie's mom, 43rd week

"Dressing, undressing, and changing are a nightmare. This happened a while ago as well. Back then, I thought the lower part of her little back might be troubling her. I started to worry more and more. So I took her to the pediatrician, but he said that her back was perfectly fine. He had no idea what could be causing it, either. But then, it cleared up by itself."

Juliette's mom, 46th week

She May Lose Her Appetite

Many babies seem less interested in food and drink at this time. Your baby may lose her appetite, or she may be very choosy, eating something only if, and when, she feels like it. Mothers are often worried and aggravated by poor appetites and fussy eating.

> "My son is not eating well. But all of a sudden he does want to breast-feed in the middle of the day, and he'll start whining and pulling at my blouse to get what he wants. He wakes up a lot during the night as well, wanting to breastfeed. I wonder whether he's getting good nutrition this way."
>
> Matt's mom, 43rd week

She May Behave More Babyish

Sometimes a babyish behavior that you thought was long gone suddenly reappears. Mothers do not appreciate such revivals. They see them as backward steps and would put a stop to them if they could. Yet a relapse during fussy periods is perfectly normal. It simply means that another huge leap forward is about to happen.

> "My daughter relapsed into crawling this week. I just hope it's nothing to do with her hips or because she started walking so early."
>
> Jenny's mom, 44th week

> "My son doesn't want to hold his bottle himself anymore but prefers to lie back in my arms and be fed like a tiny baby. A while ago, however, he insisted on holding the bottle himself. His relapse is actually bothering me quite a bit. I kept thinking, 'Cut it out, son, I know you can do it your-self.' A few times I put his hands on the bottle, but he wouldn't budge."
>
> Bob's mom, 41st week

> "Very often, I have to rock my son again before he will go to sleep."
>
> Steven's mom, 41st week

"My son doesn't want to stand anymore and immediately slumps to the floor. He's also become a lot more sluggish."

Bob's mom, 41st week

She May Act Unusually Sweet

A fussy baby can now also find nicer ways of asking for more physical contact or attention. This happens more and more often and in increasingly sophisticated ways. She may bring her parents books or toys "asking" that they play with her. She may charm you into playing games with her with a variety of ploys, such as laying her little hand on your lap, snuggling up to you, or resting her head against you. Often, she may alternate between being troublesome and sweet, whichever works best at the time, to get the desired touch or attention.

Mothers of independent babies who don't usually seek much physical contact are overjoyed at the prospect of finally being able to give them a cuddle again.

"My daughter would come up to me now and again for a cuddle. She was extremely charming this week."

Ashley's mom, 46th week

"My son was very cuddly and kept clinging to me this week."

Matt's mom, 42nd week

"When my son is in the bicycle seat or stroller, he keeps looking back to check if I'm still there, and then he'll give me his tiny hand."

Paul's mom, 44th week

"My daughter wants to sit on my lap with a book more often. When she does, she'll stay there, snuggling up wonderfully close to me."

Jenny's mom, 47th week

 My Diary

Signs My Baby Is Growing Again

Between 40 and 44 weeks, your baby may show signs that he is ready to make the next leap into the world of sequences.

❑ Cries more often and is bad-tempered or cranky

❑ Is cheerful one moment and cries the next

❑ Wants to be kept busy, or does so more often than before

❑ Clings to your clothes, or wants to be closer to you

❑ Acts unusually sweet

❑ Is mischievous

❑ Throws temper tantrums, or throws them more often than before

❑ Is jealous

❑ Is shier with strangers than before

❑ Wants physical contact to be tighter or closer

❑ Sleeps poorly

❑ Seems to have nightmares, or has them more often than before

❑ Loses appetite

❑ Babbles less

❑ Sometimes just sits there, quietly daydreaming

❑ Refuses to have diaper changed

❑ Sucks thumb, or does so more often than before

❑ Wants to cuddle toys, or does so more often than before

OTHER CHANGES YOU NOTICE

_____

_____

"My daughter keeps crawling after me. When she rounds the corner by the door, she'll give me a big smile and quickly crawl back in the other direction again. We love this little game."

Ashley's mom, 43rd week

She May Be Mischievous

Some mothers notice that their babies are more naughty than they used to be. It may seem your baby does everything that he is not allowed to. Or he may be especially mischievous at times when you are rushing to finish something and can least spare the time to deal with him.

"We're not allowed to attend to our own business. If we do, then everything we told our daughter not to touch suddenly becomes extremely interesting, such as the telephone and the knobs on the stereo. We have to watch her every second of the day."

Jenny's mom, 47th week

"My daughter keeps crawling after me. I think that's adorable. But if she doesn't do that, she makes a mess of things. She'll pull the books off their shelves and scoop the dirt out of the flower pots."

Ashley's mom, 43rd week

"Whenever my baby sees I'm busy, she crawls over to things she's not allowed to touch."

Nina's mom, 43rd week

"My son clings to me all day long, and when he doesn't, I have to keep disciplining him and taking things away from him."

Kevin's mom, 43rd week

How This Leap May Affect You

As your baby's new world expands to include sequences, his fussiness and changes that follow will affect you, too. Here are some feelings you may encounter.

You May Feel Insecure

Mothers often worry when their baby is upset. They try to find a cause for his more frequent crying. As soon as they have found one, it puts their mind at ease. At this age, they are often inclined to decide it is cutting teeth.

"I think that my son's mouth was troubling him. He wasn't his normal, easygoing self."

Ｊｏｈｎ's mom, 43rd week

"My son cried a lot. I don't think he had enough sleep."

Frankie's mom, 43rd week

"My daughter is whiny and fussy whenever I'm busy doing something. Perhaps she's having more difficulty dealing with her sisters at the moment."

Juliette's mom, 42nd week

You May (Yet Again) Be Exhausted

Mothers of babies who demand a lot of attention and need little sleep feel thoroughly exhausted toward the end of a fussy period. Some complain of headaches, backaches, nausea, and lack of concentration, as well.

"I feel that I've broken down completely because I'm not getting any support or recognition. I'd really love to have one evening of rest. At night, I keep running upstairs to the nursery and back down again. Often, this goes on into the middle of the night. To me, this is the most difficult age so far. I even kept putting off writing this diary. I just couldn't concentrate on it."

Emily's mom, 46th week

You May Become Annoyed

Toward the end of this fussy period, mothers become increasingly aggravated by their fretful little clingers. They are annoyed that they are constantly preoccupied with their demands and do not seem to have a life of their own anymore.

> "It's tedious, literally not being able to move an inch. My son constantly demands attention, or else he throws a temper tantrum, and it's slowly but surely becoming very irritating. Sometimes, I feel like he's pulling my strings, and that makes me feel rebellious. Then I get fed up. I keep contemplating if I should take him back to the day care, after all. I've kept him at home for a few weeks now. In the beginning it felt better, but now, once in a while, I can feel myself getting slightly aggressive again."
>
> Bob's mom, 46th week

> "I'm very busy, and I can't have my daughter clinging to my legs or sitting in front of the sink anymore when I'm working. Now, when I've had enough, it's off to bed with her. Perhaps I'm starting to lose my patience."
>
> Juliette's mom, 45th week

> "Even though I have the easiest baby anyone could ever wish for, when he starts crying hysterically, I notice I do get a bit impatient with him and whisk him off to bed."
>
> John's mom, 43rd week

Sometimes a mother is annoyed because deep down she knows that her baby is capable of more than he is showing and suspects that his behavior is just too babyish for his age. She thinks it's time for him to start behaving more independently.

> "When I set my son down for a clean diaper, he always starts to yell. It's the same with clean clothes, as well. This is starting to annoy me more

and more. I think he's too old for that kind of behavior. In fact, it's about time he started cooperating a little."

Bob's mom, 47th week

You May Start to Quarrel

Toward the end of every fussy period, many mothers who are still breast-feeding think about whether it might not be time to stop. One of the reasons is that the baby wants to nurse all day long. This is annoying and exhausting, and mothers begin to refuse babies sometimes. The little one, however, finds this unacceptable and before you know it, he and his mother argue.

"I keep getting more and more annoyed because I have to lull my son to sleep at my breast. I had to start doing it again when he was having so much trouble falling asleep. Now it's starting to become a habit again. Besides, he wants to nurse an awful lot and starts screaming when he doesn't get his way. I just don't feel like doing it anymore."

Matt's mom, 47th week

The good news is that for the mothers who do persist with breast-feeding, the normal feeding pattern will restore itself as soon as the fussy period is over. Once everything has settled down again, mothers seem to forget their irritations.

Another battleground is the familiar territory of negotiating a deal between mother and child about the amount of physical contact and attention.

"I'm aggravated by my son's continuous crying just so he can sit on my lap. I get terribly angry when he bites me, if I don't respond to him fast enough. It hurts so much that I automatically give him a shove. Once, he fell and hit his head really hard. That wasn't my intention, but I was so furious it just happened."

Kevin's mom, 44th week

It's critical to remember that having feelings of anger and frustration at times is not abnormal or dangerous, but acting on them is. Try to get help long before you lose control.

How Your Baby's New Skills Emerge

At about 46 weeks, you will see your baby growing calmer and attempting to do things that are brand new for him. You will see him handling his toys in a different way and enjoying new activities. He will be more precise about his actions than ever before and will pay even more attention to detail.

Your baby can now understand that sometimes one thing must follow another to make a sequence. He will realize that he can find and construct sequences in all of the senses, and as usual, your baby is unable to explore them all at once. His inclinations, preferences, and temperament will help him to select the aspects of the world that he finds most interesting and the skills that he will develop. Help him to do what he is ready to do, rather than trying to push him.

During the last leap forward, your baby realized that certain things have so much in common that they belong to one group or category. In order to categorize things, she would often examine them by breaking them down and taking them apart. For instance, she might have taken a tower of blocks apart one by one, removed a key from a lock, or loosened a handle on a chest of drawers. This paved the way for the current leap where the very opposite takes place, and she begins to experiment with putting things back together. Every baby needs to learn how to take a tower apart before she can build one. Even the seemingly simple activity of choosing the next

(continued on page 253)

My Diary

How My Baby Explores the New World of Sequences

Check off the boxes below as you notice your baby changing. Stop filling this out once the next stormy period begins, heralding the coming of the next leap.

This world is just as multifaceted as all of the others that your baby has entered in her short life. Each baby has her own ideas about what is interesting. Your baby can't experiment with everything at once. If she has always been a listening and looking baby, this may continue at the expense of more physical activities. It is perfectly normal if most of these skills do not become evident until several months later.

POINTING AND TALKING

❑ Follows and points to a person, animal, or object that you have just named, whether in real life or a picture

❑ Points out one or two items for you to name, such as persons, animals, or objects

❑ Points out and names one or two items in turn

❑ Deliberately looks through a book, making different sounds to go with one or two pictures

❑ Points to his nose when you ask, "Where's your nose?"

❑ Points to a body part, for instance, his nose or your nose, wanting you to name it

❑ Imitates the sound when you name an animal, for instance, when you ask, "What does the cat say?" he says, "Meow"

❑ Raises his arms when you ask, "How tall are you going to be?"

❑ Says "yum" when he wants the next bite

❑ Says "no, no" when he does not want to do something

❑ Uses a word in an extended way, for instance, says "yuck" for something dirty but also when he has to be careful of something because "yuck" has come to mean "don't touch" for him

WHAT GOES TOGETHER AND WHAT COMES NEXT

❑ Knows that he can push a round peg through a round hole; for example, he will choose the round peg from a pile of pegs and try to push it through the round hole of a peg board

❑ Tries to put together three pieces of a simple puzzle

❑ Tries pushing coins through a slot

❑ Tries fitting two different sizes of containers inside each other

❑ Takes a key from somewhere else and tries to insert it into a keyhole

❑ Looks at the lamp and reaches for it when you flick the light switch

❑ Tries to talk into a telephone receiver

❑ Puts objects in a container, covers it, removes the cover, removes the objects, and repeats the cycle again

❑ Tries to put a "doughnut" ring over an upright rod

❑ Pushes toy cars around, making a *vrrrm* sound

❑ Scoops up sand with a spade and then empties it into a bucket

❑ Fills bath toys with water and empties them again

❑ Takes a good look at two Primo blocks and then tries fitting them together

(continued)

Wonder Week 46: The World of Sequences

 My Diary (cont.)

❑ Tries scrawling on a piece of paper with a pencil or crayon

MAKING AND USING TOOLS

❑ Helps herself learn to walk by finding an object to push

❑ Finds something to use as a step to reach a desired place or object

❑ Points with her finger in the direction she wants to go when being carried

LOCOMOTION

❑ Clambers down the stairs or off a chair or sofa backward. In the beginning, she sometimes even starts crawling backward toward the stairs before starting her descent

❑ Puts her head down in position to initiate a somersault with help

❑ Bends her knees, then stretches her legs powerfully, so that she jumps off the ground with both feet

❑ Tries to aim before throwing or kicking a ball

❑ Looks first to see whether she can reach another supporting object within the number of steps she can take by herself

PLAYING WITH OTHERS

❑ Plays with you. Clearly expresses which games he wants to play by starting them and then looking at you expectantly

❑ Repeats a game

❑ Entices you to play with him, perhaps by pretending he is unable to do something that you have seen him doing on his own before

HIDE AND SEEK

❑ Looks for something that you have hidden by completely concealing it with something else—either as a game, or because you do not want him to get ahold of it

❑ Hides something that belongs to someone else, waits and watches, then laughs when the other person finds it

COPYING A SEQUENCE OF GESTURES

❑ Imitates two or more gestures in sequence

❑ Studies the way the same sequence of gestures looks in reality and in the mirror

❑ Copies one or two movements while you are singing a song with her

HELPING OUT WITH THE HOUSEKEEPING

❑ Hands you things that you want to put away one by one

❑ Goes and gets simple objects, if you ask her to

❑ Picks up the clothes that you have just taken off her and puts them in the laundry basket

❑ Gets her own bucket with dolls' laundry, and puts it in the washing machine

❑ Gets out a broom and sweeps the floor with it

❑ Gets a cloth out and dusts things off

(continued)

My Diary (cont.)

❏ Imitates you cooking; for example, she bangs a fork in a bowl or stirs with a spoon

DRESSING AND GROOMING

❏ Tries to undress himself; for instance, he tries to take a sock off by pulling at his toes

❏ Tries putting on his shoe or sock by himself; for instance, he holds on to his shoe or sock and his foot and puts them together

❏ Helps when you dress him. Leans toward you when you pull a sweater on or off or sticks his foot out when the sock or shoe is coming

❏ Brushes his hair

❏ Uses a toothbrush

❏ Sometimes uses a potty

EATING AND FEEDING

❏ Offers others a bite or sip while eating and drinking

❏ Blows steam off food himself before taking a bite

❏ Sticks a piece of bread on a baby fork and eats it

❏ Can scoop up food with a spoon and put it in his mouth

OTHER CHANGES YOU NOTICE

_____

_____

block and then deliberately placing it in position requires a mental leap that, until this point, your baby was not prepared to take.

As her new skills begin to take wing, your little one becomes involved for the first time in *constructing*, in *putting things together,* and *linking things*. For instance, she may now take a key off a table and try to put it in a lock. She can learn to dig sand up with a spade and then put it in a bucket. She can learn to aim a ball first and then throw it. While singing a song, such as *Pat a cake, pat a cake, baker's man,* she can begin to make different gestures successively, without you having to set the example. She can learn to scoop up food with a spoon and then put it in her mouth. She may learn to pick up her clothes from the floor and then put them in the laundry basket. At this age, babies are just beginning to be aware of sequences, and it is quite a feat if they manage to string two actions together. Although they know what belongs together, their attempts may not always succeed. For instance, your baby may try putting on her shoes by getting them out but then sit down and rub them against her feet trying to put them on.

You can also tell by your baby's reactions that she is now beginning to realize how certain events usually follow after another in the normal course of events. You will notice that she now knows what the next step is in any particular sequence. For instance, if she sees you push a doorbell, you may see your baby pause to listen for the bell.

"When a tape is finished, my son now looks up at the cassette player, not at the speaker. He now knows that I have to do something to the player if he is to hear more music."

Bob's mom, 48th week

Your baby can now also start pointing out and naming different people, animals, and objects. When she does this on her own, she may often still say *da* instead of using the proper word. When she does this together with you, she may point things out and want you to name them or have you make the appropriate sound. She might like to play the game the other way around, having you point while she tells you what she calls the object. When you are carrying her around, you may also start to notice that your baby will point in the direction that she wants you to go.

Babies who haven't been doing much in the way of talking may now begin to name people, animals, and objects, or parts of these, for the first time. The very act of naming is a way of relating a spoken word or sound to a person, animal, or object. Pointing or looking followed by a word is a sequence as well. But some babies will still put off talking in favor of other skills, such as walking.

Your Baby's Choices: A Key to His Personality

Babies can now perceive and play with sequences. This opens a new world of possibilities, and your baby will make his own choices according to his mental development, build, weight, and coordination. Some babies are very social and like to focus on skills that involve people; others prefer playthings. Some pick at every little detail and others are more interested in getting an overall impression of many different skills. You may find it irresistible to make comparisons with other babies, but remember that every baby is unique.

Watch your baby closely to determine where his interests lie. Between 46 and 51 weeks, he will select the skills he likes best from this world. Respect his choices. You will find out what it is that makes him unique, and when you follow his interests, you will help him best in playing and learning. Babies love anything new and it is important that you respond when you notice any new skills or interests. He will enjoy it if you share these new discoveries, and his learning will progress more quickly.

Every baby needs time and help to learn new skills. You can help your baby by giving her the opportunity and time to toy with sequences. You can encourage her when she succeeds and console her when she does not. You can try to facilitate her attempts and make her failures easier to bear.

Your baby will find plenty of opportunities to come into contact with sequences herself. Allow her to see, hear, feel, smell, and taste them and indulge in whatever she likes best. The more she encounters and toys with sequences, the better she will learn to understand them. Pay attention, however. She might think she knows it all. It does not matter whether she prefers learning about sequences through observing, handling toys, speech, sounds, music, or locomotion. Soon she will be able to put the expertise she has gained in one area into practice in other areas with no trouble at all.

Help Your Baby Explore the New World through Experimentation

When your baby enters the world of sequences it dawns upon him that he has to do things in a certain order, if he wants to succeed. He has observed how adults perform a particular sequence, but he has to master it himself by trial  and error. Often his "solutions" are peculiar. The sequence he performs may be correct (grabbing something and putting it into something else),

but he may apply the wrong objects to the wrong targets. He knows that dirty cloths go into a container. So why only in the laundry basket and not in the dustbin or the toilet? The sequence is much the same, after all!

> "My son pulls plugs from their outlets and then tries putting them into the wall. He also tries sticking other objects with two protrusions in the outlets. I have to watch him even closer now and take safety precautions."
>
> Bob's mom, 48th week

> "When my daughter wants to climb onto our bed, she opens a drawer of our nightstand, stands on it, and then climbs onto the bed. If she opens the drawer too far, the whole nightstand starts swaying back and forth. She makes me very nervous."
>
> Jenny's mom, 49th week

Or the sequence itself may be peculiar. For instance, your baby knows how his mother walks up the stairs. But the steps are too high for him, so he has to crawl. However, on every step he stands up.

> "My son desperately wants to climb the stairs on his own, but he behaves dangerously. He crawls on his knees to the next step, stands up, then continues upwards on his knees, stands up again, and so it goes. I don't like it one bit. I have to keep a sharp eye on him."
>
> Steven's mom, 45th week

Once he is of the opinion that he has mastered a particular sequence, it is "fixed." He will not accept it to be done in any other way and he may be quite stubborn if you try to change his mind. So always pay close attention. Your young wiseacre does not yet know the meaning of danger.

Help Your Baby Explore the New World through Independence

Many babies refuse to be helped and resist any form of interference by others. These babies want to do everything they can, or think they can, by themselves. If yours is this type of baby, try to have as much consideration for his feelings as possible. This is just the age when many little ones like to start asserting their independence.

> "My son always liked practicing walking together. But if I hold his hands now, he'll immediately sit down. Then when I leave he'll give it another try. At every successful attempt, no matter how slight, he'll look at me triumphantly."
>
> Paul's mom, 46th week

> "My son keeps trying to scribble something on paper with a pencil, just like his older brother does. But whenever his brother tries to guide his hand to show him how it's supposed to work, he'll pull his hand away."
>
> Kevin's mom, 48th week

> "When we push pegs through my son's peg board together, he'll start throwing them. But as soon as he's on his own in the playpen, he will try to copy it. To tell the truth, it annoys me."
>
> Paul's mom, 53rd week

> "My daughter will eat only if she can put the food in her mouth herself. When I do it, she'll take it out again."
>
> Laura's mom, 43rd week

At this age, many mothers spend huge amounts of time taking things away from their children and disciplining them. It's important to consider that your baby isn't necessarily disobedient. She just wants to do things by herself.

"My daughter is being troublesome and wants her own way with everything. She gets angry when I refuse her something. It's really tiresome."

Jenny's mom, 50th week

"My son tries to get things done by screaming and throwing temper tantrums."

Matt's mom, 46th week

"When I complain, my daughter screams and lashes out at everything and everybody around her, or pulls a plant from its pot. This annoys me to no end. She behaves much better with her babysitter."

Laura's mom, 49th week

Show Some Understanding for Frustrations

Many mothers see their babies' striving for independence as rebellious. But if you stop to think, it is not. Your baby simply wants to do things by himself. After all, he is becoming aware of what belongs together and the order in which things need to be done. He is convinced that he knows it all and is capable of doing anything. He no longer wants you to interfere or to tell him how things should be done. He wants to make his own decisions. But, as his mother, you are not really used to this. You naturally help him as you always have, without giving it a second thought. You know perfectly well that your baby is still unable to carry out the things he wants to do properly. And you know that he will inevitably make a mess of things if he tries.

Mother and baby often may have different views of things. This can lead to conflicts. Mother sees the baby as being difficult, and the baby feels his mother is causing all the trouble. Adolescents may go through the most difficult phases, but babies and toddlers run a close second.

"We're stuck in one of those 'no, don't touch that' and 'no, don't do that' phases now. But my son knows exactly what he wants, and he can get very angry when he doesn't agree with something. Recently, he got so upset that he didn't even notice he was standing on his own."

Frankie's mom, 49th week

Help Your Baby Explore the New World through Feedback

At this age, babies start testing the limits of how far they can go before someone stops them. If you let them know clearly when they are doing something wrong and just why it is bad or dangerous, they can learn a lot from it.

Similarly, you should let your baby know what she is doing right by praising her. This will teach her what is good and what is bad behavior. Most babies ask for praise themselves, anyway. When they do something right, they ask to be rewarded all the time. They look at you and laugh, full of pride, or call for attention. They can keep repeating behaviors many times as well, asking for a reward after each time.

"Every time my daughter puts a ring around the cone she'll look at me, grinning like mad and clapping."

Eve's mom, 49th week

If your baby is frustrated by things he is not able or allowed to do, you can still quite easily distract him with a favorite toy or game. Naturally this is different for every baby.

"This week, my son loved playing football. He'd kick really hard at the ball and then we'd run after it really quickly while I held his hands. It made him laugh so hard sometimes he had to lie down on the ground for a moment to stop laughing."

Paul's mom, 48th week

"My son keeps wanting to help out. He thinks that's the best thing ever and starts beaming. I do have to take my time with him, though. It takes me 10 times longer to put a pile of diapers away in the cupboard with his help. He'll hand me each diaper separately, but before he lets me have each one, he'll put it on his shoulder and rub the side of his chin against it."

Matt's mom, 48th week

Help Your Baby Explore the New World through Language

A baby who lives in the world of sequences may start pointing out and naming different people, animals, and objects. Pointing or looking, followed by a word, is a sequence. If you notice your baby doing this, listen to her and let her know that you understand her and that you think she is wonderful. Do not try to improve her pronunciation. This will spoil your baby's fun and will make no difference to the way she speaks.

Do make sure that you use the correct words all of the time. This way, your baby will automatically learn the right pronunciation in due time. For a while they will "translate" what you say into their own baby pronunciation.

"My daughter is starting to use words and point at whatever she's talking about. At the moment, she's in love with horses. When she sees a horse, she points to it and says 'hoss.' Yesterday at the park, a large Afghan dog ran past her. She called that a 'hoss,' as well."

Hannah's mom, 48th week

"My son suddenly said 'nana' to a toy cat. We have never used that word. He has a lot of toy animals. When I asked, 'Where's nana?' he kept pointing to the cat."

Paul's mom, 48th week

Understand Your Baby's Fears

When your baby is learning new skills, she may also perceive things that she does not fully understand yet. In a way, she discovers new anxieties—dangers that up until now she didn't realize existed. As soon as she recognizes these dangers and until she can be sure they are harmless, her fears will stay with her. So show her a little understanding.

"My daughter keeps wanting to sit on her potty. Even if she hasn't done anything, she'll take the potty into the lavatory to empty it and flush the toilet. But while she seems fascinated by flushing, at the same time she's also scared of it. She doesn't get as frightened when she flushes the toilet herself, only when someone else does. Then she doesn't like it at all."

Jenny's mom, 50th week

"My daughter is fascinated by airplanes. She recognizes them everywhere: in the air, in pictures, and in magazines. This week, she suddenly became frightened by the sound, even though she's heard it before."

Laura's mom, 46th week

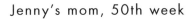

Some babies can tell you that they remember certain situations or that they have seen certain people before by using body language and sounds. If you notice your baby doing this, talk to him a lot, explain to him what you are seeing, and react to what he tells you about it later on.

"We go swimming every week. Usually, we see the same people there. One day, we saw one of the mothers on the street. Immediately, my son called out 'Oh oh' and pointed to her as if he recognized her. Then, he

(continued on page 266)

 Top Games for This Wonder Week

Here are games and activities that most babies like best now. Remember, all babies are different. See what your baby responds to best.

HELPING OUT GAMES

Your baby likes to feel needed. Let her know that you can certainly use some help from her. At this age, she will not be of any real help, but she will be able to understand the actions involved in many common activities. Plus, it is a good way of preparing her for the next leap.

DOING HOUSEWORK

Show your baby how you cook and clean. Involve him. Explain what you are doing. Give him one of your dusters. This will be much more interesting than using his own cloth. When you are baking a cake, give him his own plastic mixing bowl and spoon.

DRESSING

This is the most fun in front of a mirror. Try undressing your baby, toweling her down, and dressing her while she can watch herself sometime. Name the parts you are drying. When you notice her starting to cooperate, ask her to help out. Ask her to raise an arm or stretch her leg when you are about to put a jumper or sock on her. Praise her when she does it.

GROOMING HIMSELF

Allow your baby to groom himself. This is most fun in front of a mirror, too. This way, the baby can see for himself what he is doing, learn faster, and have more fun. Brush his hair in front of a mirror, then let him try it himself. You can do the same with

brushing his teeth. You can also see if he will wash himself. Give him a washcloth when he is in the bath, and say something such as, "Go on, wash your face." Respond with enthusiasm at every attempt. You will see how proud this makes him.

FEEDING HERSELF WITH A SPOON

Allow your baby to eat by herself with a spoon. Or give her a baby fork to eat cubes of bread or pieces of fruit. Lay a large sheet of plastic under her chair so that afterward you will easily be able to clean up the mess she makes.

NAMING GAMES

Your baby often understands a lot more than you think, and he loves being allowed to prove it.

THIS IS YOUR NOSE

Touching and naming parts of his anatomy will help your baby to discover his own body. You can play this game while dressing or undressing him or while you are sitting together. Also see if he knows where your nose is.

POINTING OUT AND NAMING

For many babies, pointing out and naming things, or making the appropriate sounds, is a fun game. You can play this anywhere: outside, in a store, or with a book. Enjoy your baby's misnomers as well.

(continued)

Top Games for This Wonder Week (cont.) - - - - - - - - - - - -

SONG AND MOVEMENT GAMES

Now your baby may want to participate actively in songs. She may start to make one or two movements that go with them by herself, as well.

PAT A CAKE, PAT A CAKE, BAKER'S MAN

Sit facing your baby and sing:

> *Pat a cake, pat a cake, baker's man*
> (Clap your hands, and let your baby follow.)
> *Bake me a cake as fast as you can*
> *Prick it and pat it, and mark it with "B"*
> (Make pricking and patting movements,
> and let your baby follow.)
> *And put it in the oven for baby and me.*
> (At the word "baby," point to her or poke her in the stomach.)

ITSY BITSY SPIDER

Sit facing your baby and sing:

> *The itsy bitsy spider*
> *Climbed up the water spout*
> (Walk your fingers up in the air or on the baby like a spider.)
> *Down came the rain and washed the spider out.*
> (Mimic raindrops coming down and make
> an action of washing water away.)
> *Out came the sun and dried up all the rain.*
> (Draw the sun in the air.)
> *And the itsy bitsy spider climbed up the spout again.*
> (Walk your fingers up in the air or on the baby like the spider
> coming back again.)

ROW, ROW, ROW YOUR BOAT

Sit on the floor opposite your child. Place your baby in between your legs. Take his hands in yours and sing while gently rocking back and forth:

Row, row, row your boat
Gently down the stream
Merrily, merrily, merrily, merrily
Life is but a dream.

HIDE-AND-SEEK GAMES

Many babies like uncovering playthings that you have made disappear completely.

UNWRAPPING A PARCEL

Wrap a plaything in a piece of paper or crackly crisp bag, while your baby watches. Then give her the parcel and let her retrieve the plaything, as if by magic. Encourage her with each attempt she makes.

UNDER THE CUP

Put a plaything in front of your baby and place a cup over it. Then put an identical cup next to the first one and ask your baby where the plaything is. Admire him every time he looks for the hidden plaything, even if he does not find it immediately. If this game is still a bit too complicated, try playing it with a cloth instead of a cup. He will be able to see the contour of the plaything through the cloth. Play this game the other way around, too—let your baby hide something that you have to find.

saw a girl in the swimming pool who lives near us and whom he's seen only a couple of times, and he reacted the same way."

Paul's mom, 49th week

"On our way to the store, we saw a large pile of stones. I said, 'Look at all of those stones.' My son gazed at them intently. The next day, he began pointing at the stones from a distance, looking at me and shouting 'eh, eh.'"

Steven's mom, 51st week

The Virtue of Patience

It's important to keep your patience with your baby as he tries to learn new skills. When you see he is not interested, stop. He will be occupied enough with other things that are more interesting to him at that moment.

"I'm very busy practicing saying 'daddy' with my boy and playing games like 'Where's your nose?' But so far, we've had little result. He just laughs, jumps around, and would rather bite my nose or pull my hair. But I'm happy enough that he's become such a lively little fellow."

Frankie's mom, 49th week

"I try to sing songs with my son, but I don't feel as if they are doing much good. He doesn't seem particularly interested. He seems to be preoccupied by his surroundings."

John's mom, 47th week

Between 47 and 52 weeks, another period of comparative ease sets in. For 1 to 3 weeks, you may be amazed by your baby's cheerfulness and independence. She may pay much better attention when you talk. She may seem calmer and more controlled when she is at play, and she may play well on her own again. She may want to be put back in her playpen—she may not even want to be taken out. And finally, she may look remarkably older and wiser. She is growing into a real toddler now.

Top Toys for This Wonder Week

Here are toys and things that most babies like best now.

- Wooden trains with stations, bridges, and sidings

- Toy cars

- Dolls with toy bottles

- Drum, pots, and pans to beat on

- Books with pictures of animals

- Sandboxes with bucket and spade

- Balls of all sizes, from Ping-Pong balls to large beach balls

- Giant plastic beads

- Stuffed animals, especially the ones that make music when you squeeze them

- Bicycles, cars, or tractors that he can sit on himself and move around

- Primo blocks

- Small plastic figures of people or animals

- Mirrors

Remember to put away or take safety precautions with electrical outlets, stairs, stereo equipment, televisions, vacuum cleaners, washing machines, pets, and small objects such as knickknacks, pins, or little pieces of colored glass.

"My daughter is getting lovelier by the day. She keeps getting better at entertaining herself. She can really keep herself occupied with something now. I got the playpen out again this week. But the thing I found most striking was that she doesn't at all seem to mind spending an hour or so in it anymore, whereas a few weeks ago she'd scream hysterically if I took her anywhere near it. It's as if she's discovering her toys all over again and enjoying the peace and quiet in the playpen."

Ashley's mom, 52nd week

"My daughter has become a real playmate for her older sister. She responds exactly like you'd expect her to. They do a lot more things together. They take their bath together as well. Both of them enjoy each other tremendously."

Hannah's mom, 47th week

"These were lovely weeks. My son is more of a buddy again. The day care center is working out fine. He always enjoys seeing the other children and comes home in a good mood. He sleeps better at night. He understands a lot more and seems fascinated by the toys he plays with. He crawls into another room on his own again, too, and laughs a lot. I'm enjoying every minute with him."

Bob's mom, 51st week

chapter 10

Wonder Week 55:
The World of Programs

*E*very child's first birthday is a significant occasion. The end of the first year means for many parents the beginning of the end of babyhood. Your little cherub is about to become a toddler. In many ways, of course, she is still a baby. She still has so much to learn about her world—which has become such an interesting place to explore. She can get around so much better now, though, and she has become adept at getting into everything that interests her.

Shortly after the first birthday, at around 55 weeks, your little one will have gone through another big change in her mental development and will be ready to explore the world of programs. This will make her seem even more like a little person with her own way of approaching the world. A watchful parent will begin to see the blossoming of a new understanding in the toddler's way of thinking.

The word "programs" is very abstract. Here's what it means in this context. In the past leap in development, your baby learned to deal with the notion of sequences—the fact that events follow one after another or objects fit together in a particular way. A program is a degree more complicated than a sequence since it allows the end result to be reached in any number of ways. Once your child becomes capable of perceiving programs, she can begin to understand what it means to do the laundry, set the table, eat lunch, tidy up, get dressed, build a tower, make a phone call, and the millions of other things that make up everyday life. These are all programs.

Note: The first phase (fussy period) of this leap into the perceptual world of "programs" is age-linked and predictable, emerging between 49 and 53 weeks. Most babies start the second phase (see box "Quality Time: An Unnatural Whim" on page 17) of this leap 55 weeks after full-term birth. The first perception of the world of programs sets in motion the development of a whole range of skills and activities. However, the age at which these skills and activities appear for the first time varies greatly and depends on your baby's preferences, experimentation and physical development. For example, the ability to perceive programs is a necessary precondition for "washing dishes" or "vacuum cleaning," but these skills normally appear anywhere from 55 weeks to many months later. Skills and activities are mentioned in this chapter at the earliest possible age they might appear so you can watch for and recognize them. (They may be rudimentary at first.) This way you can respond to and facilitate your baby's development.

The main characteristic of a program is that it has a goal but that the steps taken to accomplish it are flexible. This is how it differs from a sequence, which is the same every time. An example of a sequence is counting from 1 to 10. You do it the same way each and every time. Dusting is an example of a program. You do not necessarily have to dust an object in the same way each time—you can dust the legs of a table first and then the top, or the other way around. Every time that you dust, you can choose the sequence that you feel is best for that day, that room, that chair, and your mood. However you choose to do it, the program you are working with remains "dusting." So a program can be seen as a network of possible sequences that you can carry out in a variety of ways. The options may be limited in dusting, but if you think of examples such as "going on vacation" or "changing jobs," the programs become very complex.

Your child can now think of a goal, such as "going shopping," and know that this may mean putting on hats, coats, and boots and getting in the car. Or she may be eager to "help" you—doing the cleaning, taking the dog for a walk, and putting away the groceries. She may insist on doing things herself—washing her hands, feeding herself, even undressing herself.

As your child changes, you may feel that she is more unpredictable than ever. Interpreting her actions used to be easy when they were part of simple sequences, because one thing always led to the next in a familiar pattern. Now her world is much more flexible and any action can form part of any program. This is confusing for you both. Until you get used to the way she is operating, some of her actions may be hard to understand because you can't guess what she's trying to achieve any more. This leap will also be apparent in her play. She will begin to be interested in some of her toys all over again, and you may notice for the first time a budding imagination and more complex play.

Between 49 and 53 weeks, your child begins to perceive that her world is changing again. While she is sorting out this new complexity, she will need some extra comfort and support, and this makes her appear fussy and demanding for a while. This fussy period will often last for 4 or 5 weeks, but it can be as short as 3 weeks or as long as 6. If your baby is

cranky, watch her closely. There's a good chance that she's attempting to master new skills.

Your child may cry more easily than he did during the past weeks. Children are usually quicker to cry now than their mothers have been used to. They want to be near their mothers, preferably all day long. Some children are much more insistent about this than others are, of course. They may also seem cranky, unmanageable, and temperamental.

> "My son could be pretty bad-tempered at times. Not all the time—he would play on his own for a while, but then suddenly it was all over and he would be terribly weepy for quite some time. Then he would want me to hold him. And all of this commotion would take place in just one morning."
>
> **Bob's mom, 52nd week**

> "My daughter was very quick to cry. All I had to do was say 'no,' and she'd have an immediate crying fit. It was not like her at all."
>
> **Eve's mom, 52nd week**

Children usually cry less when they are with their mothers or when their mothers are somehow occupied with them, playing with them, or watching them.

> "While my little girl is doing things, I'm supposed to stay sitting on the sofa, preferably not doing anything myself. I long for the day when I'll be able to knit something quietly while I'm sitting there."
>
> **Emily's mom, 53rd week**

"Whenever I'm busy doing something, my son wants to be picked up. But once he's on my lap, he wants to get off quickly again, and he expects me to follow him around. He's absolutely impossible."

Frankie's mom, 52nd week

How You Know It's Time to Grow

It's still too early for your little one to tell you in words how he's feeling. But still, he is able to express the turmoil he feels inside. Here's how.

He May Cling to Your Clothes

Your little one may start clinging more to you again—many children do at this age. He may want to be carried around or cling to your legs to prevent you from walking away and leaving him behind. Others do not necessarily need physical contact, but they may keep coming back to be near their mothers for only brief moments or to touch them. Every child comes back for his own brand of "mommy refill."

"My daughter stays around me more again, plays for a moment, and then comes back to me."

Hannah's mom, 54th week

"I can't do a thing as long as my son is awake. When he's out of his playpen, he is constantly underfoot, and when he's in the playpen, I have to stay near him. Otherwise, he'll throw a screaming fit."

Frankie's mom, 55th week

"When I stand up and walk into the kitchen, right away my daughter will come after me and want to be carried. She'll really make a scene. It's all terribly dramatic. You'd think something awful was happening."

Emily's mom, 53rd week

He May Be Shyer with Strangers

When there are strangers near, your little one may cling to you even more fanatically than he often already did. Once more, many children suddenly want to have less to do with strangers now. Sometimes, this even includes their own family members.

> "This week, my daughter would suddenly become extremely upset, and she'd want only to be with me. If I put her down or gave her to my husband, she'd panic."
>
> Jenny's mom, 56th week

> "My little girl won't accept anything to eat from strangers, not even a slice of bread or a cookie."
>
> Nina's mom, 54th week

But there are also children who want only to be with their fathers.

> "My daughter was completely crazy about her father for 2 days. She didn't want to have anything to do with me then, even though I hadn't done her any wrong. If he didn't pick her up right away, she'd start crying."
>
> Juliette's mom, 53rd week

He May Want Physical Contact to Be as Close as Possible

Some children hold on as tightly as they can, even when they are being carried. They do not want to be put down—and very likely yours doesn't either. There are also little ones who do not mind being put down, as long as their mothers don't walk away. If anyone leaves, it is allowed only to be the little tyrant himself.

> "One evening I had to go away. When I set my son down to put on my coat, he started crying, grabbed me, and tugged at my hand, as if he didn't want me to leave."
>
> Paul's mom, 52nd week

"I really have to keep a close eye on my daughter. If I want to set her down to go into the kitchen for a second to get something, she'll go for the dog, pretend to pet him, while at the same time she pulls out whiskers and tufts of fur."

> Emily's mom, 53rd week

He May Want to Be Entertained

Your little one may start asking for more attention. Most children do. Demanding ones do this all day long. But even easy, even-tempered children prefer doing things together with their mothers.

"My daughter keeps coming to get me, pulls me along by my hand so we can play together, with her blocks or dolls or to look at a book together."

> Jenny's mom, 53rd week

He May Be Jealous

Some more possessive children seem to put on an act when their mothers pay attention to someone or something else. They pretend to be cranky, mischievous, or determined to hurt themselves. Others act sweetly and cuddly in an exaggerated way in order to get their mothers' attention.

"My son gets jealous when I give something to the tiny baby I look after."

> Matt's mom, 53rd week

"My friend came over with her baby. Every time I said something to her baby, mine would step in between us with this big grin on her face."

> Jenny's mom, 54th week

He May Be Moody

Your little one may be happily occupied one moment, then become sad, angry, or infuriated the next, for no apparent reason. You may not be able to pinpoint a particular cause.

"Sometimes, my son will sit and play with his blocks like a little angel, but then suddenly he'll become furious. He shrieks and slams his blocks together or throws them across the room."

Steven's mom, 52nd week

He May Sleep Poorly

Your child may sleep less well. Most children resist going to bed, have difficulty falling asleep, and wake up sooner. Some sleep less well during the day, others are restless at night, and still others simply refuse to go to bed quietly at any time.

"This week, I noticed for the first time that my toddler often lies awake for a while at night. Sometimes, she'll cry a little. If I pick her up, she goes back to sleep in seconds."

Ashley's mom, 54th week

"We'd really like our daughter to make less of a fuss about going to sleep. Right now, it involves a lot of screaming and crying, sometimes almost hysterics, even when she's exhausted."

Jenny's mom, 52nd week

"My son is awake a lot during the night, terribly distressed. He really panics. Sometimes, it's hard to get him to calm down again."

Bob's mom, 52nd week

He May "Daydream"

Occasionally, some children can just sit, staring out into nothingness, as if they are in their own little worlds. Mothers do not like this dreaming one bit. Because of this, they will often try to break into these reveries.

"Sometimes, my daughter will sit, slouching and rocking back and forth, gazing into thin air. I always drop whatever I'm doing to shake her and wake her up again. I'm terrified there might be something wrong with her."

Juliette's mom, 54th week

He May Lose His Appetite

Many little ones are fussy eaters. Their mothers almost always find this troubling and irritating. A child who is still being breastfed usually wants the breast more often, not because he really wants to nurse, but so he can stay close to his mother.

> "My daughter is suddenly less interested in food. Previously, she would finish everything within 15 minutes. She was like a bottomless pit. Now it sometimes takes me half an hour to feed her."
>
> Ashley's mom, 53rd week

> "My son sprays his lunch around with his mouth. He dirties everything. The first few days, I thought it was quite funny. Not anymore, I should add."
>
> Bob's mom, 53rd week

He May Be More Babyish

Sometimes, a supposedly vanished babyish behavior will resurface. Mothers do not like to see this happen—they expect steady progress. Still, during fussy phases, relapses such as these are perfectly normal. It tells you that progress, in the shape of a new world, is on its way.

> "My daughter crawled again a couple of times, but she probably just did it to get attention."
>
> Jenny's mom, 55th week

> "My daughter is putting things in her mouth a little more often again, just like she used to."
>
> Hannah's mom, 51st week

"My son wants me to feed him again. When I don't do this, he pushes his food away."

> Kevin's mom, 53rd week

He May Act Unusually Sweet

Some little clingers suddenly come up to their mothers for a few moments just to cuddle with them. Then they are off again.

"Sometimes, my son comes crawling up to me just to be a real sweetie for a moment. He'll lay his little head very softly on my knees, for instance, very affectionately."

> Bob's mom, 51st week

"My daughter often comes up for a quick cuddle. She says 'kiss,' and then I get one, too."

> Ashley's mom, 53rd week

He May Reach for a Cuddly Object More Often

Your little one may cuddle a favorite object with a bit more passion. Many children do so, especially when they are tired or when their mothers are busy. They cuddle soft toys, rugs, cloths, slippers, or even dirty laundry. Anything soft that they can lay their little hands on will do. They kiss and pet their cuddly things as well. Mothers find this endearing.

"My son cuddles away while I'm busy. He'll hold his toy elephant's ear with one hand and stick two fingers from his other hand in his mouth. It's a sight to see."

> John's mom, 51st week

He May Be Mischievous

Your child may try to get your attention by being extra naughty, especially when you are busy and really have no time for him.

"I have to keep telling my daughter 'no' because she seems to do things just to get my attention. If I don't react, she will eventually stop. But I can't always do that because sometimes there's a chance she might break whatever it is she's taking apart."

Jenny's mom, 53rd week

"My son is being a handful at the moment. He touches everything and refuses to listen. I can't really get anything done until he's in bed."

Frankie's mom, 55th week

"Sometimes I suspect that my son doesn't listen on purpose."

Steven's mom, 51st week

He May Have More Temper Tantrums

If you have a hot-headed little tyke, he may go berserk as soon as he fails to get his own way. You may even see a tantrum that comes out of nowhere, perhaps because he is anticipating that you may not allow him to do or have what is on his mind.

"My son wants me to put him on my lap and feed him his bottle of fruit juice again. If he even suspects it might not happen quickly enough, he'll toss his bottle across the room and start screaming, yelling, and kicking to get me to take it back to him."

Matt's mom, 52nd week

"If I don't respond immediately when my daughter wants attention, she gets furious. She'll pinch the skin right off my arm, nastily, quickly, and violently."

Emily's mom, 53rd week

"My son refuses to have anything to do with 'bed.' He gets so angry that he bangs his chin on the railings of his crib, hurting himself every time. So now I'm really afraid to put him in bed."

Matt's mom, 52nd week

 My Diary

Signs My Baby Is Growing Again

Between 49 and 53 weeks, your child may show signs that he is ready to make the next leap, into the world of programs.

❑ Cries more often and is more often cranky or fretful

❑ Is cheerful one moment and cries the next

❑ Wants you to keep him busy, or does so more often

❑ Clings to your clothes or wants to be closer to you

❑ Acts unusually sweet

❑ Is mischievous

❑ Throws temper tantrums, or throws them more often

❑ Is jealous

❑ Is more obviously shy with strangers

❑ Wants physical contact to be tighter or closer

❑ Sleeps poorly

❑ Has "nightmares," or has them more often

❑ Loses appetite

❑ Sometimes just sits there, quietly daydreaming

❑ Sucks his thumb, or does so more often

❑ Reaches for a cuddly toy, or does so more often

❑ Is more babyish

OTHER CHANGES YOU NOTICE

_____

_____

_____

"I was visiting friends with my daughter and talking with one of them. Suddenly, my daughter grabbed the cup and smashed it on the floor, tea and all."

Laura's mom, 55th week

How This Leap May Affect You

No doubt you're feeling the stress of your baby's changes as well, if only vicariously. Here are some of the signs.

You May Feel Insecure

When a mother is confronted with a little fusspot, she may at first be worried. She wants to know what is wrong with her child. But at this age, irritation soon sets in.

Also during this period, some mothers wonder why their children are not walking as quickly as they expected them to. They worry that there might be something physically wrong with them.

"We spent a lot of time practicing, and I'm amazed that my daughter can't walk on her own yet. She's been walking while holding my hand for so long now that I feel she should have been walking long ago. Besides, I think one of her feet is pointing inward, so she keeps tripping over it. I showed them at the day care center. They told me that I wasn't the only mother worried about a foot pointing inwards at this age. Still, I'll be happier when she's walking."

Emily's mom, 53rd week

You May Become Really Frustrated

Toward the end of the fussy period, parents often become increasingly aggravated by their babies' demands on them. They become increasingly annoyed by seemingly purposeful mischief and the way they use temper

tantrums to get their own way.

> "I'm so annoyed by my daughter's crying fits whenever I leave the room. I can't stand the fact that she immediately crawls after me either, clutching my leg and crawling along with me. I can't get anything done this way. When I've had enough, it's off to bed with her, I'm afraid."
>
> Juliette's mom, 52nd week

> "My son keeps pulling at the big plant to get my attention. Distracting him doesn't work. Now I get angry and push him away, or I give him a gentle slap on his bottom."
>
> Matt's mom, 56th week

> "My daughter flies into a rage every other minute whenever she's not allowed to do something or can't manage it. She'll throw her toys and start whining like mad. I try to ignore this. But if she has several tantrums in a row, I put her to bed. When she first started doing this 2 weeks ago, I thought it was very amusing. Now I'm terribly aggravated by it. Her sisters just laugh at her. Sometimes, when she sees them doing that, it brightens her up and she'll start smiling back at them, shyly. It usually does the trick, but not all of the time."
>
> Ashley's mom, 53rd week

You May Argue

During this fussy period, quarrels are usually brought on by temper tantrums.

> "I feel myself getting angry when my daughter starts bawling if she isn't getting her own way. This week, she got furious when I wouldn't immediately follow her into the kitchen. So I gave her a good smack on the bottom, after which her rage turned into real tears. I know I shouldn't have done it, but I was fed up."
>
> Jenny's mom, 54th week

It is understandable that things can get too much sometimes. But hitting or a "good smack on the bottom" does not solve anything. It unnecessarily hurts your baby and damages the trust your baby has in you.

During each fussy period, mothers who breastfeed feel a desire to stop. At this age, this is because the baby keeps wanting the breast by fits and starts, or because his demands are accompanied by temper tantrums.

"I've really given up now. My son would throw temper tantrums from just thinking about my breast. It messed up our entire relationship with him tugging at my sweater, kicking, screaming, and me getting angry. Perhaps those tantrums will start to disappear now, too. The last time he nursed was on the night of his first birthday."

Matt's mom, 53rd week

How Your Baby's New Skills Emerge

Around 55 weeks, you will notice that your little one is less fussy. At the same time, you should notice that he is attempting and achieving entirely new things again. He deals with people, toys, and other objects in a more mature way and he enjoys doing new things with familiar toys and household objects that have been there since he was born. At this point, he doesn't quite feel like your little "baby" any more but will seem to be transformed into a little toddler. This is because he is entering the world of programs where he is beginning to see that the world is full of goals and sequences of action leading up to such a goal. This new flexible world is his to discover, but, as usual, he will want to do this in his own way and at his own speed. As a parent, your help will be as vital as ever, although it may not always feel that way when another temper tantrum rolls in.

In the past leap in development, your baby learned to deal with the notion of sequences—where events follow one after another or objects fit together in a particular way. A program is more complicated than a sequence because you can reach the end result in any number of ways.

An adult's world is filled with complicated programs. Fortunately, your child's world is simpler. Instead of dealing with enormous programs like "going on a vacation," your child will be working with programs such as "eating lunch." However, operating a program entails choices at each crossroad—rather like finding your way across town. During lunch, he will have to decide after every bite whether he would rather take another bite of the same food, switch to something different, have a sip of his drink, or perhaps even three sips. He can decide whether to take the next bite with his hands or use a spoon. He can decide to finish what he has or clamor for dessert. Whatever he opts for, it will still be the "eating lunch" program.

Your toddler will as usual experiment with this new world. Expect him to play with the different choices he can make at every juncture—he may just want to try everything out. He needs to learn what the possible consequences are of the decisions he makes at different points—so he could decide to empty the next spoonful on the floor instead of in his mouth.

He can also decide when to put a program into operation. For example, he can get the broom out of the closet because he wants to sweep the floor. He can get his coat because he wants to go out and do the shopping. Unfortunately, misunderstandings are quick to occur. After all, he can not explain what he wants yet and his mother can easily interpret him wrongly. This is very frustrating for such a young person, and a temperamental child might even throw a tantrum. Even if a mother does understand her child correctly, she may just not want

Brain Changes

Your child's brain waves will show changes again at approximately 12 months. Also, her head circumference will increase, and the glucose metabolism in her brain will change.

to do whatever he wants at that very moment. This, too, can frustrate such a toddler quite quickly, for he can't understand the idea of "waiting" at this age.

Besides being able to learn how to carry out a program himself, he can now perceive when someone else is doing the same thing. So he can begin to understand that if his mother is making tea, a snack will follow shortly and he can expect a cookie—or not.

Now that your toddler can learn to perceive and explore this world, he also understands that he has the choice of refusing a program he does not like—at least in theory. If he doesn't agree with his mother's plan, he may feel frustrated and sometimes even have a temper tantrum. You may be seeing a lot of them these days.

Your Toddler's Choices: A Key to Her Personality

All toddlers will begin at this age to understand and experiment with the world of programs, a world that offers a wide range of new skills to play with. Your child will choose those things that interest her, things that she has perhaps watched others do in the world about her, but also those things that most suit her own inclinations, interests, and physique. Every little individual learns about programs in her own way. Some children will be acute watchers, studying with care the way things are done around them. Others may want to "help" all the time. Yet others will want to do it themselves, and they will let you know in no uncertain terms that they do not want any interference.

(continued on page 289)

 My Diary

How My Baby Explores the New World of Programs

Check off the boxes below as you notice your baby changing. Some of the skills in the list below may not appear until weeks or months later. Your toddler will exercise his own choices in exploring what he can do in his new world.

STARTING A PROGRAM HIMSELF

❏ Gets out a broom or duster and tries sweeping or dusting

❏ Goes to the bathroom and tries cleaning the toilet bowl

❏ Comes to you with things he wants to be put away

❏ Gets out the cookie jar and expects a snack

❏ Comes to you with coat, cap, or bag to go shopping

❏ Gets out his coat and shovel, ready to go to the sandbox

❏ Gets out his clothes and wants to put them on

JOINING IN WITH YOUR PROGRAM

❏ Throws the cushions from the chair in advance to help when you are cleaning

❏ Tries to hang the towel back in place when you are finished

❏ Puts an object or a food item away in the right cupboard

❏ Brings her own plate, silverware, and place mat when you are setting the table

❏ Tells you by word, sound, or gesture that it is time to bring out the dessert when she has finished eating

❏ Puts spoons in cups and usually starts stirring

❏ Grabs an item from you and wants to carry it herself

❑ Tries to put something on by herself while she is being dressed or helps by pulling on her leggings or sleeves

❑ Picks out a tape or CD and helps put it on. Knows which button to press for play or eject

EXECUTING A PROGRAM UNDER SUPERVISION

❑ Puts differently shaped blocks through the correct holes in a box when you help by pointing out what goes where

❑ Uses the potty when you ask him to or when he needs to. Then carries the potty to the bathroom by himself or helps you carry it (if he is not walking) and flushes

❑ Gets out pens and paper and scribbles when you help him to

INDEPENDENT PROGRAMS

❑ Tries feeding dolls or cuddly toys, copying her own eating program

❑ Tries giving a doll a bath by copying her own bathing ritual

❑ Tries putting doll on the potty, maybe after she uses it

❑ Eats everything on her plate without help; often she wants to do this while sitting at the table politely like the grown-ups

❑ Eats raisins by herself from a packet

❑ Builds a tower of at least three blocks

❑ Starts and continues a telephone conversation, sometimes dialing at the start or ending the conversation with "bye"

❑ Crawls through the room following "paths" of her own choice, under chairs and table and through narrow tunnels, and often indicates which direction she intends to go first

(continued)

 My Diary (cont.)

❑ Crawls through the room with a toy car or train saying "vroom vroom." Follows all sorts of different routes—under chairs and tables, or between the sofa and the wall

❑ Is capable of finding something you hid

WATCHING OTHERS CARRYING OUT A PROGRAM

❑ Watches a cartoon or children's show on television, which manages to keep his attention for about 3 minutes

❑ Listens to a short story on the radio or on CD

❑ Expresses understanding of what is happening in pictures —for example, by saying "yum" when the child or animal in the picture is eating or being offered something to eat

❑ Looks and listens when you play "pretend" games—feeding, bathing and dressing his dolls and cuddly toys, or making them talk and answer

❑ Studies how older children carry out a program with their toys—how they play with a tea set, a garage with cars, doll's bed, or train set

❑ Studies other family members when they are carrying out an everyday program, for instance, when they are getting dressed, eating, drawing, or telephoning

OTHER CHANGES YOU NOTICE

_____

_____

_____

You are probably getting to know the personality of your toddler quite well by now, and many of her choices will follow patterns that you've noticed previously as she has grown. She is still capable of exploring new skills and interests, however, as the opportunity presents itself. Watch your toddler carefully to determine where her interests lie. Use the list on pages 286-288 to mark or highlight what your child selects. Between 55 and 61 weeks, she will start to choose what she wants to explore from the world of programs. Remember to respect those choices and to let your child develop at her own pace. Concentrate on helping her to do what she is ready to do. Young children love anything new and it is important that you respond when you notice any new skills or interests. She will enjoy it if you share these new discoveries, and her learning will progress more quickly.

What You Can Do to Help

Help your toddler as he makes his first tentative steps toward his encounters with programs. Talk about what he's going to achieve and how he's going to do it. If he enjoys watching you, encourage this. Talk about what you are doing as you are carrying out your program. Offer him opportunities to help you. Allow him to try carrying out his own program when you notice that he seems to have one in mind.

Help Your Baby Explore the New World through Independence

If your child is interested in dressing, undressing, and grooming herself, then let her see how you do these things. Explain to her what you are doing as well as why you are doing it. She will be able to understand more than she is able to tell you. If you have a little time, let her toy with washing and dressing herself or, if she wants to, somebody else in the family.

"My daughter tries pulling her trousers up by herself or putting her own slippers on, but she can't do it yet. Then suddenly I found her walking around in my slippers."

Jenny's mom, 55th week

"My daughter likes walking around with a cap or hat on. Whether it's mine, hers, or a doll's—it's all the same to her."

Eve's mom, 57th week

"This past week, my son kept putting all sorts of things on his head: dish-cloths, towels, and, a few times, someone's pants. He'd walk around the house impervious to his surroundings while his brother and sister were on the floor laughing."

Frankie's mom, 59th week

"As soon as my daughter is dressed, she crawls over to my dressing table and tries to spray herself with perfume."

Laura's mom, 57th week

"Yesterday, when I went into my son's room to get him, he was standing up in his crib grinning like mad. He had gotten almost completely undressed by himself."

John's mom, 58th week

"My daughter feeds her dolls, bathes them, and puts them to bed. When she's used her potty, she'll put her dolls on the potty, as well."

Jenny's mom, 56th week

If your little one wants to eat on his own, let him try it as often as you can. Keep in mind that he is creative enough to want to test different methods of eating—and all of them will probably be messy. If cleaning up gets tiring, you can make cleaning easier by putting a large sheet of plastic on the floor under his chair.

"Since my son has learned how to eat his dinner by himself with a spoon, he insists on doing it completely on his own. Otherwise, he won't eat. He also insists on sitting in his chair at the table when he's eating."

> Kevin's mom, 57th week

"Suddenly, my daughter discovered it was great fun to first stir something with a spoon, then stick it in her mouth."

> Jenny's mom, 56th week

"My son loves eating raisins from a packet by himself."

> Matt's mom, 57th week

"My daughter says 'pie' when she's finished eating her food, so she knows there's more to come. As soon as she's finished her dessert, she has to be taken out of her chair."

> Emily's mom, 60th week

Bags, purses with money inside, the television set, the radio, cleaning utensils, makeup—many little persons want to use everything the same way their mothers do. Some children now leave their own toys lying somewhere in a corner. Try to work out what your little one is trying to do, even if he does not always make life easy for you.

"I saw my son pushing phone buttons for the first time today, putting the receiver to his ear, and babbling busily. A few times he said 'dada' before hanging up."

> Frankie's mom, 56th week

"My daughter picked up the phone when it rang and I was out of the room for a second and really 'talked' to her grandma."

> Emily's mom, 60th week

"My little girl knows exactly which button to press to open the cassette player. When she comes to me with a CD of children's songs, she'd really prefer to be putting it in the CD player herself."

> Jenny's mom, 57th week

"My son is in love with the toilet bowl. He throws all sorts of things in it, and cleans it with the brush every 2 minutes, drenching the bathroom floor at the same time."

> Frankie's mom, 56th week

"My son brings me newspapers, empty beer bottles, and shoes. He wants me to tidy up and put them away."

> Frankie's mom, 56th week

Help Your Baby Explore the New World through Toys

Many children now become interested in more complex playthings that allow them to imitate programs, such as a garage with cars, a train with track, a farmhouse with animals, dolls with diapers or clothes, tea sets with pots and pans, or a play shop with packages and boxes. If your little one shows an interest in such toys, offer him opportunities to play with them. Help him once in a while. It is still a very complicated world for him.

"When I sit next to my son on the floor and encourage him, he'll sometimes build towers as high as eight blocks."

> Matt's mom, 57th week

"When my daughter plays on her own and needs help, she'll call out 'Mama.' Then she'll show me what she wants me to do."

> Hannah's mom, 55th week

"My daughter is becoming increasingly interested in Primo toys, especially the little people and the cars. She's also starting to try to build things from the blocks. She fits the pieces together properly once in a while. She can continue doing this for quite a long time."

Emily's mom, 57th week

"My son is getting much better at playing by himself. Now he is seeing new possibilities in old playthings. His cuddly toys, trains, and cars are starting to come alive."

Bob's mom, 55th week

Most children are interested in seeing the "real thing," too. For example, if your baby is interested in garages, take him to see cars being repaired. If he is interested in horses, tour a riding school. And if his tractor, crane, or boat is his favorite toy, he will certainly want to see a real one working.

Help Your Baby Explore the New World through Language and Music

When he leaps into the world of programs, your child becomes fascinated by stories. You can let him hear and see them. You could let him watch a story on television, you could let him listen to a tape, or best of all, you could tell him a story yourself, with or without a picture book. Just make sure that the stories correspond with whatever your child is experiencing himself or with his interests. For some children, this will be cars, for others it will be a special flower, animals, the swimming pool, or his cuddly toys. Keep in mind that each story must contain a short and simple program. Most little ones of this age can only concentrate on a story for about 3 minutes.

"My son can really become absorbed in a toddler show on television. It's very funny. Previously he just wasn't interested."

Kevin's mom, 58th week

Also offer a budding little talker the opportunity to tell his own story when you are looking at a picture book together.

"My daughter can understand a picture in a book. She'll tell me what she sees. For instance, if she sees a kid in a picture giving a treat to another kid, she'll say, 'yum.'"

Hannah's mom, 57th week

Many little children are eager chatterboxes. They will tell you entire "stories" complete with questions, exclamations, and pauses. They expect a response. If your toddler is a storyteller, try to take his stories seriously, even if you are still unable to understand what he is saying. If you listen closely, you may sometimes be able to make out a real word.

"My son talks until your ears feel like they're about to drop off. He really holds a conversation. Sometimes he'll do it in the questioning mode. It sounds really cute. I would love to know what he's trying to tell me."

Frankie's mom, 58th week

"My son chatters away like crazy. Sometimes he'll stop and look at me until I say something back, and then he'll continue his story. This past week, it sounded like he was saying 'kiss,' and then he actually gave me a kiss. Now I pay 10 times more attention."

Frankie's mom, 59th week

Many little ones love listening to children's songs so long as they are simple and short. Such a song is a program as well. If your toddler

---

Be Happy with His Help

When you notice your child is trying to lend you a hand, then accept this. He is beginning to understand what you are doing and needs to learn to do his own share.

> "My daughter wants to help with everything. She wants to carry the groceries, hang the dishcloth back in place when I'm done, carry the place mats and silverware to the table when I'm setting the table, and so on."
>
> **Emily's mom, 62nd week**

> "My daughter knows that apple juice and milk belong in the fridge and runs to the door to open it. For cookies, she goes straight to the cupboard and gets out the tin."
>
> **Jenny's mom, 57th week**

---

likes music, she may now like to learn how to make all the appropriate gestures as well.

> "My daughter plays *Pat a cake, pat a cake, baker's man* all by herself, complete with incomprehensible singing."
>
> **Jenny's mom, 57th week**

Some children also have a lot of fun playing their own piece of music. Drums, pianos, keyboards, and flutes seem to be their particular favorites. Naturally, most budding musicians prefer grown-up instruments, but they will be able to do less harm with a toy instrument.

"My daughter loves her toy piano. Usually, she plays with one finger and listens to what she's doing. She also likes to watch her father play his piano. Then she'll walk over to her piano and bang on it with both hands."

Hannah's mom, 58th week

Help Your Baby Explore the New World through Experimentation

If your toddler is a little researcher, you could see him performing the following program or experiment: how do these toys land, roll over, and bounce? Your little Einstein can go on examining these things for what seems like forever. For instance, he might pick up different toy people and drop them on the table 25 times and then repeat this up to 60 times with all sorts of building blocks. If you see your child doing this, then just let him carry on. This is his way of experimenting with the objects' characteristics in a very systematic way. He will be able to put this information to good use later on when he has to decide in the middle of a program

Teach Him to Respect You

Many children are now beginning to understand that you can be in the middle of a program, as well, such as when you are busy cleaning. When you notice your baby starts to comprehend these things, you can also start asking him to have consideration for you so that you can finish what you are doing. At this age, however, you can't expect him to wait too long.

"When my son wants to get his own way, he'll lay down on the floor just out of my arm's reach. That way I have to come to him."

Matt's mom, 56th week

Do Remember

Breaking old habits and setting new rules are also part of developing each new skill. Whatever new rules your baby understands, you can demand from him—nothing more, but also nothing less.

whether to do something this way or that. Toddlers are not simply playing—they are working hard, often putting in long hours, to discover how the world works.

"When my son is doing something, for instance building, he suddenly shakes his head, says 'no,' and starts to do it in a different way."

Kevin's mom, 55th week

"My daughter gets out her little locomotive to stand on when she wants to get her things from the closet. She used to always use her chair."

Jenny's mom, 56th week

Good to Know

Some children are exceptionally creative when it comes to inventing and trying out different ways to attain the same final goal. Gifted children can be particularly exhausting for their parents. They continually try to see if things can be done some other way. Whenever they fail or are forbidden to do something, they always look for another way around the problem or prohibition. It seems like a challenge to them never to do something the same way twice. They find simply repeating things boring.

(continued on page 300)

Top Games for This Wonder Week --------------

Here are games and activities that most toddlers like best now. Remember, all children are different. See what your little one responds to best.

DOING A JOB BY HIMSELF

Many toddlers love being allowed to do something very mature all by themselves. Making a mess with water is the most popular job. Most children calm down as they play with water.

GIVING THE DOLL A BATH

Fill a baby bath or a washing-up bowl with lukewarm water. Give your child a washcloth and a bar of soap, and let him lather up his doll or cuddly toy. Washing hair is usually a very popular part of this game.

DOING DISHES

Tie a large apron on your child, and put him on a chair in front of the sink. Fill the bowl with lukewarm water, and give him your dish sponge and an assortment of baby-friendly items to be washed, such as plastic plates, cups, wooden spoons, and all sorts of strainers and funnels. A nice topping of bubbles will make him even more eager to get to work. Make sure the chair he is standing on does not become slippery when wet, causing the busy person to lose his footing in his enthusiasm. Then stand back and let the fun begin.

HELPING OUT

Your toddler may prefer to do things with you. She can help pre-pare dinner, set the table, and shop for groceries. She will have her own ideas about the job, but she will learn a lot by doing it with you. This helps her feel grown-up and content.

UNPACKING AND PUTTING AWAY GROCERIES

Put fragile and dangerous things away first, then let your little assistant help you unpack. You can have him hand you or bring you the groceries one by one, as he chooses. Or you can ask him "Could you give me the . . . , and now the . . . " You can also ask him where he would put it. And finally, he can close the cupboard doors when you are finished. Encourage and thank him.

HIDE-AND-SEEK GAMES

Now you can make these games more complicated than before. When your child is in the right mood, he will usually enjoy displaying his tricks. Adjust the pace to your child. Make the game neither impossibly difficult nor too easy for him.

DOUBLE HIDING GAME

Place two cups before him and put a plaything under one of them. Then switch the cups around by sliding them across the table. This way, cup A will be where cup B was, and vice versa. The object of the exercise here is not to fool your toddler but the very reverse. Make sure that your child is watching closely when you move the cups and encourage him to find the toy. Give him plenty of praise for each attempt. This is really very complicated for him.

SOUND GAME

Many toddlers love looking for a sound. Take your child on your lap and let her see and hear an object that can make a sound—for instance, a musical box. Then close her eyes and have someone else hide the object while it is playing. Make sure that your little one cannot see where it is being hidden. When it has vanished from sight, encourage her to look for it.

"When I ask my daughter, 'Do you need to use your potty?' she'll use it if she really does need to. She pees, carries it to the bathroom herself, and flushes. But sometimes she'll be sitting, then she'll get up and pee next to her potty."

Jenny's mom, 54th week

Show Understanding for Irrational Fears

When your little one is busy exploring his new world, he will run into things that he does not fully understand. Along the way, he discovers new dangers, ones that he never imagined existed. He is still unable to talk about them, so show him a little understanding. His fear will disappear only when he starts to understand everything better.

"All of a sudden, my son was frightened of our ship's lamp when it was on, probably because it shines so brightly."

Paul's mom, 57th week

"My daughter is a little scared of the dark. Not once she is in the dark, but to walk from a lit room into a dark room."

Jenny's mom, 58th week

"My son gets frightened when I inflate a balloon. He doesn't get it."

Matt's mom, 58th week

"My daughter was frightened by a ball that was deflating."

Eve's mom, 59th week

"My son gets terribly frightened by loud noises, like jet airplanes, telephones, and the doorbell ringing."

Bob's mom, 55th week

"My daughter is scared of everything that draws near quickly. Like the parakeet, fluttering around her head, her brother chasing her, and a

Top Toys for This Wonder Week

Here are toys and things that most babies like best now:

- Dolls, doll strollers, and doll beds

- Farmhouse, farm animals, and fences

- Garage and cars

- Wooden train with tracks, platforms, bridges, and tunnels

- Unbreakable tea set

- Pots, pans, and wooden spoons

- Telephone

- Primo blocks

- Bicycle, car, toy horse or engine that he can sit on himself

- Push-along wagon that he can use to transport all sorts of things

- Rocking horse or rocking chair

- Box with differently shaped blocks and holes

- Stackable containers and rod with stackable rings

- Mop, hand broom, dustpan, and brush

- Colored sponges to scrub with or play with in the bath

- Large sheets of paper and markers

- Books with animals and their young or cars and tractors

- Musical instruments, such as drums, toy pianos, and xylophones

- Cassette tape or CD with simple short stories

Remember at this time to put away or take precautions with closets and drawers that might contain harmful or poisonous things, knobs on audio and video equipment, electrical appliances, ovens, and lights and power outlets.

remote control car that belonged to a friend of her older brother. It was just too fast for her."

Emily's mom, 56th week

"My son simply refuses to get into the bathtub. He doesn't mind getting into the baby bath when it's in the big bath."

Frankie's mom, 59th week

Around 59 weeks, most toddlers become a little less troublesome than they were. Some are particularly admired for their friendly talkativeness and others for their cute eagerness to help out with the housekeeping. Most are now beginning to rely less on temper tantrums to get their own way. In short, their independence and cheerfulness assert themselves once again. With their new liveliness and mobility, however, many mothers may still consider their little ones to be a bit of a handful. That's because they think they know it all, but you know they still have to learn so much.

"My daughter is painstakingly precise. Everything has its own little place. If I make changes, she'll notice and put things back. She also doesn't hold onto anything anymore when she's walking. She will happily walk right across the room. To think I've been so worried over this."

Emily's mom, 60th week

"My son is perfectly happy in the playpen again. Sometimes he doesn't want to be taken out. I don't have to play along with him anymore, either. He keeps himself occupied, especially with his toy cars and puzzles. He's much more cheerful."

Paul's mom, 60th week

"My daughter doesn't play with toys anymore; she won't even look at them. Watching, imitating, and joining in with us is much more fascinating to her now. She's enterprising as well. She gets her coat and her bag when she wants to go out and the broom when something needs cleaning. She's very mature."

Nina's mom, 58th week

"Now that my son runs like the wind and wanders through the entire apartment, he also does a lot of things he shouldn't. He keeps putting away cups, beer bottles, and shoes, and he can be extremely imaginative. If I take my eye off him for a moment, those things end up in the trash can or the toilet. Then when I scold him, he gets very sad."

Frankie's mom, 59th week

"My daughter is such a lovely little girl, the way she plays, chit-chatting away. She's often so full of joy. Those temper tantrums seem like a thing of the past. But perhaps I'd better knock wood."

Ashley's mom, 59th week

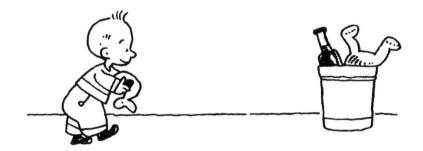

chapter 11

Wonder Week 64:
The World of Principles

After the previous leap, your little fellow began to understand what a "program" is. Your daily programs of eating, shopping, taking a stroll, playing, and washing the dishes seem normal to him at this stage. Sometimes he appears to be following your lead and other times he grabs the opportunity to show you what he can do. You also might have noticed that your little helper has a slightly different approach to household chores than that you have. He uses some string to vacuum. To mop, he uses a rag, wetting it in his mouth. And, he straightens up by using his magical powers to banish anything and everything in his way to that one special out-of-the-way spot: the bathroom, the trash or over the balcony. No more mess. Your little helper is still bound by certain strict routines, which tend to be a tad mechanical in nature. He is therefore, just a beginner in the complex world of programs. He is not yet able to adapt the program he is carrying out to different circumstances. It will require several years of experience before he becomes proficient in such matters.

We parents have the benefit of experience. You are able to adapt to change. You vary the order in which you do things. While grocery shopping, you opt for the short line at the butcher instead of joining a long line at the deli counter. Whether you are in a hurry or you want special ingredients for a recipe, you adapt. We also adapt our programs to those around us. If anyone asks your

Note: The first phase (fussy period) of this leap into the perceptual world of "principles" is age-linked and predictable, and starts between 59 and 63 weeks. Most babies start the second phase (see box "Quality Time: An Unnatural Whim" on page 17) of this leap 64 weeks after full-term birth. The first perception of the world of principles sets in motion the development of a whole range of skills and activities. However, the age at which these skills and activities appear for the first time varies greatly and depends on your baby's preferences, experimentation and physical development. For example, the ability to perceive principles is a necessary precondition for "pretending to cook for her dolls," but this activity normally appears at anywhere from 64 weeks to many months later. Skills and activities are mentioned in this chapter at the earliest possible age they might appear so you can watch for and recognize them. (They may be rudimentary at first.) This way you can respond to and facilitate your baby's development.

opinion, you measure your response in kind, given his or her status and age. You also adapt your mood or the direction you want your moods to go. You prepare a meal in different ways depending on whether you have time to relax and enjoy it or if you have to rush off to an important meeting. You anticipate everything happening that concerns you. You know what you want and how best to get it. You make sure that you achieve your goals. It is because of this that your programs appear to be so flexible and natural.

Your little angel is beginning to pick up on how he can better deal with certain situations as soon as he takes his next leap. He will land in the world of "principles." Around 64 weeks – approaching 15 months – you will notice him step up to try new things. It is a leap that has previously revealed itself to the little fellow.

Around 61 weeks – 14 months – our little tyke begins to notice that "things are a changin." A maze of new impressions is turning his reality on its head. Initially, it is quite a task for him to deal with the changes. First he will have to create some order in this new-found chaos. He turns back to familiar surroundings. He becomes clingy. He needs a "mommy refill."

This
Week's Fussy
Signs

Is your baby quick to cry? Many mothers complain that they rarely hear their baby laugh any more. They label their toddler "more often earnest" or "more often sad." The moments of sadness are unexpected, are usually short lived with no clear cause.

Do Remember

If your little one becomes clingy, watch for new skills or him attempting new things.

"This week he cried a lot. Why? I don't know. All of a sudden he burst out in tears."

Gregory's mom, 64th week, or 14½ months

Your little one could also be more irritable, impatient, frustrated or angry; for instance if he even thinks that mommy is not standing by at his beck and call, or if mommy does not understand what he wants or says, or if mommy corrects him or tells him "NO!" This could even happen if his latest building project was to topple or if a chair refuses to move or if he runs into a table.

"If she does not receive my direct attention, she sprawls out on the ground bawling."

Josie's mom, 62nd week, or 14 months

"She is more quickly irritated, angry and impatient than she was. If she wants to tell me something and I don't fully understand what she wants, she starts to scream and fuss even louder."

Eve's mom, 64th week, or 14½ months

"He was very whiny this week. His crying became louder and more insistent if he didn't get his way or if he was made to wait. The same was the case if my hands were full and I was unable to pick him up."

Kevin's mom, 65th week, or approaching 15 months

"He is really struggling. If he is unable to do something right the first time, he throws a tantrum."

Gregory's mom, 66th week, or 15 months

How You Know It's Time to Grow

She May Cling to Your Clothes

Most toddlers do whatever is necessary to be around mommy. But little kids become bigger. Occasionally, some toddlers are content if they can tempt mommy into a game of just briefly making eye contact and looking away. This is a considerable step towards independence. However, more often than not, the toddler is more like a small baby. She is only happy if sitting on a lap or being carried around. Sometimes when she is especially clingy, mother decides that transport by baby carrier is best – and the little clinger happily submits.

"He followed me constantly, dragging his toy. If I stood still or sat down, he would play at my feet or even under them. It began to wear on me."

Kevin's mom, 62nd week, or 14 months

"She constantly wanted to climb on my lap, but that was inconvenient because I was ironing. I put her in the center of the room a few times with her toys, but no, she only had eyes for my lap. The next time she went for my lap, she caught the cord of the iron bringing it down on my foot. Because she was tangled in the cord, I was unable to get the iron off my foot right away, which made me shout in pain. She then clamped on to my leg and let out a cry. By the time I had finally freed myself, she was so upset that I had to carry her with me to the bathroom so that I could put my foot under some cold running water. Lesson one: no ironing with her around!"

Julia's mom, 63rd week, or 14 months and a week

"He loves to get my attention from a short distance, just glancing at each other. He glows from our mutual relation."

Luke's mom 63rd week, or 14 months and a week

"This week he clung to me, literally. He climbed up my back. Hung in my hair. Crawled up against me. He sat between my legs and clamped on so that I was unable to take a step. All the while, making a game of it, and making it difficult to become impatient. And, in the meantime, he had it his way."

Matt's mom, 65th week, or approaching 15 months

"He crawls onto my lap more often, but doesn't stay there. Even if he is walking around he likes to be picked up for a bit."

Frankie's mom, 66th week, or 15 months

She May be Shyer with Strangers

Most children don't stray from mother's side when in the company of strangers. Some seem to try to climb back into mommy. They absolutely do not want to be picked up by another person. Their mother is the only one who may touch them, sometimes the only one who can talk to them. Even father may be too much. Mostly, they seem frightened. You think sometimes that they are getting shy.

"When we are visiting or we have guests, he stays right around me for a while before slowly venturing further. But as soon as it even looks like someone else wants to pick him up, he hurries to me to cling for a while."

Gregory's mom, 64th week, or 14 ½ months

"He is shy with strangers. If there is a group, he crawls and puts his head between my legs and stays there for a bit."

Kevin's mom, 63rd week, or 14 months and a week

"He cries if I leave him in a room with other people. If I go to the kitchen, so does he. Especially today, he never left my side, and this while his grandmother was in the room. He knows his grandmother well and sees her every day."

Frankie's mom, 63rd week, or 14 months and a week

"Even if her father wants her attention, she turns her head away. And when he puts her in her bath, she starts to scream. She only wants to be with me."

Josie's mom, 64th week, or 14½ months

She May Want Physical Contact to Be as Close as Possible

Often a small child does not want the distance between him and his mother to increase. If someone is going to go anywhere, then the toddler wants to be that one. Mommy must remain at the spot where she is and not move one bit.

"She hates when I leave. She doesn't even want me getting up for a shower. If I get out of bed in the morning and she is left with her father, then she starts shrieking. I have to take her if I want to get out of bed. She never did that before."

Laura's mom, 62nd week, or 14 months

"When I leave her at daycare and try to leave, she cries her eyes out. She only did that in the beginning though."

Ashley's mom, 65th week, or approaching 15 months

"He gets angry when I drop him at daycare and he lets me know when I pick him up. He ignores me for a while. As if I don't exist. However when he is done with ignoring me, he is really sweet and snuggles up by putting his head on my shoulder!"

Mark's mom, 66th week, or 15 months

She May Want to Be Entertained

Most toddlers don't like to play alone. They want mommy to play along. They don't want to feel alone and will follow mommy if she walks away. She is really

saying: "If you don't feel like playing with me, then I'll just tag along with you." And because mommy's tasks are usually domestic, household tasks are very popular, although not for every child. Now and then some clever little one thinks up a new strategy with a playful dodge or antic to lure mother to play. Such an enterprise is difficult to resist. Even though mother may be held up with her work, she is willing to overlook it. Her toddler is already getting big.

> "When it is least convenient, he wants us to listen to a child's CD. I have to snuggle up to him, grin and bear it. Even peeking in a magazine is out of the question."
>
> **Robin's mom, 63rd week, or 14 months and a week**

> "She hardly plays anymore, she follows me around constantly. Just wants to see what I'm doing around the house and put her nose in the middle of it."
>
> **Jenny's mom, 64th week, or 14½ months**

> "He almost never wanted to play by himself. The whole day long it was horse riding and mommy was the horse. With cute little ploys he kept me occupied, all the while thinking that I wasn't on to his little game."
>
> **Matt's mom, 65th week, or approaching 15 months**

She May Be Jealous

Sometimes toddlers want extra attention from mother when she is in the company of others – especially if the others are children. It makes them insecure. They want mommy for themselves, they must be the center of mother's attention.

"He particularly wants my attention when I'm around others. Especially if the others are children. Then he gets jealous. He does listen though if I tell him that it is time to go and play by himself, but he stays around me."

Thomas' mom, 61st week, or 14 months

"Sometimes he gets jealous if another child is on my lap. I never saw him do this before."

Taylor's mom, 62nd week, or 14 months

She May Be Moody

Some mothers notice that their little one's mood can change completely very quickly. One moment the little chameleon is grumpy, the next she is all smiles. One minute she is very cuddly, the next so angry that she sweeps her cup clean off the table, then she can become sad with gushing tears, and so on. You could say that your toddler is practicing for puberty. Little ones at this age are capable of many forms of behavior to express their feelings. And a child that is at odds with himself tries them all.

"She went back and forth from sulky to cheerful, clingy to independent, earnest to silly, unruly to compliant. And all these different moods took turns as if everything was completely normal. It was quite a chore."

Juliette's mom, 62nd week, or 14 months

"One moment he is into mischief, the next he's an example of obedience. One moment he is hitting me, the next he is kissing me. One moment he insists on doing everything himself and the next he's pitiful and needs my help."

Mark's mom, 65th week, or approaching 15 months

She May Sleep Poorly

Many little ones sleep less well. They don't want to go to bed and cry when it's time, even during the day. Sometimes mothers say their child's entire sleeping

pattern seems to change. They suspect that their child is on the verge of moving from two naps a day to one. Although the children do fall asleep, many mothers are not at peace. The poor sleepers cry in their sleep, or they regularly awaken into helplessness. They are clearly afraid of something. Sometimes they fall back asleep if comforted. But some little ones only want to continue sleeping if mom stays with them or if they can occupy the precious spot between mom and dad in the big bed.

"Because she doesn't want to take daytime naps anymore, I put her with me during the day in my bed, thinking perhaps that would help. Nope. We ended up getting out of bed again. Result: She and I were dead tired! I think she is bordering on moving from 2 naps to one."

Josie's mom, 62nd week, or 14 months

"If she wakes up during the night, she clamps herself onto me. As if she were afraid."

Jenny's mom, 62nd week, or 14 months

"Sleeping was hopeless. He slept a lot, but he was tossing and turning. I kept hearing his cries. It didn't seem like he was getting his rest."

Mark's mom, 63rd week, or 14 months and a week

"She gets very busy, bothersome and tries to bite when bedtime comes. It seems like she doesn't want to sleep by herself. It takes some doing. After crying awhile, she does finally fall asleep, but after that I'm mentally drained. Last night, she slept in between us. She spreads out with an arm and a leg on papa and an arm and a leg on mommy."

Emily's mom, 64th week, or 14½ months

"It seems like he requires less sleep. He goes to bed later. He's also awake for half an hour every night. Then he wants to play."

Gregory's mom, 65th week, or approaching 15 months

She May Have "Nightmares"

Many toddlers have nightmares more often. Sometimes they wake up looking helpless, sometimes afraid or in a panic. And other times very frustrated, angry or hot-tempered.

> "Twice this week he woke up, screeching, covered in sweat and completely in a panic. It took him half an hour to stop crying. He was practically inconsolable. This has never happened before. I also noticed that it took him a while before being at ease again."
>
> Gregory's mom, 62nd week, or 14 months

> "At night he was often awake. He seemed helpless or really in a panic. One night he slept with me because he couldn't shake his anxiety. Lying next to me relaxes him."
>
> Thomas' mom, 62nd week, or 14 months

> "I saw that she was sound asleep, went downstairs and all of a sudden I hear a thump and loud screaming. I ran back upstairs and when I picked her up to console her, she was in the middle of a fit. She rolled on the ground, kicking and screaming. I tried to hold her close to me, but she resisted with everything she had. She simply had to get rid of her rage, which took a very long time."
>
> Julia's mom, 64th week, or 14½ months

She May "Daydream"

Sometimes little ones sit staring off in the distance. It's a time of self-reflection.

> "I noticed that he was rather quiet. He sat there staring. He'd never done that before."
>
> Thomas's mom, 63rd week, or 14 months and a week

"This week he was often noticeably in dreamland. He went and laid out on the floor and was just staring."

Gregory's mom, 65th week, or approaching 15 months

She May Lose Her Appetite

Not all toddlers have the best eating habits. Sometimes they simply skip a meal. Mothers find it difficult if their child does not eat well, and this gives the little one the attention he needs. Breastfeeding toddlers, however, do seem to want to feed more often. But as soon as they have sucked a little, they let go of the nipple and look around. Or they just hold the nipple in their mouth. After all they are where they want to be: with mom.

"He hasn't eaten well this week. Especially dinner. He turned his head away at the first bite, regardless what I put in front of him."

Frankie's mom, 64th week, or 14½ months

"He wakes up often during the night again and wants the breast. Is it habit or does he really need it? I wonder because he wants to feed so often. I also wonder if I'm not making him too reliant on me."

Bob's mom, 63rd week, or 14 months and a week

She May Be More Babyish

It could seem like your toddler is a baby again. That's not really the case. Regression during a clingy period means that progress is coming. And because children at this age are capable of so much more, a regression is more evident.

"She didn't use the words she had learned! All of a sudden she called all animals 'am.'"

Julia's mom, 61st week, or 14 months

"He's crawling more often again."

> Luke's mom, 63rd week, or 14 months and a week

"She is ready for her playpen again, full of baby toys!"

> Hannah's mom, 63rd week, or 14 months and a week

"If we timed it right and asked if she needed to pee, she would generally go to her potty, but now she is back to solely using diapers. As if she has completely forgotten how."

> Jenny's mom, 62nd week, or 14 months

"I am back to giving her bottles like when she was a baby. She won't even hold it herself."

> Emily's mom, 62nd week, or 14 months

She May Act Unusually Sweet

Some mothers succumb to a generous hug, kiss or barrage of petting from their children. The little ones have certainly noticed that it is more difficult for mom to resist these displays of affection than the whining, clinging and being a nuisance. And this way they can "fill-up on mom" if need be.

"Now he climbs up behind me in the chair and proceeds on to my neck to give me a massive hug."

> Matt's mom, 63rd week, or 14 months and a week

"Sometimes she is really affectionate. She comes and hugs with one arm around my neck, pressing her cheek into mine, strokes my face and kisses me. Even strokes and kisses the fur collar on my coat. She was never this affectionate before."

> Nina's mom, 65th week, or approaching 15 months

She May Reach for a Cuddly Object More Often

Sometimes toddlers use blankets, stuffed animals and all things soft to snuggle. They especially do this if Mom is busy.

"He snuggles a lot with his stuffed animals."

Matt's mom, 65th week, or approaching 15 months

She May Be Mischievous

Many toddlers are naughty on purpose. Being naughty is the perfect way to draw attention. If something breaks, is dirty or dangerous, or if the house gets turned upside down, Mom will have to address this misbehavior. This is a covert way to get a "mommy refill."

> "She is not allowed to touch the stereo, VCR or other such devices. She knows that's off limits! She gets one warning and then a swat on her fingers."
>
> Vera's mom, 62nd week, or 14 months

> "I was really angry when he deliberately threw some things over our balcony. There's no getting the things back because they landed in the water below. After that, if he did it again, I snatched him up and put him in his playpen explaining that such things are not allowed."
>
> Luke's mom, 62nd week, or 14 months

> "She purposefully misbehaves. She lays her hands precisely where she knows that they are not allowed. She shakes the gate for the stairs (it is destroyed by now), pulled out the knitting needles from my knitting, just for starters. It is really getting on my nerves."
>
> Vera's mom, 65th week, or approaching 15 months

"He repeatedly has periods where he only does what is not allowed. I am left doing nothing but saying 'no' and keeping an eye on him."

Gregory's mom, 66th week, or 15 months

She May Have More Temper Tantrums

Many toddlers are more quickly irritable, angry and out of sorts than mothers are used to from them. These little ones roll kicking and screaming on the ground if they don't get their way, if they can't manage something first time, if they are not understood directly, or even without any clear reason at all.

"She had her first temper tantrum. It's the newest thing. At first we thought that it was teething pain. She dropped to her knees and began screeching. It turned out to be a temper tantrum. No walk in the park!"

Josie's mom, 63rd week, or 14 months and a week

"When his father put him back in bed at 5:30 a.m., he really threw a fit. He obviously had other plans than we did."

Frankie's mom, 62nd week, or 14 months

"She wanted to eat without any help and we didn't get it at first. She screamed, started kicking and practically broke her chair. I had no idea that she could be such a pain. Quite a trial!"

Nina's mom, 62nd week, or 14 months

"When we're around other people, I can't move away an inch or he'll fall to the ground and throw a fit."

Frankie's mom, 63rd week, or 14 months and a week

"If she doesn't get her way, she throws herself to the ground screeching and refuses to sit or stand up. Then I pick her up and draw her attention to something else."

Julia's mom, 62nd week, or 14 months

My Diary

Signs My Baby Is Growing Again

Between 59 and 63 weeks, your child may show signs that he is ready to make the next leap, into the world of principles.

❑ Cries more often and is more often cranky or fretful

❑ Is cheerful one moment and cries the next

❑ Wants to be entertained, or does so more often

❑ Clings to your clothes or wants to be closer to you

❑ Acts unusually sweet

❑ Is mischievous

❑ Throws temper tantrums, or throws them more often

❑ Is jealous

❑ Is more obviously shy with strangers

❑ Wants physical contact to be tighter or closer

❑ Sleeps poorly

❑ Has nightmares, or has them more often

❑ Loses appetite

❑ Sometimes just sits there, quietly daydreaming

❑ Reaches for a cuddly toy, or does so more often

❑ Is more babyish

❑ Resists getting dressed

OTHER CHANGES YOU NOTICE

_____

_____

_____

_____

How this leap may affect you

You May Become Really Frustrated

Mothers clearly have less patience with clinging, whining and provocation from a child of this age. When he was still a little baby, such behavior made them worry. Now it makes them annoyed.

> "She never had problems sleeping before. Now she does. For the last couple of nights it's been nothing but crying. I am completely annoyed by it. The evenings are my time and now she is dominating them too. Hope this doesn't become a habit."
>
> **Maria's mom, 69th week, or approaching 16 months**

The moment mothers get annoyed, they will let it show. At this age a persistent toddler will hear it when his mother disapproves of his behavior. Using words he understands, she explains what she doesn't like. Language starts to play a greater role. And a whining nuisance is quicker to land in his playpen or in his bed than when he was younger. Mother's patience is shorter. Mothers think that their child is big enough to behave better. Additionally, they think that their toddlers should learn to be more considerate of them.

> "I have arranged that she stay with a nanny. It really annoys me that she clamps on to me when we go somewhere. All the other children are running around and playing with toys. She rarely does that. Only after she's stood aside and observed long enough does she begin to let go of my dress. I only hope that she can get over the clinging when she goes to the babysitter."
>
> **Julia's mom, 64th week, or 14½ months**

> "When I am cooking, he comes and sits right at my feet. If it becomes too much and he doesn't want to move out of the way when I ask, I put him in his playpen. Then my patience has run out."
>
> **Frankie's mom, 64th week, or 14½ months**

"He constantly wants to climb on my lap and, even better, go on the nipple – preferably from sun up til sun down. It really bothers me. First, I try to get him off me a bit by playfully distracting him. But if he continues coming and pulling on me, he has a good chance of winding up in bed. It just gets to be too much."

> **Robin's mom, 65th week, or approaching 15 months**

"Sometimes he wants to be picked up at the very moment I am busy with something and that bothers me. I try to explain in simple terms why I can't pick him up. And explaining helps!"

> **Gregory's mom, 65th week, or approaching 15 months**

"I can get rather perturbed when he pretends not to hear what I say. I grab him and turn him to face me, so that he has to look at me and listen when I say something."

> **Taylor's mom, 65th week, or approaching 15 months**

"If he persists in being naughty, doesn't know what he wants, cries for any little thing and doesn't listen to what I say, I assume that he is very tired and that it's time to go to bed. I need to let off a bit of steam, because then my patience is at its end."

> **Taylor's mom, 67th week, or 15 months and a week**

You May Argue

Your toddler is getting bigger. More and more often he and mom do not see eye-to-eye. If he is not allowed to interrupt, to cling or to be unruly, he rebels fiercely. Real quarrels are the result. Such an eruption is most likely at the end of the difficult period. That's when both mother and child are quickest of temper.

"We just had a real fight! He kept grabbing the kittens and pushing them around the floor like toy cars. I had to stop him."

> **Mark's mom, 63rd week, or 14 months and a week**

"He cries even louder if he doesn't get his way instead of quitting his rant. If he doesn't stop really quickly, I put him in his playpen as punishment. But he doesn't like that at all. He throws an enormous temper tantrum. I let him go until he's run out of steam, but it's not pleasant."

Luke's mom, 63rd week, or 14 months and a week

"She's driving us nuts. She cries a lot and requires constant attention from 7 in the morning until 10:30 at night. Sometimes, a good smack on the bottom is really necessary. Trying to talk to her is like talking to a brick wall; she won't listen. Her naps are only an hour-and-a-half. We don't have time for ourselves or each other any more because she practically runs our lives. Maybe we should pay less attention to her. I'd like to know if other children are this difficult at this age. We never hear other parents complaining. We're out of ideas. At the moment we're finding parenthood a rather thankless task."

Jenny's mom, 65th week, or approaching 15 months

If your baby seeks attention in such a willful way, it can make you desperate. That is quite normal. However, you should not react in desperation. Hurting your baby or child is never a good way to teach him the rules.

"If he doesn't get his way, he gets furious and hits me. That has been bothering me for some time and now my patience had reached its end. I gave him a rap so that he could just feel it. Then I explained to him at length that the hitting must stop."

Mark's mom, 65th week, or approaching 15 months

Your child does what you do. If he cannot hit you, then you should not hit him. If you hit your child, then there's not much sense in saying that he shouldn't hit. Your words must match your actions. Hitting solves nothing and it is not good for your little one.

"She refuses to listen and that can really get tedious or dangerous. Sometimes it is necessary that she gets a rap. But a rap doesn't always work. This week as things were already heated, I said, 'Mommy doesn't like you now, go away,' and her reaction got to me. She started crying uncontrollably. She really was mortified, worse than a rap. I hope that I never say that again in desperation. I didn't mean for it to be taken so literally."

Jenny's mom, 66th week, or 15 months

How Your Baby's New Skills Emerge

Around 64 weeks—almost 15 months—you notice that much of the clinginess starts to disappear. Your toddler is a bit more enterprising again. Perhaps you already see that he is different, and acts differently. He is getting much more willful. He thinks differently. Handles his toys differently. His sense of humor has changed. You see these changes, because at this age your toddler's ability to observe and implement "principles" is breaking through. Getting this ability is comparable with discovering a whole new world. Your toddler with his talents, preferences and temperament chooses where he wants to begin. Find out where he is going and help him with it. This new ability he has acquired sometimes "gives him a headache," as a figure of speech.

"He doesn't want to sit on my lap as much, he's active again."

Thomas' mom, 67th week, or 15 months and a week

"All listlessness and bad moods have passed. She even was happy to go to daycare. The difficult period has passed."

Josie's mom, 66th week, or 15 months

"Sometimes I worry. I have the feeling that he is busy inside. In a way he keeps more to himself. But at the same time he does like to be near me. Not to do anything together, but just to be near me."

Luke's mom, 67th week, or 15 months and a week

He plays longer by himself and is calmer, more focused, more solemn, enterprising, testing, observant, and independent in the sense that he does things himself. He is less interested in toys. His interests are more towards the domestic. Furthermore, he really likes being outside just wandering and exploring. He does need you to be around, though.

Now that your toddler takes her first steps into the world of "principles," you notice that she completes various "programs" more supply and naturally. You get now what she is doing and what she wants. Principles will influence her thought process. She starts to get on top of things, just like a teacher has to be on top of things in order to be able to explain it. Your tyke is no longer "caught up" in a program, rather she can "create" or change and judge for herself what's what. She starts to think about programs. And just as when executing programs she deliberates each move and decides if she will do it this way or that, in the world of principles your tyke starts thinking about thinking. She is busier upstairs. And she feels that.

"He's feeling his way with his head. Literally. Several things he touches with his forehead: the ground, the table leg, a book, his plate and so forth. He calls to show me. I can't follow him. Certain times I think he wants to say that you can bump into these things. Other times it seems to be the start of a new way of thinking, as if he feels that he can mentally comprehend the world."

Luke's mom, 67th week, or 15 months and a week

In the world of principles your little one will think ahead, contemplate, consider the consequences of her actions, make plans and evaluate them. She will come up with strategies: "Should I ask dad or grandma to get the candy?" "How can I delay subtly?" Naturally, your toddler is not very adept in devising plans, nor are they as complex as ours. As adults, it has taken us years to master this. By practice, every one of us has learned principles by executing programs and confronting several thousand different situations. Your little rookie can not fully comprehend the meaning of so many new things. As an "Alice in Wonderland," she wanders the complicated world of principles. It begins to sink in that from morning 'til night she will have to make choices. Yes, she notices that it is unavoidable: she must choose, choose and choose again. Perhaps you have noticed your little one endlessly hesitating over what she should do. Thinking is a full time job.

> "He now realizes that the whole day through he has to make all kinds of choices. He chooses very consciously and takes his time. He hesitates endlessly if he should turn on the TV, or perhaps not. If he should throw something off the balcony, or better not. If he will sleep in the big bed or the little one, and if he will sit with his father or with me. And so on."
>
> ### Luke's mom, 67th week, or 15 months and a week

In the world of principles your child not only has to choose what she will do, but while she is doing it she must continue making choices: "Should I wreck my tower, just leave it or build it higher?" And if she chooses the latter, she must choose how to do it: "Should I put a block on my tower next or this time a doll?" With everything she does, she will have to choose: "Should I go about it carefully, sloppily, recklessly, quickly, wildly, dangerously or carefully?" If mom thinks that it is bedtime, she will have to choose whether to go along quietly or if to try to delay. Again she must choose: "Which is the best strategy for keeping me out of bed the longest? Just scampering away as fast as I can? Pull a plant out of its pot? Or pull some other stunt?" And if she knows full well that something is not allowed, she must choose whether or not to just go for it or if to wait until the coast is clear. She contemplates, chooses, tests and makes mom desperate.

With all these choices, it dawns on your toddler that she, too, can manage, just like mom, dad and everyone else. She becomes possessive as well. She doesn't readily share her toys, especially not with other children. She now counts as a person. She is queen of her own world. Her own will is on overtime. One moment she decides to place a full cup on the table carefully and the next she lets the cup fall down and spills the contents. One moment she tries to get a cookie off her mother with kisses and caresses. The next moment she opts for a less subtle approach. And mom has no idea that she is after a cookie! Your toddler is full of surprises. By using her whole arsenal and by studying your and others' reactions, your tyke discovers that the various strategies she employs give different results. So, your toddler discovers when she can best be friendly, helpful, aggressive, assertive, careful or polite. And that's not all. Your child thinks up some of the strategies herself, others she imitates: "Oh, that kid hit his mother, should I try that?" Your toddler wanders around in the world of principles and really needs mom and others in her learning process.

We adults already have years of experience in the world of principles. By trial and error we have become skilled in this world. We know for example what justice, kindness, humanity, helpfulness, ingenuity, moderation, thriftiness, trust, frugality, caution, cooperation, care, empowerment, assertiveness, patience and caring mean to us. We know what it means to be considerate of others, to be efficient, to cooperate, to be loving, respectful and we know how to put others at easy. Yet we don't all interpret these principles in the same way. We know, for instance, that it is polite to shake hands when we introduce ourselves—that is, in our culture. However, in England, a handshake is not expected; there, a nod and a greeting is sufficient. And in Tanzania, both hands are expected; one hand is just a half-offering. We fulfill our principles according to our personality, family and the culture in which we have grown up.

In general, you could say that when pursuing a certain goal, a principle is a common strategy that we use without having to go through all the specific steps one-by-one. The previous examples are mainly moral principles, which deal with standards and values. But there are other types of principles that concern the way we do things. For example, there are the strategies you use when playing a board game. Another example is that when planning a weekend trip you plan

for enough time to sleep. Yet another example is the principle that when writing an article, you must take into account your intended audience. Or the principle of keeping dual accounting, or the development of a musical "theme." Then there are the laws of nature that dictate how things move, chemical equations describing how complex matter is built up by simple elements, or the geology that describes the movements of the earth's crust. All these belong to what we call the world of principles.

Your toddler is naturally nowhere near being ready for such adult applications of principles, such as strategy in chess, laws of nature or grown-up standards or norms. Those are all very big words that we don't usually associate with toddlers. But in her own rudimentary way, your tyke gets started in the world of principles. She has already devised strategies to be able to stay up longer! And some toddlers spend all day playing with toy cars, watching them descend an incline.

There can be stark differences with the way in which an adult sorts out a principle in practice. We constantly ready ourselves for the changing conditions that present themselves. Thus we are not always patient, careful or thrifty, and as caring, careful and respectful towards everyone in the same way. That wouldn't be prudent. Sometimes for instance we find it less important to be open with someone, other times we find it more important to take into account another's situation or age. Suppose your spouse and your toddler both give you a drawing of an ape and look at you full of expectation. You will most likely be more honest with your spouse. You might even tell him that he should stick to his day job. But you praise the little scribbler for her effort. Even if you can't tell what it is, you say that this is the most charming ape you've ever seen. And as a show of appreciation, you put the ape up on the fridge. Without even thinking about it, you took the maker's age into account. It would not have

been beneficial if you had been forthcoming with your toddler. You might have permanently destroyed her will to draw.

At this age your toddler can not yet prepare herself for all the various conditions. She has yet to acquire the subtleness. She is still attached to the strategies that she first learned. This is because she has just gotten her first whiff of principles and she is only able to apply them in

fixed ways. Only after she has made her next leap will you notice that your child begins to become more adaptable to her surroundings. She adapts her strategy. Just like your tyke was able to grasp the programs after making her leap into the world of principles, your toddler will, after the next leap, grasp that she can choose what she wants to be: honest, friendly, helpful, careful, patient, resourceful, efficient, just, caring or frugal. And that she can choose not to be any or all of those. She begins to understand that she can pay attention to grandpa, or that she doesn't have to. That she can comfort a friend, or choose not to. Or, that she can treat the dog gently, or she can be rough. That she can be polite to the neighbor and cooperate with mom, or not...

"Nora snuck off! Grandma was cooking and she was playing sweetly with her doll and things. Slowly she expanded the bounds of her territory to the hall. But she was not planning on stopping there. She must have closed the hall door very quietly and with the same skill opened the front door. Grandma found it all too quiet in the hall. She looked around and the closed door made her fear the worst. She ran outside before knowing what to do. Two streets down she saw her. She was running like a rabbit behind her buggy with her baby doll into the wide world, far away from Grandma's house. When she saw Grandma, she was very startled and began a loud protest: 'Nora doesn't like this! Nora doesn't like this!' She wanted to continue on wandering on her own.

She couldn't stand getting caught. From now on Grandma's front door will be locked."

Nora's mom, 87th week, or 20 months

"She has been wanting to give the bathroom a good going over, but had yet to succeed. All of a sudden she found a solution for her cleaning urge. Suddenly, we heard the door to bathroom lock and this enormous cleaning sound emerged from the smallest room. There was scrubbing, flushing and waist bins rattling. A flush, and another and another. The splashing of water brought the whole family knocking and calling at the door. But however grandpa, grandma and I begged, the door remained locked with the continuing sound of cleaning from inside. Slowly some water seeped under the door. But the door stayed shut. Some twenty

minutes later the door opened and out came the little cleaning lady. Soaking wet, proud and satisfied: 'All done,' she said and walked away. Everything was wet—the walls, the commode, the floor. The rolls of toilet paper lay in the toilet and sheets of toilet paper were stuck on the wall. And on the floor lay a pan, a brush and a towel. She had prepared well for the job."

Angela's mom, 92nd week, or 21 months

Brain Changes

From U.S. research on 408 identical twins it was concluded that around 14 months of age there was clear hereditary influence upon mental development. The development concerned both non-verbal skills as well as speech comprehension.

Your Toddler's Choices: A Key to His Personality

All toddlers have been given the ability to perceive and uphold principles. They need years in order to completely familiarize themselves with the wide range of new skills to play with, but as toddlers they take their first tender steps in the world of principles.

At this age for example your toddler chooses how he will go about things: carefully or recklessly. He chooses whether or not to pay heed to mother or to try to get his way with a fit of obstinacy. In short, he chooses which strategy he will use to reach the goal he set for himself. And like every other toddler, first he chooses that which best suits his talent, mobility, preferences and his particular circumstances. The very first choices become apparent when he is 64 weeks or almost 15 months old. Don't compare your child with other toddlers. Each child is unique and will choose differently.

Take a good look at your toddler. Establish what his interests are. Use the list in My Diary on pages 332-333 to mark or highlight what your child selects. You may also have a look for yourself to see if there are some principles that you think your child could use or learn. Stop marking when your child begins with the next leap. That is usually when he is 71 weeks old, or 16½ months.

In the world of principles your toddler will discover that there are several ways to accomplish a goal. All the strategies he can utilize: "Should I do it carefully, recklessly, pushy or sweetly? Or should I try a prank?" Your tyke is becoming

---
Toddlers are like this

Anything new to him, your toddler likes the most. Therefore, always react especially to new skills and interests your toddler shows. In that way he learns more pleasantly, easier, quicker and more.

(continued on page 334)

 My Diary -

How My Baby Explores the New World of Principles

EXERCISING HER OWN WILL

❑ Chooses consciously

❑ Takes initiative

❑ Wants a say if others do something

❑ Feels more need to belong, to be accepted

❑ Possessive with toys

❑ What I have noticed otherwise:_____

_____

COPYING AND IMITATING

❑ Observes grownups

❑ Observes other children

❑ Imitates sweet behavior

❑ Imitates aggressive behavior

❑ Imitates overt physical actions, like somersault, climbing

❑ Imitates subtle motor skills, like holding a pencil

❑ Imitates "oddities," like limping, walking like a hunchback

❑ Imitates what he sees on TV or in a book

❑ What I have noticed otherwise: _____

_____

PRACTICING STRATEGIES, EXPLORING THE LIMITS AND BE-
COMING RESOURCEFUL

❑ Experiments with motor skills

❑ Experiments with stashing and recovering objects

❑ Experiments with crawling in or behind something and getting out again

❑ Experiments with manipulating things with caution and care

❑ Experiments with making choices: what shall I choose?

❑ Experiments with the meaning of "Yes" and "No"

❑ Experiments with fooling mom; acts like he is disobedient

❑ Experiments with ramps and rises; feels with his finger and studies them or runs his cars up and down them

❑ What I have noticed otherwise: _____

IMPLEMENTING STRATEGIES AND TACTICS

❑ Is helpful (more often) or tries to be so

❑ Is obedient (more often) or does his best to be so

❑ Is (more often) careful and caring or tries to be so

❑ Accepts (more often) that he is still small, requires help and therefore must obey. Grasps for instance that streets are dangerous and he therefore must walk hand and hand

❑ Makes fun to get something or to get others to do something

❑ Is (more often) extra sweet to get his way

❑ Tries (more often) to get his way by being pushy

❑ Shows (more often) his feelings in a fit of obstinacy

❑ Does (more often) what he feels like, goes his own way

❑ Makes use of others to get something done he otherwise was unable and that mom disapproved of; for instance, "perhaps dad will give me a cookie?"

❑ What I have noticed otherwise: _____

OTHER CHANGES YOU NOTICE

more resourceful. He owes this to the fact that he is quickly growing sharper in all areas. He begins walking more adeptly and is able to quickly make his way. He understands you better and can sometimes answer back. He practices playing with his emotions and not always around you. He can think ahead and knows that his person counts, too. He is increasingly better at eating and drinking, with cleaning up, building towers, putting things together, pushing and kicking other kids. His throwing aim has improved, as have other things. Everything comes more naturally to him in the coming weeks. And, he will continue to use new strategies to get to his objective. Of course, not every strategy your child thinks up achieves its desired effect. That requires time and practice. By trying, your toddler realizes that various strategies bring different results. Some are a smashing success, others the converse and most are just so-so.

Give your child the opportunity to experiment with all sorts of strategies, testing them out and reflecting on them. He will learn to behave in certain situations only by being resourceful, by gauging your reaction and through lots of practice.

Skillfulness

Physical antics

When your toddler is trying to make his way in the world of principles, he will also want to know what his little body is capable of—in other words, how to use his body when he wants to be quick, slow, careful, funny or clever. Your little one will be experimenting with his body. He tests its capabilities. Which stunts can my body do? Can I fit between there? How do I climb the stairs? How do I go down? How do I go down the slide? Is that a good spot to lie between the toys and furniture? How strong am I? In short, your tyke is getting resourceful with his body. He sometimes appears reckless, which frightens mom.

"She goes upright up and down a step. She practices that the whole day through. Now I keep my eyes open for other objects of different heights so she can develop this skill."

Hannah's mom, 67th week, or 15 months and a week

"We put a mattress on the ground so that she can jump around on it. She loves galloping over it; she dives on the mattress and tries a somersault. She keeps testing how far she can go on the soft surface."

Josie's mom, 66th week, or 15 months

"Thomas likes to stay on the couch the whole day. He climbs up the back rest using the wall to get up."

Thomas' mom, 66th week, or 15 months

"Every day he discovers new games. He has found a small tunnel behind his bed and chest of drawers and loves going back and forth behind them. He slides under the couch and studies how far he can go before he gets stuck. And he gets a kick sliding around the room on his knees instead of using his feet."

Matt's mom, 70th week, or 16 months

"She practices different ways of walking. Walking backwards, turning circles, fast walking, walking slowly. She is very studious about all these tricks."

Eve's mom, 64th week, or 14½ months

"She lies in and on everything: in the doll's bath, in the doll's bed and on the cushions spread on the floor."

Ashley's mom, 64th week, or 14½ months

"He laughs as he rolls himself in the curtains."

Matt's mom, 69th week, or approaching 16 months

"All of the sudden he is picking up chairs and benches."

Kevin's mom, 70th week, or 16 months

Getting acquainted with the outdoors

Many toddlers enjoy browsing around outside. They look like they're just fumbling about, but in fact they are surveying the area. This is not saying that they don't need mother: they do! Many question endlessly about everything: what is this and what is that called. And all children absorb what you say and what they see with the utmost concentration.

"She was startled when she walked through a puddle and got wet. She walked back to look at and investigate the puddle."

Ashley's mom, 64th week, or 14½ months

"He finds it interesting to splash through the puddles. It really pleases him."

Matt's mom, 71st week, or 16 months and a week

"She stood eye-to-eye with a real live cow and was really at a loss. This was at the children's zoo. She wasn't ready to pet the animal yet. Even when she was in daddy's arms. On the way home she was quiet as she mulled it over. That was the impression left on her by the living version of the cow from the book."

Victoria's mom, 61st week, or 14 months

Getting skillful with things

Your child will become ever more resourceful with games and objects in the world of principles. He only eats properly if he can feed himself. Helping when it's not wanted could result in everything ending up on the floor. He manages quite well building things or with his game of rings and puzzles. But beware!

He tries to open the faucet, bottles and jars with twist-off lids on a regular basis. Your toddler is above all interested in testing which of the strategies works best when he needs it. He contemplates and experiments. What will happen if I drop the key chain behind the cabinet? What if I put it under the bed? And what will happen with the key chain if I let it slide down between the couch and the wall? And how will I make it reappear? And if I am unable to reach it, can I get to it with a pole? In short, he is learning how to hide something, put something away and recover it. Later, if he is skillful enough or thinks himself to be, he will use his tricks perhaps to amuse you with a prank. He could also hide a game if, for instance, he doesn't want one of his friends to play with it. Do watch what your tyke is up to. Put dangerous items out of reach and keep an eye on your little explorer.

"We do puzzles together. Now he likes it and participates gladly. Not that it always goes well, but it's a start."

Kevin's mom, 65th week, or approaching 15 months

"Now his ring game is popular. He sees clearly if he puts the wrong ring onto the pole and says: 'No.' If he gets it right, then he is very proud, looks at me and expects applause."

Harry's mom, 64th week, or 14½ months

"He stashes the ball and the balloon way behind something. The consequence is that he can no longer reach it."

Luke's mom, 66th week, or 15 months

"She throws things on the floor when you are least expecting it. She studies the effect her throwing has on the object."

Josie's mom, 64th week, or 14½ months

"He likes playing with his cars. This week he tried to see how well they stack up on top of each other."

Robin's mom, 72nd week, or 16½ months

"When she is vacuuming with her battery powered vacuum, she prefers to go for the most impossible spots. She does those spots as if her life depended on it: under the cabinet, between the chairs and table legs, in open cupboards. She skips the easy large open spaces."

Victoria's mom, 61st week, or 14 months

"Again and again she pulled open my desk drawer, so I locked it. She then tried several ways to get it open. Squatted and pulled, sat and pulled, the standing pull. It completely frustrated her."

Laura's mom, 65th week, or approaching 15 months

"She wanted candies that were on the fireplace mantel. I wouldn't give them to her. She then went into pushy mode. When she wouldn't stop, I put her in the hall to cool off. I had hoped that she would forget about the candy, but I was wrong. The minute she returned to the room, she dragged a chair from the dining room to the den. It took her 15 minutes. When the chair reached the fireplace, she asked her brother to lift up the chair. He realized that was a no go, so he laughed at her. She then gave up. Grandpa was visiting that evening and he was playing with her. He has a real sweet tooth and when he saw the candy, he just had to help himself. She got one, too. Later when I came back into the room, she walked victoriously towards me and showed me her spoils. She prevailed in the end."

Victoria's mom, 61st week, or 14 months

"She was unable to get something out of the basket of magazines. When she finally managed after trying pulling and yanking five or six times, she laughed contentedly to herself. She'd never done that before."

Emily's mom, 68th week, or 15½ months

Becoming skillful with language

In the world of principles your toddler is continuously getting a better grasp of what the big people around him are saying to each other and to him. He is also getting better at understanding brief instructions and often carries them out with much enthusiasm. He feels like he counts for something. He also has fun pointing to parts of the body when you name them. The same goes for various things in the home, whether they are on the floor, the walls or ceiling. Many mothers think that their little one should be speaking more, given that they already know so much. But that is not the case. Only after the next leap does your toddler's speech really take off. Your child is 21 months by then. In the world of principles most children are content with pronouncing single words, imitating animal sounds and reproducing all sorts of other noises.

Get your child to play a game of pointing and naming with you. You name something and let your child point to it, whether it is a toy, a body part or whatever. And try to see what your child thinks of a game of calling each other. It is best if your child starts by calling you. Call his name to get him to call your name. Call out his name again. For many children it gives them a sense of pride and importance that their egos count.

> "He understands more and more. Unbelievable how quickly a child picks up new words. Yet he picks out only a few to use in his speech. He prefers words that begin with 'b' like his favorite things: ball and boy. He pronounces the words well and completely. It seems like he knows how to pronounce the words but he doesn't have the coordination."
>
> **Harry's mom, 69th week, or approaching 16 months**

> "She points perkily to her foot, toe, eye, ear, nose, stomach, hand and hair. She also knows that you wash your hair with shampoo as well what bottle it's in."
>
> **Juliette's mom, 69th week, or approaching 16 months**

> "She cried 'daddy' when her father was busy in the kitchen. The calling out automatically evolved into a language game. Taking turns, the two

called out each other's name: 'Anna...,' 'Daddy...,' 'Anna...,' 'Daddy.' Endless. Now it happens all the time if one of them goes out of the other's sight."

Anna's mom, 70th week, or 16 months

Imitating others

In the world of principles your toddler will observe how adults or other children do things and what effect their actions have. "How does he do that so skillfully?" "That kid gets immediate attention from everyone if she bites grandma." "Mom and dad regularly sit on the toilet. That must be a part of being 'big.'" "He keeps kicking the leg of the lady from next door; she laughs so kicking must be funny." Just for starters. He copies, imitates and tries out what he sees. The people around him are his role models. Also the behavior he sees in books and on TV gives him an inexhaustible source of ideas.

React to your tyke's behavior. Let him know what you think of his behavior. Only in this way your toddler will learn what is right and wrong, and if he can do things better, quicker, more efficiently or nicer.

"Imitating is now his main occupation. He imitates every behavior he sees: someone stamps her feet, he stamps his feet; someone hits, he hits; someone falls, he falls; someone throws, he throws; someone bites, he bites."

Thomas' mom, 63rd week, or 14 months and a week

"Everything that I do, he wants to do too. Also what other kids do, he directly absorbs. Even if he sees something only once, he picks it straight up. He copies pleasant and not-so-pleasant behavior."

Paul's mom, 64th week, or 14½ months

"She spends more time and is ever more attentive to books and TV. One child on TV stuck his tongue out at another and she copied him directly."

Josie's mom, 64th week, or 14½ months

"She wants to brush her teeth by herself. She brushes up and down once and knocks the toothbrush on the edge of the sink – knock, knock, knock – slide the toothbrush again up and down in her mouth and knocks again – knock, knock, knock. And on she brushes. The funny thing is that she is imitating me. I knock the toothbrush on the edge of the sink, but only after I am completely finished and have rinsed my brush. I do it to shake the water off my brush."

Victoria's mom, 61st week, or 14 months

"Initially she would turn her vacuum on with her fingers. Then she saw that I use my foot to turn mine on. Since now she uses her foot to start hers, too."

Victoria's mom, 61st week, or 14 months

Replaying

In the world of principles your child replays the daily domestic business done indoors and out. He "cooks," "shops," "takes walks," "says goodbye," and "takes care of his doll children." Naturally, he does all of this in his toddler way. Yet you start to recognize better what he is up to. Above all you see whether or not he does his best to be careful or helpful or if he is just being bossy, or if he's sweetly sucking up. He may do

that simply because he thinks that it is part of his role or because he is imitating the people around him.

Give your child the opportunity for him to settle into his role. Play with him once and a while. Your tyke then feels like he counts and that what he does is important. Many toddlers at this age are very keen for signs of appreciation. They really want to be understood.

"She 'cooks' for her doll. I lay out some actual food, because that's what she wants. She puts everything in a small bowl, feeds her doll and then removes the food."

> Emily's mom, 68th week, or 15½ months

"He bakes mud pies: scoops and scoops buckets full to dump them out again. He finds it all very interesting."

> Thomas' mom, 66th week, or 15 months

"For the past few days he has been pouring water from one bucket into the other. This is keeping him busy. Now and again I get a request to fill up a bucket. Otherwise, he seems to have forgotten me and is consumed with his special brew."

> Steven's mom, 63rd week, or 14 months and a week

"She strolled proudly upon the premises of the petting zoo behind her doll carriage. A goat blocked her way and she began an extensive discussion with the inattentive animal. Unfortunately incomprehensible. It sounded as if she was calling him to order."

> Hannah's mom, 64th week, or 14½ months

"He often plays 'saying goodbye.' He picks up a bag, walks to the door and says, 'Bye Bye.' He waves while doing so."

> Frankie's mom, 64th week, or 14½ months

"He often snuggles, kisses, comforts and caresses his dolls and bears. He also puts them to bed. Really loving."

> Luke's mom, 66th week, or 15 months

Sometimes a child imitates being father or mother. He studies how it is to be dad or mom. When a little girl wants to be mom, the real mom is actually in the way. They then seem to be competing. Naturally, the same happens if father is home and he wants to walk in dad's shoes. And if a little boy is playing dad, he wants to know how mom reacts to this new dad.

Grasp what your child is doing. Give him the opportunity to play his role and play along. Your little one learns much from this. He feels the need to express himself in this way and to experience how it is to be mom or dad.

> "He goes and spreads out on his father's bed and looks around as if it is his. Also, just like his father, he goes and sits in his chair to read the paper. It is important to him to do as dad does. He wants my reaction to it all as well."
>
> Jim's mom, 66th week, or 15 months

> "As soon as I take off my shoes, she's in them. And then she follows up by taking a walk around in my shoes. She also regularly wants to sit in my chair. I have to vacate it for her. She starts pulling and yanking me and if I don't concede, she throws a tantrum."
>
> Nina's mom, 69th week, or approaching 16 months

Practicing with emotions

In the world of the principles, many toddlers experiment with their emotions. How does it feel if I am happy, sad, shy, angry, funny or emotional? And when I greet someone, what does my face do then? What does my body do? And how can I use those emotions if I want others to know how I feel? And how should I act if I want to have or do something badly?

> "He walks around laughing very artificially like he is experimenting with how it feels to laugh. He does the same with crying."
>
> Bob's mom, 63rd week, or 14 months and a week

> "This time she greeted Grandpa very differently than she used to. Normally, she threw herself onto him putting her head on his neck and shoulder. When she had been still for a bit, the greeting had run its course and she began to play with him. But this time she stood up straight looking at him, only to launch herself onto him again. She repeated this a number of times. Then she gave him a cautious kiss and looked at him again. This, too, repeated itself a number of times. Never before had

she greeted Grandpa in such a studious way. She was clearly experimenting with a greeting."

Victoria's mom, 61st week, or 14 months

"She wanted to read a certain book again for the eighth time and noticed that I had had enough of that. She sat there a bit with her head facing downward. Very quietly she practiced a pout. When she thought she had the right expression, she looked at me with a perfectly pouting lip and passed the book back to me."

Josie's mom, 65th week, or approaching 15 months

"Suddenly he's become shy. If I brag about him for instance, he shies away almost in shame. I've never seen that before. Yet he's quick to notice if I talk about him."

Luke's mom, 68th week, or 15½ months

Thinking ahead has begun

In the world of principles your toddler can think ahead, contemplate and make plans. He now understands that mom can and does, too. You soon notice this by the reactions from your tyke. He realizes what the consequences are from something that mom does or wants him to do. And all of a sudden he comments on something that he used to find quite normal or even liked. Remember though that he is not unruly. His development has just made a leap. It is progress!

"Now she has a hard time when I leave for work. Up until recently, she ran to the front door to give me a send-off. Now she protests and holds me back. I think this is because she now understands the effects. Sending someone off can be fun, but when mom leaves, she is gone for at least a few hours. And that's not so nice."

Eve's mom, 67th week, or 15 months and a week

"Thinking ahead has started! I brush her teeth after she has had a go. That always leads to terrible shouting matches. Up until recently when she heard 'time to brush our teeth,' she came running. Now she throws the toothbrush in the corner when I hand it to her, because she knows what follows after the fun of doing it herself."

Laura's mom, 67th week, or 15 months and a week

"Sometimes she walks away having forgotten her pacifier. She then says: 'Oh, no,' and turns around to go get it."

Ashley's mom, 69th week, or approaching 16 months

"Now he remembers where he has hidden or left behind his things, even from yesterday."

Luke's mom, 63rd week, or 14 months and a week

"When he realized that he would have to get on the bike for the second time today in the freezing weather, he got really cross. He clearly recalled how cold it was and repeating the outing in such severe weather conditions didn't sit well with him."

James' mom, 67th week, or 15 months and a week

"This was the first time that I was able to see that she had a clear expectation. We had finger-painted and she had decorated the mirror. While she was bathing, I snuck off to clean the mirror. I shouldn't have done that. When she got out of the bath, she walked right to the mirror looking for her decoration. Very sad."

Josie's mom, 65th week, or approaching 15 months

Nagging and getting one's way

The Drama Class

Does your little one try getting her way by screeching, rolling, stamping and throwing things? Does she lose her temper for the slightest of reasons? For example

if she doesn't get direct attention, if she's not allowed to do something, if her play is interrupted for dinner, if her building topples over, or just out of the blue without you detecting that anything is wrong? Why does a toddler put on such an act? Because mom and the toys aren't reacting the way she thinks they should. She is frustrated and needs to express it. She does so using the most obvious strategies: getting as angry and making the biggest fuss possible. She has yet to discover and practice more successful, quicker, sweeter strategies in order to persuade you to do what she wants, or to build a better building. Your nagging toddler is only able to make her wishes known by acting like she does. Grasp your toddler's frustration. Let her blow off some steam if she needs to. And help her to discover that there are other and better strategies that she can use when she wants to get something done, ways that are more receptive and more successful.

"She only wants to eat if she can feed herself. A saga when we didn't get it! Everything flew through the air."
Juliette's mom, 65th week, or approaching 15 months

"At the slightest little thing or if things don't go as she has in mind, she throws herself on the floor. She lands on the back of her head with a thud, then lies on the ground stamping her feet and screaming."
Julia's mom, 65th week, or 14½ months

"He has an inordinate number of tantrums. He screams and throws things if he is corrected or if he 'bites off more than he can chew' or if his playtime is interrupted. If I distract him quickly, though, he doesn't shed any tears. But if it takes too long then his temper turns into a sad bout of tears."
Matt's mom, 68th week, or 15½ months

"He's thrown a number of temper tantrums this week. One was so bad that he went completely limp. If he doesn't get his way, he gets really angry and then it's a real battle. He is really in his own world! At the moment he doesn't listen well at all."
James' mom, 67th week, 15 months and a week

"She throws an increasing number of temper tantrums. Yesterday, I got her out of bed and for no reason she threw a temper tantrum. This one lasted quite a long time, complete with rolling on the floor, banging her head, kicking and pushing me away, and screeching the whole time. Nothing I tried helped, not cuddling, not distracting or stern words. After a while, I went and sat perplexed on the couch, leaned back and watched while she rolled around on the floor. Then I went into the kitchen to carve an apple. She slowly calmed down, came to the kitchen and stood next to me."

Julia's mom, 65th week, or approaching 15 months

He wants his say

In the world of principles your little one discovers that he counts, too, just like all the big people. He begins to speak up for himself. But sometimes it goes too far: his will is law and he will not be swayed. This happens because it is becoming ever clearer to him that he can impose his will. He counts, too! He realizes that just like mom or dad, he can decide if, when or where he does something, how he will do it and when he will finish. On top of that, he wants to put in his "two cents worth" if mom wants to do something. He wants to help decide how it is done. And if he doesn't get his way or if it doesn't go according to plan, he becomes angry, disappointed or sad. Show him

 ## The gender gap

Boys express their sense of impotence and displeasure more often than girls do. This is often because parents accept this type of manifestations more easily from boys than they do from girls, so girls learn to suppress these feelings of impotence and displeasure. Consequently they may also become more easily depressed.

understanding. He still has to learn that what he wants to do will not always be possible right away, and that he also has to learn to consider the wishes of others, even though he wishes to stand up and assert himself.

"She emphatically wants to choose which breast she takes. She hesitates a bit, looking which breast to take, points to the winner and says 'tha.' Sometimes it looks as if she is deciding between two different flavors."
 Juliette's mom, 65th week, or approaching 15 months

"If he gets something into his head, it's impossible to change his mind. It's like talking to a brick wall. He just goes on to the next room and gets up to no good. The toys in his brother's and sister's drawers were this week's target. He really had designs on the modeling clay. He knows full well what he is allowed, but he is less concerned with what I think of it all."
 Frankie's mom, 65th week, or approaching 15 months

"If he does not wish to listen, he shakes his head 'no.' These days, he walks around the whole day shaking his head, meanwhile just going about his business. Recently, when he was fishing through the garbage can, I got angry at him. A bit later, I saw him sulking in the corner crying."
 John's mom, 70th week, or 16 months

"All of a sudden she's developed her own will! We picked out a book in the children's book store. It was really fun. When I decided that it was time to go, she had other ideas. First she screamed her head off in the store and then kept on screaming when we went outside. On the bike she kept standing up in her seat. I had to keep pushing her down in her chair. We almost got into a real fight. She didn't want to leave the bookstore, and I had no say in the matter. I'm still amazed."
 Josie's mom, 68th week, or 15½ months

"Three weeks ago we went shopping for Thomas. He needed a 'big boy's suit' for a party. When we had chosen a suit, he came tip-toeing back with a pair of shoes – dainty, shiny, black patent leather. He tried to convince dad that he needed these shoes. Dad didn't think that that was such a good idea and put the shoes back in the rack.

A week later, Thomas and I went back to the shoe store. He was getting his first pair of shoes. I went straight for the macho gear. It seemed a 'shoe-in' that my big boy would want the same, but he had other ideas. On the girls' rack, he found a pair of shiny lace-up boots with feathers. He loved them and had to have them. With his prize in hand, he came wobbling up to me. I was astounded. There was my boyish Thomas with a pair of dainty patent leather boots in his slightly less dainty hands, beaming. They  were exactly the princess boots that I loved so much as a child, it was bewildering that my little guy would fall for the same thing. I quickly recommended a series of boyish styles while sneaking the shiny boots back were they belonged. Thomas looked at the boy's rack and quickly found something much to his liking. 'Vroom, vroom,' he cheered and grabbed a pair of thick-soled shoes with trucks sticking out the sides of the shoes. This made them shoes on wheels. As a true car-lover, they caught his eye. He wanted them and was very content; as was I. But when I was paying for the shoes on wheels, he nudged me. There he was trying to put something onto the sales counter. It was the boots."

Thomas' mom, 69th week, or approaching 16 months

"She is increasingly insistent. When she won't cooperate, we get into a fight. While getting dressed, eating or if I'm in a hurry. Yesterday, it happened again. I lost my cool and ended up screaming and cursing at her."

Julia's mom, 66th week, or 15 months

"Sometimes if she sees something in my hand, like a knife, she must have it. This can result in real altercations."

Nina's mom, 67th week, or 15 months

Aggression

Many mothers say that their sweet toddler sometimes turns into an aggressive tiger. This makes
mothers uneasy. Yet it is an understandable
change. In the world of principles, your child
tries all types of behavior. Being aggressive is one
of those. Your toddler studies how mom, other
adults and children react if he hits, bites, pushes
or kicks, or if he deliberately breaks something.

Show your child what you think of his behavior. This is the only way that
he will learn that being aggressive isn't sweet, interesting or funny. This way he
learns that it is hurtful and that adults are not amused by aggressive or destruc-
tive behavior.

*"She hit me in the face. I said 'don't do that' and she did it again and
started to laugh. It really bothered me. It's tough laying down ground
rules."*

Hannah's mom, 70th week, or 16 months

'He bit a kid at daycare. For no apparent reason."

Mark's mom, 70th week, or 16 months

Mine and yours

In the world of principles your little one discovers that some toys in the house are
his and only his. Just like big people, he is suddenly the proud owner of his own
stuff. This is quite a discovery for a toddler. He also needs time to grasp what
"mine and yours" means. While figuring this out, things aren't easy for him. Some
children find it disturbing if another child grabs something out of their hands
for no reason without recognizing them as owner. Such lack of understanding

Tips on aggression

Research has shown that shortly after the first birthday mothers report the first physical aggression. At 17 months, 90 percent of the mothers report that their child is sometimes aggressive. Physical aggression peaks just before the second birthday. Thereafter, this type of behavior recedes. By the time children have reached school age, it will have mostly disappeared under normal circumstances.

Of course, some children are more prone to aggressive behavior than others. Yet, a child's surroundings are also very important. They help determine how long a child remains aggressive. If children live with adults and children who are aggressive, then they can assume that "being aggressive" is normal social behavior. However, children can also live in an environment where aggression is not tolerated and where sweet and friendly behavior is rewarded. The result is that the child will not start hitting and kicking when he is frustrated, wants something or is corrected. He uses more acceptable ways of expressing himself.

starts them crying. Others become very wary and protect their territory as best they can. They come up with all sorts of strategies to prevent others from getting close to their things. They especially don't trust children. Your toddler still has to learn to lend, share and play with others.

"She is developing a certain urge to own. When we have guests, she comes and proudly shows her possessions. If we go over to play at a friend's house, she grabs her things and gives them to me for safe keeping. She hopes by doing so to prevent her friend from playing with them."

Eve's mom, 64th week, or 14½ months

"Suddenly, he is very possessive of my breasts. If his father comes close, he tries to protect his territory. He clamps his mouth on to a nipple and covers the other with his hand so that dad can't get to it."

Thomas' mom, 65th week, or approaching 15 months

"Every time his little friend snatches one of his toys, he bursts out in tears."

Robin's mom, 68th week, or 15½ months

"He doesn't let anyone take anything from him. You can't even tempt him with a 'good trade' either. If he's got a hold of it, he's keeping it. He's keen, though, to snatch things from others. There he has no scruples at all."

Kevin's mom, 65th week, or approaching 15 months

Being nice and placating

The joke strategy

In the world of principles, tricks and antics play an ever increasing role. Your toddler may start making his first jokes and he will get the biggest kick out of them himself. You might notice that he appreciates others' jokes also. Many toddlers do. They enjoy gags, and if people or animals do something out of the ordinary, whether in real life or on TV, it makes them laugh. They find it exciting. Some tykes pull gags to try getting around the rules.

You may notice that "being funny" is used as a strategy to do something that would otherwise be frowned upon. Something pleasant and unexpected is ever more successful in getting on mom's good side than a temper tantrum. Give your child the opportunity to be creative while making fun and pulling gags. Be very clear when he oversteps the bounds. He is unable to know the differences without you.

"He is constantly kidding around and has a great time doing it. He and his friends have a barrel of laughs acting silly. He really cracks up if he sees an animal do something silly or unexpected."

> Robin's mom, 68th week, or 15½ months

"He loves just being silly. He giggles and if his sister joins in, he really bursts out laughing."

> James' mom, 69th week, or approaching 16 months

"Cartoons really make him laugh , especially if something sudden or unexpected happens. He even loves the monsters in 'Sesame Street.' He really starts giggling when they talk and move around."

> Robin's mom, 70th week, or 16 months

"He loves for me to chase after him saying, 'I'm gonna get you.' However, when I want to put on his jacket, he runs away squawking and making a game of it."

> James' mom, 70th week, or 16 months

"She cracks up when she ignores me, is disobedient or is making fun of me, or when she hides something from me and it is hard for me to get at. She thinks she is very clever."

> Laura's mom, 66th week, or 15 months

"She loves playing pranks. When we get to the front door, she doesn't wait for me to put the key in the lock, she just continues walking to the next door. She really thinks she's funny."

> Ashley's mom, 70th week, or 16 months

Negotiating and bargaining

It used to be that mom laid down the law. Children had to obey. Adults didn't take kindly to back-talk. Everything changes. Nowadays it is generally assumed that children who have learned to negotiate grow up being better able to think

for themselves. When your toddler lands in the world of principles, you could see a budding negotiator.

Does your toddler experiment with the words "yes" and "no?" They sometimes do so nodding or shaking their heads, occasionally pronouncing aloud "yes" or "no." They also try nodding while saying no and shaking while saying yes, which is very funny to them. His stuffed animals have mandatory "yes" and "no" lessons. Other times he practices on his own while building something or wandering through the house just looking for something to get into, but mostly he practices his yes and no routine with his mother. She is also good for trying out his jokes on.

Give your child the opportunity to be inventive with the concepts of yes and no. This type of practice allows him to learn to use a yes or a no to his advantage. How does mom do it? He can find the best yes and no strategy for various situations. He discovers which strategy is best suited to meet his needs.

"He is able to answer all sorts of questions with just a yes or no. He sometimes makes a mistake. He says 'yes' when he means 'no' and if I act upon his answer, he smiles and quickly changes to a 'no,' in a tone of 'not really.'"

Luke's mom, 65th week, or approaching 15 months

"She says 'yes' and 'no' with increasing authority, but she likes to try to trick me using yes and no."

Juliette's mom, 66th week, or 15 months

"She tests the words yes and no on me continuously: Is her 'yes' a real yes and will her 'no' remain a no? Perhaps I can find a way to cheat? She tests me to see how far she can go."

Nina's mom, 70th week, or 16 months

"He knows what he wants and is getting better at answering with a definite 'yes' or 'no.' He also has different yes's and no's. Some indicate very clearly where his boundaries lay. When he reaches his limit, I know that he is dead set. His other yes's and no's lack finality. I know then that I can press him for a better deal."

Paul's mom, 71st week, or 16 months and a week

Asking for help

Your toddler can be inventive in trying to put someone on the spot. He can do it in a clever, sneaky or sweet way. He still requires some practice in learning the tricks of the trade.

Just watch your little one go to work on you or someone else when he needs to get something done. Tell him what you think. Your child is still researching in the world of principles. He learns from your feedback.

"When he asks me to get something for him and I ask where I should put it, he walks to a spot and points where I should put it down. Then he is very friendly and easy going."

Steven's mom, 65th week, or approaching 15 months

"She is getting better at expressing her wishes. She takes my hand and leads me off if she needs a new diaper. She grabs my finger if she needs me to do something for her with my finger, like pressing a button. She also leads me to where she doesn't want to go alone. It doesn't matter if I'm in the middle of something or not. She wants things done right away."

Josie's mom, 67th week, or 15 months and a week

"He points at things more and more. He also points to the things he wants you to get for him. This week he lured his grandmother to the kitchen, walked to the cabinet where the cookies are and pointed to the top shelf."

Frankie's mom, 63rd week, or 14 months and a week

"With a sly look on her face, she pointed to an egg and then a plate. She meant, 'put that egg on my plate.' She was so cute that no one could refuse."

Hannah's mom, 62nd week, or 14 months

"These past weeks he has been commanding like a general. He cries out loudly and forcefully: 'Mom! Mom!' when he wants something. When I look at him, he sits there with his arm outstretched, pointing at the toy of his choosing. He wants them  brought and when he gets his request, he pulls his arm back and carries on playing. Giving orders has become second nature to him. This week was the first time I really noticed it."

Matt's mom, 68th week, or 15½ months

"Today she showed me what she wanted when we were visiting someone. She took my hand and walked to the door, behind which were our coats, opened the door, went to our coats and pointed while looking at me with a questioning look on her face. I didn't know what hit me."

Emily's mom, 67th week, or 15 months and a week

Cooperation

In the world of principles your child has choices: "Am I going with the flow or against it?" "Do I care what mom says or not?" In addition to that, your toddler is growing ever more outspoken and more capable. Small assignments are getting easier for him, like: "Get your shoes," "Go get your bottle," "Throw that in the trash," "Give it to daddy," "Put it in the hall," or "Put it in the hamper." You might have already noticed that you sometimes don't have to say what to do. Your little fellow already grasps what you want and is working along. It is increasingly easier to lay down certain ground rules.

Try involving your child in day-to-day business and getting involved in his day-to-day, too. It makes him feel understood, appreciated and important. His ego is growing. Praise him too, if he is thinking ahead for you. He is demonstrating that he knows what needs to be done.

"Every time before we go somewhere, she gets her own jacket."
> **Josie's mom, 65th week, or approaching 15 months**

"He now understands that he needs to stay with me when we're on the sidewalk."
> **Luke's mom, 66th week, or 15 months**

"She puts two and two together. When I say: 'Go find your bottle,' she returns after her expedition and makes a gesture of 'gone.'"
> **Eve's mom, 72nd week, or 16½ months**

"When she needs changing, she walks with me to her dresser. She lays still and practically helps me."
> **Laura's mom, 63rd week, or 14 months and a week**

"She knows that she is not allowed to take the nuts from the bowl on the table. So she thought of a trick so she could eat the nuts and still conform to the rules. She got her

own plate and a spoon and scooped some nuts onto her plate. She then ate her winnings with her spoon. This way she could have some nuts and eat them, too, without breaking the rules in her eyes."

Ashley's mom, 68th week, or 15½ months

"When we are discussing practical things, he follows the conversation, fully focused. When the conversation is finished, he smiles exuberantly to demonstrate that he could understand some of what was said even though it was not directed at him. After that, he likes to prove it with one feat or another. It's almost like we just had a conversation. It really makes his day when we understand each other so well."

John's mom, 63rd week, or 14 months and a week

"She keeps trying to involve one of us in her games."

Jenny's mom, 72rd week, or 16½ months

Being helpful

When toddlers land in the world of principles, most of them are particularly interested in all the goings-on about the house, although there is a big chance that your little one is no longer content just watching mom do her thing. He wants to help. He wants to lighten your load.

Let your child do his part. He really wants to believe that he is a big help and that without him things would be a huge mess or that dinner wouldn't be any good. Be sure he receives a well-deserved compliment.

"He constantly wants to help me. Whether it is straightening up, cleaning, going to bed or somewhere else, it doesn't matter. He wants very much to take part in the day-to-day routine on his own accord. When he is taken seriously, it gives him profound contentment. Understanding one another is central these days."

Jim's mom, 64th week, or 14½ months

"She helps me set and clear the table as well as do the vacuuming. She just started one day and it disappoints her if she doesn't get the necessary time and space to be creative."

Josie's mom, 62nd week, or 14 months

"She gladly helps making drinks. Sometimes, I let her make her own drink. She uses all kinds of ingredients. When she drinks it, she goes around murmuring, 'yum, yum, yum.'"

Juliette's mom, 68th week, or 15½ months

"As soon as I grab the vacuum cleaner, she grabs her battery-powered one. She wants to help oh so badly. So what happens is that my vacuum is the one she wants to use because it's better. Therefore, I begin with hers and when she takes it back, I can peacefully go on with the real one."

Victoria's mom, 61st week, or 14 months

"She used to like to watch me doing my thing. Now she wants to help. When she sees me slice a lemon, she runs to the counter to be picked up so that she can put the lemon in the citrus press. If she sees dirty dishes, she hurries over to the counter to do the washing up."

Nina's mom, 64th week, or 14½ months

Being careful

Does your toddler experiment with being "rash" or "careful?" "Should I fling my cup on the ground or should I carefully place it on the table?" Reckless behavior seems to be very popular. Running, climbing, wild horseplay and reckless treatment of objects seem to be the favorite pastime. But realize that by experimenting and getting your reaction to such behavior, your little one learns what it means to be reckless or to be careful.

"He practices his balance. Outside, he reaches for the sky, inside he reaches for the ceiling. He climbs onto chairs and tables so that he can reach higher and does seem to understand that space is out of reach. While reaching he all of a sudden lets himself fall down."

Luke's mom, 64th week, or 14½ months

"When you're least expecting it, she throws her bottle away, for instance when we are cycling, and then she studies our reaction to her behavior out of the corner of her eye."

Hannah's mom, 64th week, or 14½ months

"He climbs like a monkey. He climbs on everything. He climbs on chairs a lot. I also constantly find him on the dining room table, claiming that he can't get down! He is careful. He is aware of the danger, but sometimes he falls pretty hard."

Frankie's mom, 66th week, or 15 months

"Wrestling with his brother is now the top draw. Sometimes they get really rough."

Kevin's mom, 69th week, or approaching 16 months

"She spilled a few drops of her drink on the floor. I grabbed an old sock that was lying around and mopped up. She looked at me shocked and amazed, went purposefully to the baby wipes, took one out of the box and mopped all over again. When she had finished, she looked at me as if she wanted to say, 'That's how it should be done.' I was taken aback at the level of cleanliness, and I praised her for it."

Victoria's mom, 61st week, or 14 months

"She is very capable in expressing that something is dirty. She repeatedly says 'poo' to the slightest smudge in bed. I hope that this is temporary and she doesn't stay such a 'neat freak.'"

> Josie's mom, 64th week, or 14½ months

"When her brother was looking through her dolls in search of a special robot, he swept all her dolls onto the floor. Even Elisabeth's baby doll. She immediately ran to her fallen child and picked her up, hurried to me and thrust the doll to my breast. She then gave her brother a dirty look."

> Elisabeth's mom, 63rd week, or 14 months and a week

Show Understanding for Irrational Fears

When your toddler is busy exploring her new world and working through her newfound ability, she will encounter things and situations that are new and foreign to her. She is actually discovering new dangers, dangers that until now did not exist for her. She isn't able to talk about it yet. Only after she comes to understand things more fully will her fears disappear. Show sympathy.

"He was mad for batteries. All batteries had to come out and be put back in, out, in, out, in; it was endless."

> Steven's mom, 61st week, or 14 months

"He is scared of his sister's ducky. He walks way around it if it's in the way. When he grabs it, he drops it immediately."

James' mom, 66th week, or 15 months

"It looks as if she is afraid to sit in the bathtub by herself. Yelling and screeching. We don't know the reason. She wants to get in provided one of us joins her. She's not afraid of the swimming pool. She likes getting in there."

Josie's mom, 67th week, or 15 months and a week

"She is not afraid of new things, but you do notice that she is not completely convinced."

Josie's mom, 68th week, or 15½ months

Learning the rules

Whining and whimpering to get one's way, childish behavior like constantly needing to be entertained and always wanting a pacifier, being messy without any cause, not being careful and expressly hurting others, going out of the way to be bad – you probably wonder if you're the only one that is having such trouble with your little one's behavior. No, certainly not. Your toddler is no longer a baby. Time has come to lay down some ground rules. Your toddler is ready for you to start asking and expecting more from her. What's more: she is searching for these boundaries. Now that she has entered the world of principles, she yearns for rules. She is looking for chances to familiarize herself with them. Just as she must satisfy her appetite by eating, so too she must satisfy this yearning for rules. Most rules she will only discover if they are presented to her by you. Social rules in particular are important. You must show her what is acceptable and what is not acceptable socially. There is no harm in laying down the law. On the contrary, you owe it to her, and who better to do so than someone who loves her?

"I think that he should be able to put things on the table neatly. It really annoys me if he throws his sandwich and bottle when he's finished with them. He has to stop that. He's capable of putting things down properly."

Thomas' mom, 67th week, or 15 months and a week

"She still whines and whimpers to get her way, making it difficult to be consistent. It seems that this is the point where she needs guidance. It's much easier to give her what she wants, because she stops whining then. If I don't give her what she wants, then all hell breaks loose. Then there's a power struggle, which she easily wins. I've never been quite so aware of power as I am now."

Josie's mom, 68th week, or 15½ months

"Sometimes he does something he's not supposed to on purpose. He throws rocks, puts batteries in his mouth or smears his food on the floor. I scold him, while taking everything he has in his hands and putting it out of reach. This sometimes ends in an argument."

Paul's mom, 69thweek, or approaching 16 months

"Is my child the only one that rolls around on the ground kicking and screaming when she doesn't get her way? I don't hear the other parents complaining much. Do I let her get away with too much? Do I cater too much to her needs? Is it because she goes to daycare more often? What am I to do? Right, lay down clear ground rules, that's what I will do."

Vera's mom, 70th week, or 16 months

"I teach him that he is not allowed to just take things away from other children."

Thomas' mom, 70th week, or 16 months

(continued on page 368)

 Top Games for This Wonder Week - - - - - - - - - - - - - - -

Here are games and activities that most 15-16 month toddlers like best now and that help develop their new abilities. Remember, all children are different. See what your little one responds to best.

Skillfulness

In the world of principles toddlers have surpassed programs and thoroughly enjoy endlessly practicing variations and experimenting with these programs. By doing so, they become skillful and discover how and when they can best get things done. They are also keen observers.

PHYSICAL ANTICS

Your toddler will like running, climbing, chasing other kids, jumping on the bed, doing somersaults, rolling on the ground, wrestling with other kids, playing "I'll get you," walking stairs without holding on, walking on walls, jumping from walls, the list is endless. Take the time to give her the opportunity to do it.

EXPLORING THE GREAT OUTDOORS

Roaming around outside, doing nothing in particular while scouting about is often the favorite pastime: at the petting zoo, on the playground, or in the zoo. Even just being carried on mom or dad's back at a festival, is doable for several hours.

POINTING GAMES

Challenge your little one to play a pointing game. You say a word and have your child point to where the object, toy, or body part is.

GAMES USING HANDS AND FEET WITH SINGING AND RHYMING

Use rhymes or songs which involve using hands and feet. For instance, they love: "The Wheels on the Bus Go 'Round and 'Round" or "If You're Happy and You Know It, Clap Your Hands" or "Itsy Bitsy Spider" or "Head, Shoulder, Knees and Toes."

CALLING GAMES

See how your child likes playing a "calling game." It's best to start with your child calling you. Then call her name out and get her to call back at you. Call her name out again. Most children feel proud upon hearing their own name called out. It makes them feel like they belong.

Kidding around

In the world of principles, kidding and joking will start to play a more important role. By now, your toddler has figured out a bit how things work. So when things get out of whack, she really gets a kick out of it, whether it's someone acting funny or bending the rules.

JUST BEING SILLY

Your toddler loves acting silly: funny faces, funny walks or odd sounds. Especially if she is not expecting it. It's a real mess when the little ones get together. It cracks her up when her brother and

(continued)

Top Games for This Wonder Week (cont.)

sister join the antics. She and her little friends also have the greatest time acting silly.

THE JOKE AS STRATEGY

Your toddler uses silliness to get something or get something done by someone. Pleasant surprises are far more effective in getting something out of mom than temper tantrums. Some tykes employ various antics in order to bend or get around the rules. Not listening, being unruly or teasing mom are all cause for laughter. Give your kid the opportunity to play the clown. But be clear and correct her if and when she oversteps the bounds. She won't yet always know if she has gone too far.

CARTOONS, MONSTERS AND ANIMALS

Animals that do something silly or unexpectedly are favorites with toddlers. For instance, the monsters in "Sesame Street" are really funny. Cartoons really make her laugh, especially if something happens that catches her by surprise.

Household games

In the world of principles, your child re-enacts the daily business in and around the house. Give her the opportunity and play with her sometimes. It makes your toddler feel she is part of the club. It's great if she can actually help out. Here below are a few examples, but you are bound to come up with more.

COOKING PRACTICE

Give her some small bowls, some real food and a bowl of water, so she can cook to can feed her doll.

VACUUMING

There are toy vacuum cleaners that are exact replicas of the real thing. Vacuuming together can be fun!

DOING THE DISHES

The water goes everywhere, but that's what mops are for.

DOING EXACTLY AS MOM DOES

Leave your shoes lying around, so that she can put them on.

Games with emotions

Your toddler will be experimenting with emotions, such as varying her expressions when she greets people or when she wants something. Pay special attention and play along with the drama. For instance, you can imitate her and play pitiful. It will probably make her laugh.

Hide and seek

PEEK-A-BOO

Peek-a-Boo is a classic that always works.

HIDE AND SEEK

With each leap playing "hide and seek" becomes slightly more advanced. By this age, your toddler is already good at staying hidden in one place.

Top Toys for This Wonder Week

Here are toys and things that most 15-16 month old toddlers like best now and that help develop the new ability:

- Jungle gym, slide
- Balls
- Books
- Sandbox
- Tea set with water or cold juice in cups or mugs
- Puzzles
- Plastic bottles
- Cleaning utensils
- Toy vacuums
- Toys on a string
- Sesame Street
- Cartoons

Be careful with the following:

- Garbage cans
- Toilets
- Baseball bats, hockey sticks in the hallway

After the Leap

Around 68 weeks, or approaching 16 months, most toddlers become a little less troublesome than they were. They are bigger and have grown wiser and are living right along with the rest of us. You sometimes forget that they are still very little.

"He looks slimmer, less stocky, his face thinner, he is growing up. I sometimes see him sitting calmly, focused on his food. He seems rather mature then."

Luke's mom, 66th week, or 15 months

"Everything comes easier to her now, from feeding herself to cleaning up. She is really just like the rest of us. I keep forgetting that she is still a very small child."

Eve's mom, 67th week, or 15 months and a week

"All of a sudden, she seems wiser and more mature. It seems that she has taken a giant leap forward. She has entered the wide world, full of confidence and fearing nothing and nobody. She is doing extremely well, is easy-going and sweet, and at night she falls asleep much easier."

Josie's mom, 70th week, or 16 months

chapter 12

Wonder Week 75:
The World of Systems

$\mathcal{S}$ince the previous leap, your toddler has started to understand what "principles" are. Because she has risen above the previous confines of "programs," she has shed their mechanical character. For the first time she was able to evaluate existing programs and even to change them. You could see her constantly changing a program, then studying the effects. You could also see her performing physical antics, exploring the great outdoors, getting skillful with objects and language, imitating others, replaying the day-to-day, trying out emotions, beginning to plan, staging her own drama class, insisting on taking part, using aggression, learning what's hers and what's not, using gags as a strategy to an end, experimenting with "yes" and "no," being resourceful in putting people on the spot, learning to cooperate, wanting to help out around the house and experimenting with being reckless and being careful.

Just as her programs were mechanical before she had risen to new heights, so too were her principles lacking a certain flexibility. She was only able to apply them in a set way, always the same, regardless of the situation.

We adults are capable of adjusting our principles to fit different circumstances. We are able to see a bigger picture. We see how certain principles are linked and form a whole system. The concept "system" encompasses our idea of an organized unit. We use the term "system" if the parts it consists of are interdependent and function as a whole. There are tangible examples, like a grandfather clock that needs winding, an electrical network or the human muscle system. These systems form a

Note: The first phase (fussy period) of this leap into the perceptual world of "systems" is age-linked and predictable, and starts from 71 weeks onwards. Most babies start the second phase (see box "Quality Time: An Unnatural Whim" on page 17) of this leap 75 weeks after full-term birth. The first perception of the world of systems sets in motion the development of a whole range of skills and activities. However, the age at which these skills and activities appear for the first time varies greatly and depends on your baby's preferences, experimentation and physical development. For example, the ability to perceive systems is a necessary precondition for "being able to point the way to the supermarket or park," but this skill normally appears at anywhere from 75 weeks to many months later. Skills and activities are mentioned in this chapter at the earliest possible age they might appear so you can watch for and recognize them. (They may be rudimentary at first.) This way you can respond to and facilitate your baby's development.

coherent set of principles on, respectively, gear ratios, electric amps and volts, and balanced muscle tensions.

There are also less tangible examples. Take human organizations: They are arranged on the basis of principles that you cannot always put your finger on. There are rules (or agreements) for duties assigned to certain positions, rules for social behavior like being on time, and rules for learning the goals that your boss imposes. To name just a few examples of human organizations, take the scouts, the family, the drama club, the police station, the church, our society, our culture, and the law.

When your toddler makes her next leap, she will land in the world of systems. For the first time in her life she will perceive "systems." Of course, it's all new to her. She will need a number of years before she understands what our society, our culture or the law really entail. She starts with the basics and stays close to home. She develops the idea of herself as a system, and together with mom and dad she forms a family. And her family is not the same as that of her little friend, nor is her house the same as that of the neighbors.

 Do Remember

If your toddler is clingy, watch her closely. There's a good chance that she's attempting to master new skills.

Just as your tyke learned to be more flexible with programs after she made the leap into the world of principles, your toddler begins to be more flexible in applying principles after leaping into the world of systems. Now she begins to understand that she can choose what she wants to be: honest, helpful, careful, patient, and so forth. To be or not to be, that's the question. She applies principles less rigidly and starts to learn how she can refine her approach to all sorts of different circumstances.

Around 75 weeks, or 17 months and more than a week, you usually notice that your little one starts trying new things. However, she already felt the leap into the world of systems coming at an earlier age. From week 71, or just over 16 months onwards, your toddler has noticed that her world is changing. A maze of new impressions turns reality on its head. She cannot process the novelty all at once. First she will have to create order out of chaos. She returns to a familiar and safe base. She gets clingy. She needs a "mommy refill."

In this last chapter we no longer describe in detail the clues that your baby is about to make a developmental leap. By now these will be familiar to you. For this reason we include just the "My Diary" section below for you to remember. A useful memory aid is the three C's: CRYING, CLINGINESS and CRANKINESS. Remember that your toddler is only

after two things – being near you and having your undivided attention. She is also bigger and smarter now and more capable of finding new ways to these same goals.

How You Know It's Time to Grow

Which one or all of these signs did you notice as your baby started with this leap?

My Diary

Signs My Baby Is Growing Again

❑ Cries more often and is more often cranky or fretful
❑ Is cheerful one moment and cries the next
❑ Wants to be entertained, or does so more often
❑ Clings to your clothes or wants to be closer to you
❑ Acts unusually sweet
❑ Is mischievous
❑ Throws temper tantrums, or throws them more often
❑ Is jealous
❑ Is more obviously shy with strangers
❑ Wants physical contact to be tighter or closer
❑ Sleeps poorly
❑ Has nightmares, or has them more often
❑ Loses appetite
❑ Sometimes just sits there, quietly daydreaming
❑ Reaches for a cuddly toy, or does so more often
❑ Is more babyish

OTHER CHANGES YOU NOTICE

_____

_____

How This Leap May Affect You

Initially you were solely concerned that something was wrong with your baby when she became clingy, cranky and cried more often. By the time she was 6 months old, you began to become increasingly annoyed when it became clear that nothing was wrong, but generally you let it pass. After all she was so tiny then. After her first birthday, you started to take action if annoyed and that resulted sometimes in an altercation. You were able to enjoy the true pleasures of parenthood! All parents report that they quarrel with their "teenaging" toddler. Teens have been known to be able to make life rotten for their parents. Toddlers can do it, too. It gives one a preview of what is to come ten years later. It's part of the bargain.

You May Become Really Frustrated

"If she asks me with a whiny voice if I want to do something, I say very friendly: 'Yes, mommy do you want ...' Then she repeats very sweetly: 'Mommy, do you want ...'"

> Anna's mom, 71st week, or a good 16 months

"I was really annoyed this week. He didn't want to take his nap. If he doesn't want to, then he doesn't have to. It's easier and it saves me a lot of trouble. Nor does he want to wear a diaper, so I often let him go without."

> Taylor's mom, 73rd week, or approaching 17 months

"It was difficult for me when she completely dominated my time. She was driving me nuts. I thought, 'What am I doing wrong?' I try to relax and not to make plans and take things as they come, but it's not easy."

> Ashley's mom, 73rd week, or approaching 17 months

"Once in a while this week I put him in his playpen, although he was whining and what-not. He was constantly being pushy and impatient. He wanted to get his way all the time."

> Frankie's mom, 74th week, or 17 months

"I was afraid again that I had created a terribly spoiled monster."

Elisabeth's mom, 74th week, or 17 months

"I tried time and again not to give in, but she always ended up back on my lap."

Josie's mom, 74th week, or 17 months

You May Argue

"We regularly get into it. When she sees candy, she wants some but doesn't always get it. She gives up when she sees that she is not getting any. I don't get the feeling that this upsets her."

Julia's mom, 72nd- 74th week, or 16-17 months

"On several occasions, we have had big spats. He's not allowed to rearrange the kitchen in the vacation house as he does at home. It went fairly well last week, but now he's stopped listening, so I put him outside with the door open so that he could come back inside, but he didn't like it one bit."

Luke's mom, 74th week, or 17 months

How Your Baby's New Skills Emerge

Around 75 weeks, or 17 months and a good week, you will notice that a large part of the clinginess disappears. The temper tantrums and quarreling with your "teenaging" toddler subside. She's back to her enterprising self. You may notice that she has changed, that her behavior is different, that she is becoming very aware of herself as a person, that she thinks differently, and that she has a better sense of time. She plays with her toys differently and her use of fantasy takes off. Her humor has changed. This change in toddlers is evident because at this age your toddler's ability to perceive systems and to apply the concept of system is emerging. This new ability is the equivalent to a new world opening up. Your toddler, with

her talents, preferences and temperament, chooses where she will begin to explore. Try to see what she is doing and help her. But watch out! She wants to do it all by herself.

> *"His father claims that he has more patience."*
>
> ### Gregory's mom, 74th week, or 17 months

> *"Things went much easier with her, although she is very pig-headed and needs a lot of attention."*
>
> ### Juliette's mom, 75th week, or a good 17 months

When your toddler enters into the world of systems, he is now able to see clearly over the world of principles. He no longer applies principles as rigidly as before. He is able to adjust his principles to changing circumstances. For instance, he is now able to choose to apply a moral principle, or not. From off this age you can see him develop the earliest beginnings of a conscience, by systematically upholding his norms and values.

> *"She jumps when we catch her doing something she's not allowed. Then she blurts out 'no.'"*
>
> ### Jenny's mom, 73rd week, or approaching 17 months

The system your toddler lives with day in and day out is the one he knows the best – himself. He is his own person. When the world of systems opens up to him, he starts to develop his notion of self. This has several consequences. Your toddler now discovers that he owns and controls his own body. He also discovers that he can orchestrate things, that he can do things himself, that he can control things, and that he can make decisions, all things that stem from his growing concept of self.

"Now he expressly does things differently than is expected or is asked of him. For instance if you ask him: 'Give mom a kiss?' he gives everyone a kiss, walks to me and says: 'Hahahahaha' and doesn't give me a kiss. It seems to me that he wants to show that he is his own person. That he is no longer one with me, but a separate person. That's all."

Thomas' mom, 80th week, or a good 18 months

Your toddler begins to understand that mom and dad are separate people. He starts using terms as "you" and "me" and is also very interested in both mom's and dad's physique. He discovers that he has a penis just like his father, and that mom doesn't. He sizes up all the similarities and differences to a tee. For the first time in his life, your toddler can put himself in someone else's place, now that he realizes that not all people are alike. For the first time he sees that not everyone likes the same things as he does. That would have never occurred to him when he was younger. We can sum this up with one elegant word, he has become less egocentric. That has all sorts of consequences. He is now able to comfort someone. He is at his high point in mimicry. He copies anything and everything around him. His imagination comes to life.

Your explorer is also fascinated by other living creatures: ants, dogs and so forth. They are all systems, too.

Your "teenaging" toddler starts realizing that he is part of a family, that his family is different from his little friend's family, whom he visits twice a week. After all, his family is the first human organization he gets to know from the inside, and he makes no mistake about noticing that his little friend's family doesn't necessarily have a salad with dinner like his own family. In his family they have a different set of rules.

Just as your toddler recognizes his family as a system, he begins to distinguish his family from others. He already does the same with his friends, house and neighborhood. He is getting better at finding his way around in the familiar surroundings outside of his house.

He starts paying great attention to his clothes. He can be quite vain and is very possessive of his toys.

Your little artist starts to create art with a capital A. He no longer scribbles, now he draws "horses," "boats" and "himself." He also begins to appreciate music – that, too, is a system.

Your toddler starts to develop a sense of time. He is now better able to recall past experiences and to understand better what the future will bring.

He will now begin forming his first sentences. Not every toddler does this, though. Just as with other skills, children differ greatly in the age at which they start. All toddlers now understand much of what you say to them, but some are not ready to start speaking. Others use several words and constantly mime, but do not yet produce sentences. A few, though, do speak in sentences. Whether or not your toddler does depends on how you interact with him.

Some examples from the adult world will help to clarify what we mean by a system. Take, for instance, practicing mathematics. On the level of programs, we think, use logic and handle mathematical symbols. On the level of principles, we think about thinking and therefore we think about how we make use of mathematics. On a system level, we look at mathematics as a whole, as an intellectual system.

In a similar way, the science of physics is a large system consisting of carefully discovered principles. This also applies to the science of biology and the theory of evolution and the accompanying principles of natural selection. This applies to other sciences as well.

World views or outlooks on life are also systems. Our everyday lives also offer examples of systems. Our approach to diet leads us to formulate principles regarding food, which in turn determines our eating programs. Another example of a system is democracy. Just as with other human organizations, some aspects are tangible and demonstrable, while others are very cursory. By the time someone else is able to see something the same way you do, the situation could have changed completely. We can point to government, the annual budget, or employee hiring practices. What we are unable to do is point to authority, cooperation, back-room politics, compromises or organization in general. You can point to what you think is evidence of its existence, but you can not demonstrate it as easily as you can something simple and tangible, like a rock.

Other examples of human organizations as systems are family, school, church, the bank, a factory, the army, the government, the soccer club and the bridge club. Such social institutions have the important task of encouraging their members to familiarize themselves with their goals, norms and values. Some institutions insist on it. In the family, it is called socialization. There the learning of values, norms and other principles is practically automatic because toddlers imitate anything and everything they see. There are also countless learning opportunities, where such things are often not emphasized, but acted out as a matter of course.

It may seem different from a system like physics or mathematics. "That's way too advanced for such a little fellow," most people will

say. "He won't learn that until high school." But if you observe him playing, if you see how he holds a ball under water again and again to see it fly up out of the water, if you watch him endlessly rolling things down an incline or running up and down an incline himself again and

again, you cannot ignore that he is experimenting with the fundamental principles of physics to establish systems of his own in his mind, which puts him in good company. It was Newton himself who once experimented with something as simple as a falling apple. Perhaps it wouldn't be a bad idea for physics teachers to seek advice from toddlers at play to come up with a few nice demonstrations for their classes.

This applies to other systems as well as those of math and physics. A toddler is also interested in basic architecture. He can watch builders for hours or imitate his father making cement. He mixes water and sand the whole day long and then he starts "plastering walls." His Lego buildings have also become more complex. For instance, he can lay down train tracks and run his trains on them.

Brain Changes

Between 16 and 24 months, the number of synapses in the cerebrum vastly increases, both within the various subareas of the cerebrum and in between those subareas. In the second half of the second year, a part of the cerebrum behind the forehead matures (the orbitofrontal lobe), and a cascade of new skills emerge. The right half of the brain develops in leaps and bounds in the first year and a half. Then development in the left half of the brain, where the language centers reside, takes over. As far as the comprehension of single words is concerned, at 20 months, a confinement takes place from the whole cerebrum to a few small areas in the left half.

Your Toddler's Choices: A Key to Her Personality

All toddlers have been given the ability to perceive and control systems. They need years in order to completely familiarize themselves with the wide range of new skills to play with, but as toddlers they take their first tender steps in the world of systems. For instance, at this age, a toddler chooses to work on getting the hang of using her body and leaves speaking for later, using just a few words and no sentences. Or, she may be very busy with her family, friends, house and neighborhood. Or she might prefer the arts, drawing endlessly and listening to music. Just like every toddler, she chooses what best suits her talents, mobility, preferences and circumstances. The very first choices become apparent when she is 75 weeks, or 17 months and a good week. Don't compare your child with others. Each child is unique and will choose accordingly.

Take a good look at your toddler. Establish what her interests are. Already you can readily see which talents and preferences she has, as well as her strong points. If your toddler has a high musical intelligence, that will now become clear. Use the list in "My Diary" on pages 384-389 to mark or highlight what your child selects. You may also have a look for yourself to see if there are some systems that you think your child could use or learn. Stop marking when your child begins with the next leap. That is usually when she is approximately 20-21 months old.

Toddlers are like this

Anything new to her, your toddler likes the most. Therefore, always react especially to new skills and interests your toddler shows. In that way she learns more pleasantly, easier, quicker and more.

(continued on page 390)

How My Baby Explores the New World of Systems

THE CONSCIENCE

❏ Jumps and blurts out a loud "no" when caught

❏ Tests you by doing what's not allowed

❏ Imitates behavior from TV

❏ Is hurt and confused by unjust sanctions

❏ Is able to "lie"

❏ What I have noticed otherwise:_____

THE NOTION OF SELF

❏ Me and my body

❏ I control my body

❏ I can do things on my own

❏ I have my own will

❏ I can decide for myself

❏ I want power

❏ What I have noticed otherwise:_____

OUT OF SIGHT BUT NOT OUT OF MIND

❏ Hides and wants to be found

❏ Looks for people without just going back to where they were

❏ What I have noticed otherwise:_____

ME AND YOU

❏ Grasps that mom and dad are not the same person

❏ Sizes up similarities and differences to a tee

❏ Wants to be recognized as his own person

❏ Can put himself in the place of others

❏ Can realize that another child wants something different

❏ Can console another

❏ Is at his high point in mimicry

❏ Imagination takes off

❏ Starts treating toys as autonomous agents

❏ What I have noticed otherwise:_____

OTHER LIVING CREATURES

❏ Waves at birds and planes

❏ Smells the plants

❏ Likes feeding the chickens

❏ Is interested in bees, ants, ladybugs and the like

❏ Laughs at nature films with animals doing unusual things

❏ Wants to water the plants

❏ What I have noticed otherwise:_____

(continued)

My Diary

THE NUCLEAR FAMILY

❑ Grasps that members of his nuclear family are separate people but still belong together

❑ Plays the whole day long with stuffed animals, feeds them and puts them to bed

❑ Grasps that there are other nuclear families with other moms and dads, brothers and sisters

❑ What I have noticed otherwise:_____

_____

FAMILY AND FRIENDS

❑ Grasps the difference between his family and that of his friends

❑ Knows exactly who belongs to who

❑ Wants to phone Grandma and Grandpa

❑ Wants to visit Grandma and Grandpa

❑ What I have noticed otherwise:_____

_____

HOUSE, NEIGHBORHOOD AND FINDING THE WAY

❑ He has a good idea of the lay of the land in his surroundings

❑ Knows exactly where to find things in and around the house

❑ Recognizes his own house and that of Grandma & Grandpa

❑ Can point the way to the supermarket or the park

❑ Recognizes things even if they are in a less familiar surrounding

❑ What I have noticed otherwise:_____

OWNERSHIP

❑ Knows perfectly well which clothes belong to whom when sorted out of the washing machine

❑ Knows exactly which bag and jacket belongs to which kid

❑ Knows exactly which toy belongs to whom and what is off limits

❑ Wishes no longer to share his toys with other children

❑ Collects things and insists they are not to be thrown away

❑ Doesn't like mess. Wants everything systematically put away

❑ What I have noticed otherwise:_____

PUZZLES AND LITTLE THINGS

❑ Is now good at doing puzzles. Puzzles consisting of 7, 12 or at the most 20 pieces

❑ Motor skills are increasingly more refined

❑ Finds the sewing kit interesting, or a vast assortment of buttons

❑ Is a stickler for detail

❑ What I have noticed otherwise:_____

MAKING UP HIS OWN GAMES

❑ Makes up a game with its own rules

❑ Makes up his own magic tricks

❑ What I have noticed otherwise:_____

(continued)

 My Diary ---------------------------------

ART

❑ Grasps that toys symbolize real world things or people

❑ Starts drawing in a completely different way. Random scribbling makes way for circles, squares and the like

❑ Draws horses, boats, planes, the dog, Grandma, Grandpa and himself

❑ Likes it when you draw, too

❑ Music lovers can listen to music for quite a long time

❑ Likes playing the keyboard

❑ Erects more buildings

❑ What I have noticed otherwise:_____

SENSE OF TIME

❑ Remembers past experiences

❑ Predicts familiar, daily events and programs

❑ Reminds you the whole day long of your promise to go to Grandma and Grandpa's house

❑ Makes plans; if you promise to do something and forget, he is upset and insulted

❑ Remembers in the morning what we did the night before

❑ What I have noticed otherwise:_____

BASIC PHYSICS

❑ Holds a ball under water to watch it pop up

❑ Is endlessly busy pouring his special mixture from one container to the next

❑ Pays attention to colors

❑ Found his first snow intimidating

❑ Is frightened of the electric toothbrush

❑ Is busy with basic phenomena of physics

❑ What I have noticed otherwise:_____

BASIC ARCHITECTURE

❑ Watches builders for hours

❑ Imitates making cement by mixing sand and water

❑ Imitates plastering walls

❑ Lays down Lego train tracks

❑ Tries building with Lego blocks

❑ What I have noticed otherwise:_____

LANGUAGE

❑ Understands most of what is said

❑ If he's exposed to different languages, he can distinguish between them and can ignore one

❑ Produces more and more words

❑ Sooner or later is able to combine words to form sentences

❑ Imitates animal noises

❑ Mimes a lot. Is able to communicate with gestures

❑ Loves books. Listens attentively to short stories til the end

❑ What I have noticed otherwise:_____

what You Can Do to Help

In the world of systems, your toddler will discover that she can choose her principles. She will discover herself, her family, her friends, her house, her neighborhood, her art and more. Give your toddler the opportunity to experience all sorts of systems. Just from her ingenuity, from seeing your reactions, and through much practice, she learns how the world of systems is made up.

Me and My Conscience

The conscience is a system of moral principles, of values, norms and rules. The development of a conscience is not to be taken for granted. Your toddler has to construct her conscience by using the examples she takes from you. You must demonstrate right and wrong. It takes time, much time, before your toddler has seen enough examples from which to draw conclusions. Hopefully, your actions have been consistent. If you say one thing one time and something else the other, then it will take your toddler much longer. The same applies if the signals you give her are confusing. She will have a hard time figuring it all out. From this age on, your little one tries to discover a system in everything, also in values, norms and rules. She craves rules and tests the boundaries. Just as she is entitled to her daily meals, likewise is she entitled to her daily portion of rules.

"She knows that the things on the top shelf of the closet are her brother's. Now she climbs in the closet to grab and sneak something out. If she's seen, she drops it and looks at you with a look of 'How did that get there?'"

Victoria's mom, 76th week, or 17 months
and a good week

"He tests us by doing what he's not allowed."

Harry's mom, 77th week, or 17½ months

"He laughs when he surprises his father or me by suddenly doing something un-expected and expressly forbidden. He also laughs when we catch him."

> **John's mom, 79th week,**
> **or 18 months**

"He imitates everything he sees on TV. For instance, he falls to the floor on purpose, and in one film, he saw children fighting. He observed this and hit himself."

> **Thomas' mom, 80th week, or a good 18 months**

"I also noticed that he wouldn't listen and his bad behavior. I've never seen him like this. He hit someone on the head for no reason and threw another to the ground by his shirt. It is very irritating and a couple of times I have gotten really angry. I keep explaining that it hurts if he does that. Maybe I talk to him too much, so that he only listens when he wants. It has no effect on him if I tell him he can not do something or I ask him to help with something. I figured out that I need to tell him that we can do this chore together. Like putting a bottle back where it belongs instead of just throwing it."

> **Jim's mom, 81st week, or 18½ months**

"I noticed if he falls down, he doesn't cry too quickly and takes his lumps well. But if he thinks that he is corrected unfairly, he is very hurt and confused. For instance, he bawled because he wasn't allowed on the bed with his boots. I said it was fine because they were clean, but the nanny didn't know and didn't understand. I could tell from the way he cried that it really upset and hurt him, even though it wasn't that big of a deal. I rarely hear him like that. I do hear the same cry after he has been staying with his father who tells him yes where I say no."

> **Taylor's mom, 81st week, or 18½ months**

"We changed the routine for going to bed. She used to not go to bed until 10 and then she wanted to fall asleep on our lap first, and only then could we put her to bed. Last Saturday, we put her to bed at 8 o'clock, after she had been very tiresome. She yelled her lungs out for 45 minutes before she finally fell asleep. Since that night, she goes to bed between 8 and 8:30. We sing songs with her, her father talks with her a little bit more and then she falls asleep and sleeps through until 7 the next morning. Dad does have to put her to bed though."

> Jenny's mom, 84th week, or 19 months

"The latest fad is making things up. He finished playing a flight simulator game on the computer with his dad and told me that his dad didn't do well and that he had crashed upon landing. This was not at all the case, as it turned out, but he said it on purpose. He likes that he can make things up. He laughs heartily when dad sets the record straight."

> Jim's mom, 85th week, or 19½ months

"He is now able to 'lie.' For instance, he eats a cookie and his mouth is full of chocolate when the next round of cookies is handed out. When it's his turn he puts his hand behind his back with cookie in hand and says that he hasn't gotten one yet. If he is allowed to take another one, he laughs and then shows the one he already had in his hand."

> Thomas' mom, 87th week, or 20 months

Me and My Notion of Self

The system with which your toddler most comes in contact is herself. That is what she gets to know first, and it has all sorts of consequences. Your toddler discovers that she is the owner of her own body and that she has control over her own body. She also discovers that she can make things happen, that she has her own will and can make her own decisions, and that she has power to influence. She thinks in terms of me, me, me.

Me and My body

"He is very interested in his 'weenie.' He plucks at it and rubs it wherever he can. I often let him walk around naked."

> Mark's mom, 72nd week, or 16½ months

"It seems as if she has rediscovered her toes. She studies them bit by bit, for minutes at a time."

> Victoria's mom, 73th week, or a good 16½ months

"She calls herself Mita. She gave herself that name."

> Victoria's mom, 75th week, or 17 months

"Often he hits his head hard against the wall. It makes me feel ill. I would like him to stop. I think he does it to experience his notion of self."

> Kevin's mom, 76th week, 17 months and a good week

"She cracked up at a silly doll in the supermarket."

> Maria's mom, 81st week, or 18½ months

"She is obsessed with angels. I asked: 'Is that you?' 'Yes,' she said."

> Nina's mom, 82nd week, or a good 18½ months

"No one is allowed to touch him. Not the doctor while weighing and measuring him, nor the hairdresser, even though she was a friend. Not even his Grandma while getting dressed."

> Matt's mom, 82nd week, or a good 18½ months

"She also says: 'Is me.'"

> Hannah's mom, 83rd week, or 19 months

"If anyone says to him: 'Nice curls,' he runs his hands through his hair like the star in the movie Grease."

> Thomas' mom, 86th week, or approaching 20 months

"She is really busy with putting on and taking off her clothes. She even puts her slippers, her socks and pants on. She is also very vain. When she has on new clothes, she gets on our bed in front of the mirror to examine herself better. Once she insisted on putting on a dress when I tried to get her in pants. She loves getting her hair done at the hairdresser."

> Vera's mom, 74th - 87th week,
> or 17-20 months

I Have Control Over My Body

"He walks the stairs erect taking big steps. Right foot on one step and the left foot on the next and so on."

> Bob's mom, 72nd week, or 16½ months

"I already got angry once this week. She climbed up a dangerous flight of stairs after I had already forbidden it."

> Eve's mom, 74th week, or 17 months

"He pulls himself up on a bar, swings back and forth a bit then drops to the ground laughing."

> Paul's mom, 74th week, or 17 months

"He climbs on everything. Nothing is too much. He is careful however. He is aware of the dangers."

> James' mom, 76th week, or approaching 17½ months

"She finds all kinds of ways to get to where she is not allowed. I have put certain things away and protected others. That is no use anymore. She finds a way to get to them. Even if she needs to drag over a chair or get a ladder."

> Victoria's mom, 76th week, or approaching 17½ months

"She climbs like an acrobat. She climbs on me while holding my hands. She pushes off my stomach diving backwards."

> Laura's mom, 80th week, or 18 months and a week

"He went down the plastic slide at MacDonald's for the first time on his stomach."

> Steven's mom, 81st week, or 18½ months

"She learned to somersault, slide down the slide by herself and climb back up by herself. She now gets in and out of bed by herself."

> Nora's mom, 81st - 83rd week, or 18½-19 months

"He likes to jump from high places if he thinks he can do it. When he can't, he says 'scary' and sticks his arms out, which says: 'It's too high for me, can we do it together?' He also likes to walk along little walls, practicing his balance. He enjoys it if the wall is about four feet tall. I act calm, but inside it scares me."

> Luke's mom, 83rd - 86th week, or 19 to almost 20 months

"Since a month ago, the new thing is to try to make her fall while crossing the waterbed."

> Eve's mom, 82nd week, or approaching 19 months

"She enjoyed shooting little blocks away with her mouth, it made her laugh. Running down the sand dunes and chasing after the dog on the beach was the best thing."

> Hannah's mom, 86th - 88th week,
> or approximately 20 months

I Can Do It Myself

"She peels and eats an orange by herself, opens doors and can say her own name. She winds up her toy radio herself and goes around listening to it."

> Juliette's mom, 72nd week, or 16½ months

"She grasps that she can use her potty to do her business. Twice she went and sat down with a diaper and relieved herself."

Josie's mom, 73rd week, or approaching 17 months

"She doesn't want to sit in her highchair much anymore. She wants to sit in a normal chair at the dinner table. Also she doesn't want to wear a bib and she wants to feed herself."

Julia's mom, 73rd - 75th week, or around 17 months

"This week he walked around with napkins. He used them as a bib or towel, but particularly as an oven glove. I mean, when he goes to pick something up, he puts it on top and then picks it up. He primarily did this in the kitchen with the grips on the drawers."

Paul's mom, 74th week, or 17 months

"Now he is busy with spatial aspects. Putting things in or under something is very interesting to him. It's not so much that something fits somewhere, it's more that he is the one putting things in and taking things out. He is more interested in researching his own potential, instead of the qualities of the things themselves. He now has a renewed urgency to look into the pans. Now it's not about me showing him what we are eating and telling him what it's called, but that he looks and identifies it himself. Playing with the bucket with the shape-sorting lid has taken on a new twist. It's now about him putting the pieces in as he wants. He purposefully tries to ram the forms through the wrong holes. If he accidently puts one in the proper hole, he quickly pulls it out. He wants to put the pieces in as he sees fit, not according to the rules of the game."

Frankie's mom, 76th week, or approaching 17½ months

"This week he likes drawing. I think it's because it's something he does himself. He makes something by himself."

John's mom, 77th week, or 17½ months

"She makes drawings and then laughs about it herself."

Maria's mom, 77th week, or 17½ months

"These days he wants to feed himself dinner. That's not without its problems, but in general, he does well. He imitates more and more. He cleans the floor with a sponge, he blows his nose with a handkerchief and vacuums with the vacuum cleaner attachment. He now knows exactly what things are for."

James' mom, 77th week, or 17½ months

"If I ask, 'Do you want mom to do it?' she says: 'No, Anna.' Even if she has broken something and we ask who has done it, she says: 'Anna.' She is very conscious of herself. She laughs if she drops something or throws something on the ground."

Anna's mom, 77th week, or 17½ months

"This week he came walking up proudly with a full potty. I was just as proud as he. If he goes around without a diaper, he is indicating that he wants to use his potty or that he has used it before I even know. He waits to pee until he has the potty. He uses all his might to BM and every little bit must be done in the toilet. Endearing. Then he says 'more.' That means that he wants to use it again. When he's all done he says 'finished.'"

Mark's mom, 78th -79th week, or approaching 18 months

"Now she releases her belt and climbs out of her chair herself."

Ashley's mom, 80th week, or 18 months and a week

"He can now function as an 'errand boy'. He gets whatever is asked of him. He gets the remote control, the TV guide, the socks. He turns on the washing machine, 'medium heat please.' He gets the shoes. Gets the cleaning products. And if he and dad are playing the flight simulator on the computer, he follows his commands: 'Gas!' 'Landing gear!' 'Eject!'.

I am proud of my big little boy. He really gives it his all and does everything asked of him right away. But I feel for the poor child. He really gets put to work."

>   Thomas' mom, 80th week, or 18 months and a week

"She is an expert with the toy doctor's instruments."

>   Elisabeth's mom, 81st week, or 18½ months

"She did her business on the potty. She says 'poo-poo' if she goes in her diaper, which means that she wants a clean diaper. Now and then she does her business on the toilet."

>   Nina's mom, 80th -83rd week, or a good 18 to 19 months

"He likes to walk around naked after his bath. Then he crouches down and strains to go pee. Once, he peed in his closet."

>   Robin's mom, 82nd week, or approaching 19 months

"It never ceases to amaze me how well she understands what's going on. Now and again, she has it all figured out. For instance, if she can't reach something, she goes to the bathroom, gets a stool and puts it where she needs it. That's just one of the many moments I see her solving her own problems."

>   Vera's mom, 82nd week, or approaching 19 months

"She colors with crayons now."

>   Laura's mom, 83rd week, or 19 months

"She is able to arrange the colors. She saw that one of the markers had the wrong color top on it."

>   Victoria's mom, 84th week, or a good 19 months

"He tells me ahead of time that he needs to use the bathroom."

>   Taylor's mom, 84th week, or a good 19 months

"Now and again she wants to use her potty. She sits down for a second and goes to wiping furiously, but has yet to do anything on the potty."

Eve's mom, 85th week, or 19½ months

"He is increasingly more helpful and he imitates more. He brings his cup to the kitchen and puts it on the counter or grabs a plate. He also likes to play like he is hammering something. He wants to drink out of a big person's cup and not a bottle or baby's cup."

Bob' mom, 86th week, or approaching 20 months

"She did a little business once on the toilet."

Anna's mom, 87th week, or 20 months

"She gets onto the potty herself if she's already naked. If she's wearing pants, she does it in her pants, but alerts us directly."

Hannah's mom, 87th week, or 20 months

"Completely potty trained. After only 3 nights, she completely stopped wetting the bed."

Emily's mom, 87th week, or 20 months

"He can blow his nose. Now he tries to blow his nose into everything, even the coasters."

Gregory's mom, 88th week, or 20 months

I Have My Own Will

"The last few months he has been naughty and has been testing the waters to see what's allowed and what's not, as well as the consequences. At the moment, he knows full well what's allowed. Now he is just naughty to show: 'I do what I want. So what are you going to do about it?'"

Harry's mom, 76th week, or approaching 17½ months

"He doesn't listen to warnings anymore. It looks as if he is proclaiming that he knows what he's doing. Experimenting has taken priority: falling down, heat, strong spices, etc. He decides what he eats, when and how."

Matt's mom, 76th week, or approaching 17½ months

"He really goes his own way. Preferably looking for trouble."

James' mom, 77th week, or 17½ months

"She wanted a lot of attention if she wasn't allowed something or if getting something took too long. She kept tugging on me, was very stubborn, whiny, pig-headed, naughty, hot-tempered and uncontrollable."

Josie's mom, 77th week, or 17½ months

"He gets into everything, but I have to keep a close watch on him. It's too dangerous to leave him unattended because he is always defying the rules. I really got angry when he tried to light the stove with a hot pan on it. It really made me jump. Fortunately, he only received slight burns, and there was only minimal damage, but he certainly got a physical warning. I hope it has sunk in that he is not allowed to touch the gas. It is really fun to cook together, but if he hasn't learned his lesson we will no longer be able to."

Steven's mom, 78th week, or approaching 18 months

"Recently she has abandoned her toys for the things that she is not allowed to touch, like the DVD player."

Laura's mom, 78th week, or approaching 18 months

"I have to accompany him everywhere. He is very enterprising and quite the prospector. Everything must be turned upside down and inside out with me present. We had a run-in because he makes a mess faster than I can clean it up."

Luke's mom, 79th week, or 18 months

"He is a real clown. He pays no mind to anything, just does his own thing. He loves to kid around. We call him the 'little elf.'"

James' mom, 80th week, or a good 18 months

"She's increasingly independent. She goes off by herself or along with others. A quick wave and off she goes."

Elisabeth's mom, 80th -81st week,
or a good 18 to 18½ months

"The last few days he has been playing with cars. Wednesday I ended up with a half hour all to myself. He played happily with his blocks and cars and I didn't hear him for a whole half hour."

James' mom, 81st week, or 18½ months

"She put her finger in the hot tea. Ouch!"

Julia's mom, 84th week, or a good 19 months

"Now and then she really amuses herself well. She plays by herself if I'm around, but I am not allowed to read. I sometimes get a bit of reading in, which is more than I used to."

Nina's mom, 83rd -86th week, or 19 to almost 20 months

"Her personal awareness grows daily. She indicates what she wants and what she doesn't want. She blows kisses when bidding farewell and if she gives something to you, it is a conscious decision."

Ashley's mom, 83rd - 86th week,
or 19 to almost 20 months

"She doesn't want me to brush her teeth, but if she does it, she doesn't brush but eats the paste and then she's finished. One time when I went ahead and brushed her teeth for her, she was angry with me for the next half hour."

Anna's mom, 86th week, or approaching 20 months

I Can Decide For Myself

"She starts to laugh already when she's planning something naughty."

Eve's mom, 76th week, or approaching 17½ months

"He announces everything he does. He always points to himself."

Kevin's mom, 76th week, or approaching 17½ months

"She really knows that it's 'bah' if she has messed her pants. She comes up and says 'bah.' If she can choose the spot where she gets changed, then she doesn't make a scene and will consent to it. She finds the strangest spots to be changed. Changing clothes is the same: 'Find your spot,' and there she goes."

Nora's mom, 86th week, or approaching 20 months

"He wants to pick out his own clothes these days. He really has certain preferences. His comfortable jogging pants with mice print is 'out.' Sometimes he puts Daddy's jacket on with a tie and goes and wakes Mom up."

Thomas' mom, 86th week, or approaching 20 months

I Want Power

"The temper tantrums have really picked up. She can really scream loud. Short but powerful. She also watches her brother very carefully when he misbehaves. It looks like she is taking mental notes."

Victoria's mom, 72nd week, or 16½ months

"If she doesn't agree, she starts to scream. The rolling around on the ground has lessened. She tries to get her way by screaming."

Jenny's mom, 72nd week, or 16½ months

"He scares me with snakes and mice and does the same to the girl next door."

Frankie's mom, 74th week,
or 17 months

"He tries putting oversized cars into his tiny toy garage. He didn't ever try this before."

Robin's mom, 76th week, or
approaching 17½ months

"He constantly hits and sometimes pinches if he doesn't get his way. If he's angry, he punches hard, softer when he's joking. The general idea is I try to break his bad habit by calmly correcting him, and offering him a pillow to pound or by urging him to calm down. I do sometimes get angry if he really hurts. This makes him sad and then he starts handing out kisses."

Luke's mom, 76th week, or approaching 17½ months

"He insists on eating and drinking what I have, even if he already has the same. He wants what I have. He takes my food and drink from me. We fight that out like two children."

Gregory's mom, 76th week, or approaching 17½ months

"She screams so loudly and in a high pitch if she doesn't get her way or she fails at something. That really annoys me and I want to break her of that soon. We have had several squabbles this week because of this."

Juliette's mom, 77th week,
or 17½ months

"A couple of times a day she gets in a rage, especially if she doesn't get her way. It generally blows over all by itself. Sometimes, I have to intervene in order to calm her down. She is quite fierce."

Maria's mom, 77th week, or 17½ months

"He has gotten notably rougher. He also forcefully throws things and really can't stand not getting his way. He sometimes throws things at the cat, like the alarm clock."

Matt's mom, 77th week, or 17½ months

"He is very well tempered and exceedingly energetic. He is so very busy with what he seems to need to do, that he doesn't even flinch when I express my displeasure at certain things. He throws and hits with anything he can get a hold of, with all his might. I think he flings things like that because he feels a certain power of his possessions. The same goes for hitting. I try to make it clear to him when I take action against him by threatening punishment. If he persists in throwing and hitting, I put him in his playpen. He sits there quietly waiting it out, only to pick up where he left off, throwing and hitting. The only thing that helps is to distract him. It seems like we are dealing with a new learning pattern."

Kevin's mom, 78th week, or approaching 18 months

"If he doesn't get his way he gets angry. For instance, if he wants to go outside, he points to his jacket. If I say no, he gets angry. He also gets angry if he doesn't get more candy or if his friend isn't home."

Robin's mom, 77th week, or 17½ months

"If she has to come inside from the garden, she cries and stamps her feet. In these cases, I give her a time-out."

Vera's mom, 79th week, or 18 months

"Sometimes I doubt whether or not I can manage his headstrong, dynamic activities."

> Harry's mom, 79th week, or 18 months

"He throws everything to the ground and away from himself. He bites and hits. I really got angry this week when he smeared his food and drink all over the floor."

> John's mom, 79th week, or 18 months

"I try anger and demanding obedience, insisting that he has to stop, but nothing helps. He is not at all impressed. It is difficult when he acts this way. If he is tired, it is even worse. Then it really is overwhelming."

> Paul's mom, 79th week, or 18 months

"If I leave the room briefly or neglect her in the slightest, she starts digging in my plant."

> Laura's mom, 80th week, or a good 18 months

"She was very annoying this week. She kept insisting on getting her way. If she didn't get her way, then she started screaming and threw herself on the ground. If we just left her, she would come around on her own."

> Emily's mom, 81st week, or 18½ months

"If she can't get something, has to go to bed or doesn't get her way, she cries and stamps her feet."

> Ashley's mom, 84th week, or a good 19 months

"The throwing and hitting seem to be lessening. But the biting is sometimes very serious. Harsh scolding, explaining, a spanking: nothing seems to help."

John's mom, 83rd -86th week, or 19 to almost 20 months

"He terrorizes the cats. He constantly keeps tabs on where they both are. Then he has to be able to pet them."

Jim's mom, 83rd 86th week, or 19 to almost 20 months

"She doesn't want to be seen as 'small.' We went to get ice cream in a nice place, where the scoops are pricy. Dad said: 'Elisabeth can have some of ours.' When the ice cream came, she could lick it but she wasn't allowed to hold it. That brought on a temper tantrum. She wanted to leave. She was insulted that she was thought to be small. Dad then went to a lesser ice cream parlor for some more ice cream. She held it but didn't eat it. Her tantrum continued all the while. She was deeply insulted. For the next half hour to 45 minutes, she was no fun. She hit dad, too."

Elisabeth's mom, 86th week, or approaching 20 months

"She is very willful, which is sometimes difficult. She cries if she isn't allowed something or she doesn't get her way. Real tears are reserved for when she falls or hurts herself."

Julia's mom, 87th week, or 20 months

I Am Out of Sight But Not Out of Mind

Because your toddler now understands that he is a separate system, he also understands that the same principles that apply to the people and objects around him also apply to him. He understands that they continue to exist, even though they may not be in his field of vision. He also understands that he still exists for mom and dad when they can't see him. Furthermore, he now understands that other people do not necessarily remain where he last saw them. It starts to dawn on him that they can move about and change their positions. When he looks for dad, he now understands that he not only needs to look where he last saw him.

"He likes to crawl into closets and shut all the doors."

Steven's mom, 81st week, or 18½ months

"She hides in the closet, slides the doors shut and then calls 'mom.' It really makes her laugh when we finally find her."

　　　　　Josie's mom, 85th week, or 19½ months

Me and You

Now that your toddler sees himself as an individual, he will start using terms like "me" and "you." He grasps that mom and dad are individuals too who lead their own lives. He starts to compare himself with them and maps out the similarities and differences to a tee.

"She has discovered that her father has a penis. She calls it 'Pino.'"

　　　　　Victoria's mom, 72nd week, or 16½ months

"His own weenie is really an item. So is his father's and the absence of mine."

　　　　　Bob's mom, 73rd week, or approaching 17 months

"These days he points first to himself and then to me, as if he wants to point out the difference."

　　　　　Mark's mom, 75th week, or a good 17 months

"If I propose: 'Shall we go out together?' she points to herself as if she would say: 'You mean me?' as if there are other people in the room."

　　　　　Nina's mom, 75th week, or a good 17 months

"He loves it when I make special reference to him. He points to himself to distinguish himself from me and as a confirmation that it is for him."

　　　　　Luke's mom, 77th week, or 17½ months

"If I imitate certain stereotypical statements or behavior of hers, it makes her laugh."

　　　　　Hannah's mom, 78th week, or approaching 18 months

"He is very interested in his father—in the shower, in bed, on the 'john.'
He follows him everywhere and always talks about him."

Frankie's mom, 79th - 86th week,
or 18 to almost 20 months

"She learned the terms 'me' and 'you.'"
Juliette's mom, 86th week, or approaching 20 months

Now that your toddler can distinguish between himself and others, he
can also put himself in another person's position. In a simple experiment,
it was shown that toddlers of 13 to 15 months were unable to fathom
that another person could make a choice that was different from theirs.
At 18 months they will be able to do this for the first time. That has all
kinds of consequences.

The Dangling Carrot

"We came out of the store and there stood a
helicopter ride for the kids. If you put money in,
it moves around for a while with lights flashing.
Nora loves it and was allowed to go on once.
But there was already a kid in it, who didn't want
to get out after his turn. Nora looked around and
ran to a mini-shopping cart and started pushing it
around. The other kid came out of the helicopter
right away and wanted to push that cart around
too. Nora shot over to the helicopter and got in."
Nora's mom, 87th week, or 20 months

I Can Console

"She says to us that we have to cry and then she will give us a kiss and
a gentle caress."

Jenny's mom, 79th -80th week, or 18 months

Me and My Mimicry

"He reenacts moods. He says for instance 'stop!' in a way that a girl does, a bit sassy. He imitates certain gestures, like turning his head and body and putting his hand up, and talking to the hand."

> Taylor's mom, 80th week, or a good 18 months

"Imitating certain postures and movements is a favorite pastime. She even tries to imitate the cat."

Maria's mom, 83rd – 86th week, or 19 to almost 20 months

"He observed the monkeys and how they open nuts. We collect hazelnuts in the neighborhood and at home he really gets in to shelling them."

Bob's mom, 83rd - 86th week, or 19 to almost 20 months

"She imitates the other children quite a bit. If they climb a fence, she tries too. If they knock on a window, she does the same. If they do it, she copies it."

> Vera's mom, 87th week, or 20 months

Me and My Fantasy Play

In his make-believe play he starts to treat his toys like they play along too, like people capable of doing things.

"She grabbed an imaginary something from her hand and put it in her mouth. She did it a couple of times. It was very peculiar. It looked like her first game of make-believe."

> Josie's mom, 71st week, or a good 16 months

"Suddenly she has become more independent. She plays by herself very well. Now and then it looks like she is in a dream world. She fantasizes. I had yet to see her do that. She plays the game with her doll. Sometimes she tells me her fantasies."

> Victoria's mom, 75th week, or a good 17 months

"He made a drawing of a turd and then stamped on it. I don't allow him to stamp on turds in the street."

Paul's mom, 77th week, or 17½ months

"After having seen his baby pictures one afternoon, he decided that all his animals were his babies and played with them the whole afternoon in his bed."

Gregory's mom, 84th week, or a good 19 months

"She indicates much more clearly what she wants and gets frustrated if I don't get what she means. Playing make-believe has much to do with it. She gives me a dog and I have to understand that the dog needs to be breast fed."

Emily's mom, 86th week, or approaching 20 months

"He does play make-believe a lot. Having a tea party. Sitting together in his Lego car, on the steps. He pats the ground beside him in the most inviting way and loves if we sit there together."

Thomas' mom, 86th week, or approaching 20 months

Other Living Creatures

Other living creatures are all separate systems with their own behavioral rules and programs. Your toddler is fascinated by this.

"This week she was very interested in birds. She laughed if a bird she was watching returned from out of sight. She laughed more when she saw where the sounds came from, the sounds she had heard before even seeing the bird. It is the same with airplanes. She also likes to investigate how plants smell."

Eve's mom, 73rd week, or approaching 17 months

"She waves at planes and birds and sometimes to people."

Eve's mom, 74th week, or 17 months

"This week he liked feeding the chickens. He stayed with his grandfather on the farm."

Jim's mom, 77th week, or 17½ months

"He saw a snail in the street and then before I noticed it, he said that the snail was dead. It turned out that he and his father had covered this topic a few times."

Harry's mom, 79th week, or 18 months

"He enjoyed the bees with his grandfather, the beekeeper."

Steven's mom, 83rd week, or 19 months

"She cracked up when she saw a snake eat a mouse in a nature film."

Laura's mom, 84th week, or a good 19 months

"This week he was really interested in an ant outside in the garden."

Matt's mom, 84th week, or a good 19 months

"She is really into bugs this week – ladybugs and ants."

Anna's mom, 85th week, or 19½ months

"She likes watering the plants these days. She starts by making smacking noises as if the plants are hungry: 'The plants want to eat.' Preferably, she feeds them twice a day. For Ashley, it is the filling up and pouring out of the watering can that makes her feel she has done her deed for the day."

Ashley's mom, 85th week, or 19½ months

"At the beach he was able to play endlessly in the sand, digging and pushing shells into the sand and then pronouncing them dead."

Kevin's mom, 87th week, or 20 months

I am Part of a Nuclear Family

The nuclear family is a system like other human organizations. And it is the first human organization which your toddler experiences from the inside, right from the start. However, it is only now that he begins to see that a nuclear family is a unit, a system.

"She now has a strict division of tasks. Mom gets her glass and dad fills it."

Victoria's mom, 73rd week, or approaching 17 months

"She now grasps that we are a family, a group. If I just use the names Xaviera, Marko and Thomas in a sentence, she corrects the omissions of Mita (Victoria) and Kitan (Christian)."

Victoria's mom, 74th week, or 17 months

"She is busy with her dolls and stuffed animals all day long. One goes in the highchair. If she gets something to eat, she first gives some to her 'friends.' She also puts them all to bed in her doll wagon and then goes and lays in the big bed."

Elisabeth's mom, 74th -75th week, or 17 months

"She knows exactly who belongs with who or who gave her what."

Vera's mom, 75th week, or 17 months

"She laughs when we play with the cats or if the cats get riled up."

Jenny's mom, 71st -76th week, or a good 16 til almost 17½ months

"He points to his father, to me and to himself. Then I am supposed to say that we all are separate people and yet we belong together. Then he nods approvingly 'yes' and sighs from contentment."

Frankie's mom, 76th week, or approaching 17½ months

"Nowadays, he is a real 'pal.' He asks me to accompany him in the Lego car. He wants to read together. He wants to color together."

Thomas' mom, 78th week, or approaching 18 months

"When we would take her brother to school or pick him up, she had a hard time with me calling other women 'mom of so-in-so.' There was only one mom and that was me. Now she understands that there are other families and that those women are mothers of other children. She still protests though if she hears them called 'mom.' The only unequivocal mom is her mom."

Victoria's mom, 79th week, or 18 months

"If his older brother or sister is on my lap, he gets angry, and remains that way until my lap is vacated."

James' mom, 82nd week, or approaching 19 months

"This week he enjoyed getting in bed and snuggling with mom and dad."

Gregory's mom, 83rd week, or 19 months

"He is very bold and already teases his brother and sister, sometimes getting on their nerves."

James' mom, 83rd week, or 19 months

"Now she grasps that ours is not the only family. Recently, we went to pick up her brother who was playing at a friend's house. We stayed to have coffee. She was clearly upset and kept calling the name of the boy's sister and asking where she was. But the sister was playing at a friend's. The family was incomplete without the sister and that troubled her. She saw that as being wrong."

> Victoria's mom, 84th week, or a good 19 months

"James sometimes gets left out by his brother and sister when they want to play a game. They put him in the hall and shut the door in his face. He comes to me shattered and needs to be consoled."

> James' mom, 87th week, or 20 months

"She knows her father is called Hank and her mother Miko."

> Julia's mom, 87th week, or 20 months

Me and My Family or Friends

Just as a nuclear family is a system, so too is the extended family and the circle of friends. Your toddler starts to recognize that now as well. He also learns the differences between his family and his friends' families.

"She came to me with the telephone and a picture of her grandparents and signaled that she wanted to call them."

> Juliette's mom, 78th week, or approaching 18 months

"If I speak about his friend, he knows who that is and he says his name with enthusiasm. He certainly knows his friend."

> Steven's mom, 78th week, or approaching 18 months

"We are really close. He follows my conversations and interactions with others. He reacts to statements, even if they are not directed at him. When my friend called her son, who was pretty far away, she said that he doesn't listen to her, so my son rushed out to go get him. He tried to drag him along, but his friend got him in a hold which resulted in a screaming match, because my son does not like to be pinned down."

> Luke's mom, 79th week, or 18 months

"When the neighbor went home to cook, he wanted to go with her. That was fine and I waved him off. I had expected that my boy would want to come back soon. That wasn't the case. After an hour-and-a-half, I got worried and went to see what was going on. But Thomas didn't want to come home. He wanted me to stay, too. Then he showed me everything he had seen there, the refrigerator, the grapes, etc. He has a great time there because he is allowed to do what he wants. While she was cooking, he sat on the kitchen counter with his feet in the sink playing in the water."

Thomas' mom, 80th week, or a good 18 months

"Grandma and Grandpa live around the corner. We stop by often and naturally we don't always go inside. If we pass by, she always calls out 'ama' or 'apa.'"

Victoria's mom, 82nd week, or approaching 19 months

Finding My Way Around My House and My Neighborhood

Your own home is a system as is the surrounding neighborhood. Your toddler learns to recognize that now and starts learning how to find his way. He constructs a map in his head of his surroundings. Such a mental map is actually a system, too.

"He is finding his bearings. Even when he is not in familiar surroundings, he looks for other points of recognition and he is very pleased when he finds them. He wants to share this immediately, as well as what is coming up."

Harry's mom, 74th week, or 17 months

"A month ago he didn't notice the sea while at the beach. This time he shouted for joy when he spied the sea from the top of the dune. He was practically overcome with joy when he saw the sea. Day after day, a constant reminder."

> Bob's mom, 74th week, or 17 months

"He knows where we are going. If I ask him, he answers correctly."

> John's mom, 79th week, or 18 months

"He knows the way from the campground to the sea."

> Jim's mom, 80th -81st week, or approaching 18½ months

"Taylor and I have moved to another floor in the same building. Taylor felt at home in his new abode and after settling in, started going around with his buggy. He was familiar with the house because the previous inhabitants had two kids of their own. He seemed already used to it."

> Taylor's mom, 82nd week, or approaching 19 months

"A few times she didn't want to come with me inside to visit, regardless if they were strangers or Grandma and Grandpa. Really strange, she's never done this before. When she finally made it in, she was fine."

> Maria's mom, 82nd week, or approaching 19 months

"He has a good map of the vicinity in his head. He knows exactly where to find things, at home, outside, or at dad's work. He can point me the way to the grocery store or the way to dad's work as well as the way inside the building to his office. He also knows the next door neighbor's house very well. He knows where everything is. The grapes and so on. She usually has them. He gets disappointed, though, if they are not in the right place."

> Thomas' mom, 83rd week, or 19 months

"If we let the dog out in the neighborhood, she asks 'ama' or 'apa' [Grandma or Grandpa] and points in the right direction to their house, even though the house is still out of sight around the corner. Clearly she wants to visit."

Victoria's mom, 86th week, or approaching 20 months

"This summer, my friend and I went to the beach regularly. Our two boys got along well. They are still good friends. Jim had expected to meet up with his friend before we went. He kept asking where he was. This time they were waiting for us at the beach."

Jim's mom, 87th week, or 20 months

Me and My Belongings

In a nuclear family system there are all sorts of principles, among which there are values, norms and rules. Consider for instance "we will share fair and square" or "thou shalt not steal." There are rules for what belongs to whom and what we are entitled to. Your toddler learns these rules by doing. Sometimes he picks it up unnoticed and it's a pleasant surprise to find out what he's learned on his own. Other times it takes some persuasion.

Me and My Clothes

"She knows exactly which bags, coats and what-not belong to which kids and when we leave she fetches our things."

Nina's mom, 82nd week, or approaching 19 months

"When I empty the washing machine, I lay out every piece on the machine and pull them into shape before I put them into the dryer. She

is right on top of everything, sorting things in her own way. She knows precisely what belongs to who: 'is Thomas,' 'is mommy,' 'is Mita.'"

(Mita)/Victoria's mom, 83rd week , or 19 months

"He seems aware of his new clothes, underwear and undershirt instead of one-sies. He finds it very interesting. He loves his new shoes."

Paul's mom, 83rd-86th week, or 19 to almost 20 months

Me and My Stuff

"While visiting a friend, Robin played with one of his toy cars, which wasn't allowed to go home with him. He cried the whole way back to the house and at home threw away his own cars."

Robin's mom, 76th week, or approaching 17½ months

"She remembers where she left things. If I ask where something is, she remembers."

Emily's mom, 78th week, or approaching 18 months

"She finds one 'diamond' after the other. Her brother collects nice stones and lays them out in his room. So she scavenges for rocks too. Pieces of gravel go into her pocket one after the other and absolutely none of them can be thrown away."

Victoria's mom, 78th week, or approaching 18 months

"One day she came up to me, took my hand and led me to the room where all the toys are. She pointed: 'Is Thomas, is Thomas, is Thomas... and Mita?' This was a hefty protest. Recently, Thomas didn't allow her to touch his toys, because she had broken some things. And indeed, this left her with very little to play with!"

Mita/Victoria's mom, 83rd week, or 19 months

"When Lisa (now 25 months) comes to visit, it's terrible. Lisa isn't al-lowed to play with anything. If Lisa has anything in her hands, Hannah grabs it right from her."

Hannah's mom, 87th week, or 20 months

"He no longer wants to share his toys with other children. He gets angry and passionate if they grab his toys."

Robin's mom, 88th week, or a good 20 months

No mess

You've never seen anything like it before. He can't stand a mess. Enjoy it while it lasts. It lasts until the next leap and won't be back for a number of years – if it ever does come back. He wants everything arranged systematically.

"He can't handle messiness. It upsets him. So I said to my parents, 'What you never managed to achieve, my son did. Now, I always clean up.' In the evening we always clean up the Legos. Every time we have finished reading a book, he puts it back before taking another one."

Thomas' mom, 86th week, or approaching 20 months

Doing Puzzles

A puzzle is a system too—an organized unit that is a whole due to the interdependence of the components from which it is made up.

"What he likes to do is put animal puzzles together. One is twelve pieces the other is seven. He knows exactly how to do it; he does it quickly and has no patience for putting the pieces in well. He even recognizes the back side of the pieces."

Kevin's mom, 72nd week, or 16½ months

"Her motor skills continue to improve. This week she enjoyed putting beads on sticks and then the sticks in holes. She also likes to take my money out and spread it out."

> **Anna's mom, 73rd week, or approaching 17 months**

"She does the puzzles herself."

> **Laura's mom, 75th week, or a good 17 months**

"He is good at puzzles with a bit of help. Even puzzles he has not seen yet."

> **Matt's mom, 76th week, or approaching 17½ months**

"I pretended that I couldn't do the puzzle. Every time I went astray he said: 'No, no' and then told me where I should put the piece. After repeating this act several times, I had had enough. I pulled the puzzle apart and put it back together in a flash. I acted like I was very proud and said: 'See, I can do it too.' He responded with: 'No.' It turned out that a tiny corner of a piece of the puzzle was sticking up. He pushed it in and then it was right!"

> **Thomas' mom, 80th week, or a good 18 months**

"All of a sudden he did the puzzle right. He turns them so that they fit well. Not always, but mostly."

> **Frankie's mom, 82nd week, or approaching 19 months**

"She enjoys the box of buttons and all the various tops."

> **Jenny's mom, 82nd week, or approaching 19 months**

"She does many puzzles now. Her first puzzles, the easier ones, are no longer fun. Now she has a difficult one, 13 pieces."

> **Julia's mom, 86th week, or approaching 20 months**

"He pays attention to the minutest of details. Like the smallest piece of the puzzle that is not quite right. He seems rather nit-picky. For instance, in the fairy tale 'Snow White' the expectant mother says that she would like to have a baby girl. One with skin as white as snow and lips as red as blood. The mother had just pricked her finger and there was a tiny drop of blood visible on the picture. He noticed this even though he had never seen anything like 'pricking a finger.' He pointed to the picture where the nice red was."

Thomas' mom, 86th week, or approaching 20 months

"All of a sudden she did a 20-piece puzzle without batting an eye. She had not done the puzzle before. After that she had no more interest in puzzles."

Xaviera's mom, 87th week, or 20 months

Creating a Game

A puzzle is a system devised by someone else. Your toddler is now able to think up systems by himself, for instance a game where he makes up the rules. Or a magic trick.

"He made up a game himself, taking turns throwing dice. One person throws, the other has to pick it up. He is strict in keeping the sequence. He keeps looking for tight corners to throw the die."

Mark's mom, 83rd -86th week, or 19 to almost 20 months

"Today she did a magic trick she had come up with herself. She watches her brother doing tricks a lot. She put a marble into a bottle and said: 'Uh, oh.' She shook the bottle up and down and said: 'No.' She meant that the marble was stuck. Then she turned in a circle (like a magician does) and held the bottle upside down. Tada!"

Victoria's mom, 83rd week, or 19 months

Me and My Art

After a year-and-a-half, your toddler starts to use toys in a way that signifies that she knows what the toys stand for, what or who they represent. In her play it shows that she is familiar with the people, the objects and the situations from everyday life that are represented by the toys. The toys symbolize someone or something from the real world. Your toddler can play with these symbols in her imagination.

Her ability to symbolize enables her to create drawings that are completely different from the earlier drawings and that represent something from that real world—for example a car, a dog, or even herself. This new ability to symbolize did not come gradually. It came into being all of a sudden with a leap and is a new quality. Art is born. If your little artist loves making drawings, you will have a hard time keeping her supplied with paper. The beginning of a huge collection is at hand. If she experiences something exciting, like fireworks at New Year's Eve, it is likely that she will make a drawing to capture the moment.

Not only does she start making drawings, but she starts building constructions as well. And if you have a little music lover, she will be playing her keyboard and can listen to music for quite a long time and enjoy it.

"Her drawings are very different now. The scribbles have made way for small circles, tiny tiny. She is really into details."

Victoria's mom, 78th week, or approaching 18 months

"She now colors in her drawings. She is very precise and hardly colors outside the lines."

Victoria's mom, 79th week, or 18 months

"He draws horses and boats now and this morning he meticulously drew a circle and a square and then pointed to himself. He had drawn himself."

Luke's mom, 79th week, or 18 months

"He has started building more, whereas he used to be more into destruction."

Taylor's mom, 83rd week, or 19 months

"He drew a car. It was a good drawing of a car. He can only do this if he is lying down on his side with his head resting on his other outstretched arm. What does his car look like? It's two circles, the wheels, with a line in between. Circles are 'vroom vroom'. He also draws airplanes and just recently, legs. A spiral is a steering wheel – a steering wheel turns."

Thomas' mom, 83rd week, or 19 months

"She likes to draw, especially if I draw a bear, rabbit or a pet."

Juliette's mom, 84th week, or a good 19 months

"She has a Bambi book. In it is a picture of possums hanging by their tails from a tree branch. 'Hey,' Elisabeth thought, 'that's not right.' So she turned the book upside down, so she could see it better."

Elisabeth's mom, 85th week, or 19½ months

"He loves music. He likes playing his electric keyboard. He puts on a certain rhythm to accompany his lead. At the store, he listened to practically a whole CD of classical music. It lasted almost an hour. He was upset when I disturbed him half way through to go on with our shopping. He had to listen to the end."

Thomas' mom, 86th week, or approaching 20 months

That toddlers in Japan can play the violin fairly well at the age of two is not without reason. Of course, they use special, small violins. In Western culture, not many people are eager to drill their toddlers this early in life in

pursuit of such mastery. "Freedom and happiness" is the motto. However, we are not addressing cultural differences here. The fact is that toddlers at this age normally have the ability to learn such things.

"He said that he was going to draw Grandpa. He drew a head four times and said: 'Wrong.' He was not yet satisfied. The fifth time, when he got the goatee in the right spot, he was satisfied and said: 'Grandpa!'"

Thomas' mom, 101st week, or 23 months

" wrong ~ wrong . . wrong . . . . wrong . . . Grandpa "

 ## The Evolution of Art

Art appeared late in the evolution of our species. While we easily consider our evolution to be a matter of millions of years, most evidence for the emergence of art is dated as recently as 35,000 years ago. About that time so many artifacts were found that there was talk of an art explosion. All of a sudden there was a surplus. We are talking about cave drawings, small stone carvings and musical instruments. A very rare find of the remains of a flute dates back 90,000 years. Art is characteristically human. The emergence of art was preceded by a massive increase in our brain size. We are, however, still in the dark about how this came to be. But the notion of self, fantasy and language certainly play a large role, just as the increase in the size of the frontal lobe placed just behind our forehead does.

Me and My Sense of Time: Past, Present and Future

Your toddler starts to develop a sense of time now. Her memory of past experiences improves and she gets better at anticipating the future.

"I can't tell her anymore in the morning that we are going to do something fun in the afternoon. She reminds me otherwise the whole day until it happens: 'Now apa ama [Grandma Grandpa] to?'"

> Victoria's mom, 78th week,
> or approaching 18 months

"She makes plans. When we sit down for dinner, she asks if she may draw. I tell her that first we're going to eat. Then she tells me where her pen and paper will need to be. I am supposed to say that I understand and that it will happen. If I forget after dinner, she gets very angry, and she is offended."

> Victoria's mom, 80th week, or a good 18 months

"He remembers promises. If I promise that we will do something after his bath, he reminds me. When he wakes up in the morning, he refers to what we did before he went to sleep."

> Gregory's mom, 82nd week, or approaching 19 months

Basic Physics

If you observe his play well, you cannot ignore that he is busy with the basic phenomena of physics.

"He dunks things like a ball under water to experience their resistance. He also disassembles a small electric telephone. Now he looks at it differently than he did before, when it just made noise. It doesn't work

anymore after his experiment. He finds throwing things and taking them apart really interesting. He tries things out."

Harry's mom, 77th week, 17½ months

"She can spend hours pouring some liquid from one vessel into another. She uses bottles, glasses, plates or cups. While she's busy she likes to add the necessary commentary."

Ashley's mom, 78th week, or approaching 18 months

"She pays close attention to colors: green, red, yellow. Red and yellow together. I was kidding with her when I told her that it is supposed to be that way."

Josie's mom, 78th week, or approaching 18 months

"It snowed at Easter. It was his first snow. He was a bit weary and out of sorts. He just couldn't place it. Wanted to be alone after taking in all the new impressions."

Thomas' mom, 80th week, or a good 18 months

With principles, we have seen how your toddler started to "think about thinking." When he has entered the world of systems, for the first time he can hone his principles into a system, principles that he has learned through experience. It is quite possible that he is doing this while taking his "thinking break."

"Sometimes he likes to be alone. He says: 'bye' and goes in his room to be alone. He is pondering life. Sometimes he does that a half hour at a time with a toy. Other times he stares and thinks for ten minutes like a 50-year-old. He just wants a bit of peace after having such fun playing. After he has taken his break to collect his thoughts, he returns cheerful, says 'hi,' wants to nurse a bit and then goes to sleep or to play a bit. He really needs his privacy."

Thomas' mom, 80th week, or a good 18 months

"Initially, he was afraid of the electric toothbrush, but now that he has gotten used to it, it's fine and he says 'on.'"

John's mom, 83rd week, or 19 months

"She grasps that the train takes batteries, and that they were drained. She went and found new ones."

Hannah's mom, 86th week, or approaching 20 months

"When playing the flight simulator on the computer, he doesn't treat the joystick carelessly like he used to; he is very aware. He puts the landing gear down right. He checks to see if it happened like he wanted by having the plane climb a bit and then back down."

Jim's mom, 86th week, or approaching 20 months

Basic Architecture

His interest in the phenomena of physics extends to more systems than just physics. He is also interested in basic architecture. He can spend hours watching builders, and you will notice that his play will produce more structures since his latest leap, like towers of cups pushed together, and more elaborate structures.

"My husband cemented the fish pond this week. He explained to my eldest son how to mix cement. He then explained the same to Victoria. Now they are together the whole day long mixing sand and water for cementing. She does everything he does. She looks up to Thomas."

Victoria's mom, 79th week, or 18 months

"Cars have fallen out of favor. Now it's more the alternative transportation, like motor bikes, semis, dump trucks, trolley cars. He loves to watch the builders."

Mark's mom, 80th week, or a good 18 months

"She was chosen as a test person for new Lego toys for toddlers. She was rewarded for her efforts with an electric train for 3-year-olds. Much to everyone's surprise, she quickly laid down the rails for the train. She approaches it like a puzzle. The straight pieces are easy. The curved pieces are a little more of a chore. She doesn't complete the track. It is one track with a beginning and an end. When she's finished with the track, she put the crossing guard arm on the train and went riding around. It struck me as strange and I said that to her. She didn't change anything though, which surprised me, until I discovered that she had copied this from the picture on the box, which showed the guard arm on the train just as she had done. She isn't really interested in running the train, though. She prefers to lay track. She constantly takes the track apart and starts over."

Emily's mom, 82nd week, or approaching 19 months

"He tries putting the small Lego blocks together theses days. He can't quite manage because it takes a bit of strength. But he tries. He doesn't use the bigger blocks."

Matt's mom, 86th week, or approaching 20 months

Me and My Talking

Between 17 and 22 months, toddlers start using the adult language system with an explosive increase in the spoken vocabulary and the average duration of a speaking turn. They also start combining words to form sentences. They are now able to distinguish two different languages from each other and ignore one of the two. Furthermore there is an impressive increase in verbal language comprehension around 18 months.

There is large individual variation in the budding development of speech. Some toddlers don't use many words (approximately six) about the time this leap takes place. The parents know that they actually know and understand many more words, which causes some irritation. Other children use many words, repeating after you (sometimes just the first syllable) or taking the initiative, but no sentences yet. They can make themselves understood, though, literally with hands and feet. They mime their part. A third group already produces sentences, while they are still miming.

Understands All, Few Words

"The words he now uses are limited: 'cookie,' 'bottle,' 'ouch,' 'thank,' 'mom,' 'dad,' 'bread' and 'pel' (= apple; he only pronounces the last syllable). He understands everything and follows instructions well."
> **James' mom, 76th week, or approaching 17½ months**

"He puts his arms up in the air at 'hip, hip, hooray' and shouts something like 'oora!' He knows all the gestures too like 'clap your hands.' And if he doesn't succeed he says 'oot' (shoot)."
> **Robin's mom, 76th week, or approaching 17½ months**

"She uses more and more words. Not yet very clearly pronounced, mostly the heavy syllables."
> **Anna's mom, 79th week, or 18 months**

"He says three words: 'di dah' is tick-tack, 'moo' is moon, and 'hi hi' is horse."
> **Robin's mom, 80th week, or a good 18 months**

"She repeats more and more. If she picks up the phone, she says 'hello.' The words she says now are 'daddy,' 'mommy,' 'up,' 'hi,' 'bottle,'

'bread,' 'cookie,' 'apple,' and 'out.' She shakes her head 'no' if she doesn't want something. She nods her head 'yes' if she wants something."

> Laura's mom, 80th week, or a good 18 months

"He doesn't say much yet, but he understands everything! And he communicates exactly what he wants."

> James' mom, 81st week, or 18½ months

"Now she says 'cheese,' 'boom,' 'daddy,' and 'mommy.'"

> Anna's mom, 82nd week, or approaching 19 months

"He understands everything you say and ask. He is very enterprising, always doing something, walking through the house all day long singing or mumbling something."

> James' mom, 83rd week, or 19 months

"She is using some more new words."

> Laura's mom, 83rd week, or 19 months

"He uses more and more words, although his vocabulary is limited. He speaks his own language a lot. This week he clearly said 'grandma' to get her attention. The words that he now occasionally uses are 'grandma,' 'grandpa,' 'ow,' 'hi,' 'bottle,' 'bite,' 'sit,' 'me,' and 'look.'"

> James' mom, 84th week, a good 19 months

"He picks up more and more words. Now he knows 'dad,' 'mom,' 'cheese,' 'ouw,' 'boom,' 'ant,' 'more,' 'di dah,' 'moon,' and 'sars' (= stars)."

> Robin's mom, 84th week, or a good 19 months

"She imitates animal sounds."

> Laura's mom, 85th week, or 19½ months

"He definitely uses more words now. He answers sometimes now with 'yes.' 'Eese' (=cheese) and 'food' are now part of his repertoire. In general, he's not yet very talkative. By pointing and a few oohs and ahs we understand him. He gets what he needs."

James' mom, 86th week, or 19½ months

"She talks a lot and repeats a lot."

Anna's mom, 86th week, or 19½ months

Understands All, Many Words, A Lot of Mime, No Sentences

"The most understandable word at the moment is 'cheese.' 'Ird' (= bird) is also clear. 'Papa' he says like he spent the summer in Italy. It's charming."

Taylor's mom, 72nd week, or 16½ months

"He talks more and more. Now he likes to make noises with his tongue: 'Illl.' We play a lot of language games. He loves that."

Luke's mom, 72nd week, or 16½ months

"A great moment this week was the comprehensive contact we had when we were playing a game making noises. It was really funny. We tried to stick our tongues in and out of our mouths while making noise. Later we tried to push our tongues against the back of our front teeth to produce the 'Ill' sound as in: 'Lala.' She found it exciting and challenging and wanted to do what I did. At the same time, it looked like she was thinking 'I'll get you.' I saw so many different expressions in her face. We both loved it and the laughter grew, especially when she said 'lala' spontaneously with a kiss."

Ashley's mom, 73rd week, or approaching 17 months

"His manner of talking has changed again. Even though his speech is for the most part incomprehensible, it does seem that he is forming

more sentences, and I think: 'Heck, I'm getting this!' He explains clearly through gestures and words what has happened to him in my absence. For instance, when he was at Grandma's in the kitchen and I asked him what he had done. He said something I couldn't understand with the word 'cheese' in it, which led me to understand that he had gotten a piece of cheese from Grandma. When asked, he nodded yes."

Taylor's mom, 74th -77th week , or 17 to almost 18 months

"It looks like she's talking. She has been curious for a long time what everything is called, but it seems that she has developed in some way. She asks the name intending to repeat the name to herself. Some are perfectly pronounced. Most are only with the first syllable: ball is 'ba,' water is 'wa,' and breast is 'bre.' It is great to hear the sound of her voice. She is proud, too, and repeats when requested."

Elisabeth's mom, 74th week, or 17 months

"His way of communicating this week was interesting. He seems to be forming sentences in his own language. He keeps it up until I understand him. An example: we walk across the street to the sea for the second time, Luke on Daddy's back. I had the bag with gear and the sand shovel was sticking out. All of a sudden he shrieks: 'da, da, da.' It takes a bit before I get that he means the shovel. When I say 'the shovel?,' he says 'Ya' and points from the shovel to the sea. I repeat in words: 'Yeah, we're going with the shovel to the beach.' He sighed contentedly and leaned back. We have this type of conversation often."

Luke's mom, 74th week, or 17 months

"We can now actually have a dialogue. We communicate extensively. What she most wants to communicate to me is her world plan. For instance, track down dirt and then say 'bah, bah,' to show that she can find dirt and that she knows what it is and what to do with it."

Elisabeth's mom, 75th week, or a good 17 months

"She makes sentences that seem like a long word missing some letters. But I can understand her if I pay close attention. She saw that the stop light was red and pointed to it. I hadn't seen it yet, but heard her say it, and she was right, although I don't know exactly what she said. Rather strange! It was like she didn't know herself what she was saying, but did utter some sounds that seemed to fit the picture."

Ashley's mom, 76th week, or approaching 17½ months

"I can keep him occupied with stories while changing his diaper."

Luke's mom, 76th week, or approaching 17½ months

"He uses a lot of words. He repeats them or starts them himself. He says the first syllable and that is usually good. He doesn't really try sentences. He jabbers on sometimes."

Bob's mom, 76th week, or approaching 17½ months

"This week it was interesting to witness his desire to give everything a name. What an endless desire to learn a language is buried inside such a little person. Another gem is how he can communicate so well. He literally uses his hands and feet to get his message across. He is a mimic. Even when I am talking with other people, he chimes in. He mimes his part."

Luke's mom, 76th week, or approaching 17½ months

"She is interested in repeating words and practicing with me more than before."

Ashley's mom, 77th week, or 17½ months

"He uses a lot of words, especially the first syllable. More and more words I don't have to cue. The joy he gets from speaking is touching."

Bob's mom, 77th week, or 17½ months

"Communicating about what he does and wants to do and about what he has done is central. He is very creative in saying what he wants with body language that he cannot say yet in words. He enunciates much better. Words are not trimmed at the root. He is starting to use words that have not been cued. From memory."

Kevin's mom, 78th week, or approaching 18 months

"She knows new words: 'horse,' 'cow,' and 'melon.' She also knows the name of the children with whom she has played. 'Nina' she can pronounce best."

Ashley's mom, 80th week, or a good 18 months

"I think that he basically can repeat everything I say first. It depends on his mood if he will or not."

Taylor's mom, 81st week, or 18½ months

"She uses many words now. She starts them with the proper letters but puts them in the wrong order, like 'flower' becomes 'fowler.' Every day brings new words. She practices for a while until she has the letters right. With some letters that is very difficult, like the 'h' and the 'r'."

Ashley's mom, 82nd week, or approaching 19 months

"The way he expresses himself is very creative. He points to his eyes if he wants to peek in the diaper that I whisk away."

Kevin's mom, 82nd week, or approaching 19 months

"If I don't understand him and he doesn't know the word, he refers back to words that have been used in that context before. Usually we are able to figure it out."

Luke's mom, 82nd week, or approaching 19 months

"He now uses the word 'nice.' He comes with a book in his hand, points to the cover and says: 'Nice.'"

Taylor's mom, 83rd week, or 19 months

"He comes up to me with his index finger pressed to his thumb and that means 'money.'"

Taylor's mom, 84th week, or a good 19 months

"All of a sudden he gets an idea and says words completely. When I praise him, he's proud as can be. He still doesn't take the trouble to make sentences. He prefers body language. It happens a hundred times a day that he wants to see something I'm doing or something I prohibit. He points to his eyes. That means 'I just want to have a look.' His other sensory needs he broadcasts in the same way, by pointing to the relative sense."

Kevin's mom, 83rd -86th week, or 19 to almost 20 months

"He says something if he is scared. Whether or not he understands the word 'scary' I'm not sure, but things he doesn't like or that are overwhelming, such as loud noises or being physically held down, he calls scary. He

finds some animals scary, and some dangerous situations, like if he almost falls down. 'Scary' doesn't always mean 'run away.' He tries to overcome his fears by confronting what's scary."

Luke's mom, 83rd - 86th week, or 19 to almost 20 months

"He doesn't enjoy repeating words anymore. But he is still improving. There are more and more words he repeats as well as more and more words with more than one syllable."

Luke's mom, 83rd -86th week, or 19 to almost 20 months

Understands All, Many Words, and Sentences, Too

"She is starting to sing. For instance, when I sing 'Kitty Meow,' I sing 'kitty' and she sings 'meow.'"

Jenny's mom, 73rd week, or approaching 17 months

"She really 'reads' books now. She tells a story while she looks at the pictures. Can't understand a word, but very touching. Moreover, she can speak in intelligible sentences, too."

Victoria's mom, 75th week, or 17 months

"If she wants the cat to come to her she calls: 'Wittie, come here.'"

Jenny's mom, 75th week, or 17 months

"She repeats every word we say and knows exactly what is what. She doesn't repeat it unless she knows what she is saying."

Emily's mom, 76th week, or a good 17 months

"Recently he's been having some nightmares. Towards the end of his REM sleep, he uttered many new words. I think he is very frustrated because he really wants to talk. He dreams now out loud. After his visit to the petting zoo, he imitated all the animals."

> Thomas' mom, 80th week, or a good 18 months

"She says several things together, like 'that's good,' 'not now' or 'mommy and daddy.'"

> Emily's mom, 81st week, or 18½ months

"He wanted the soap. But I didn't feel like reacting to 'eh, eh' and said: 'Tell me what you want?' Then he said: 'Yes, that that, me.'"

> Thomas' mom, 82nd week, or approaching 19 months

"In the garden center, he had another nice sentence: 'That....nice.'"

> Thomas' mom, 82nd week, or approaching 19 months

"She now puts two and three words together."

> Emily's mom, 83rd week, or 19 months

"She keeps making headway with speaking. She sometimes puts three words together. For instance: 'Daddy sit me.'"

> Jenny's mom, 84th week, or a good 19 months

"He loves his books. Now he listens to and reads fairy tales. Those are little books with very short stories that he got when he visited the amusement park. When I read to him, I always let Prince Thomas play the lead role. He listens all the way to the end of the tale."

> Thomas' mom, 86th week, or approaching 20 months

"She already speaks in complete sentences, one after the other."

> Emily's mom, 87th week, or 20 months

Show Understanding for Irrational Fears

When your toddler is busy exploring his new world and elaborating his newfound ability, he will encounter things and situations that are new and foreign to him. He is actually discovering new dangers, dangers that until now did not exist for him. Only after he comes to understand things more fully will his fears disappear. Show sympathy.

"She is afraid of thunder and lightning. She says: 'scary, boom.'"

> Maria's mom, 71st week, or a good 16 months

"He really disliked the vacuum cleaner and a running tap. They had to stop."

> Paul's mom, 72nd week, or 16½ months

"He is scared of balloons. He also won't go between the sheep and goat at the petting zoo. He wants to be picked up then. Nor does he like sitting on an animal at the carousel. He does like to watch though."

> Matt's mom, 73rd week, or approaching 17 months

"She is afraid of loud noises (trains, airplanes, drills) and of the dark."

> Nina's mom, week 75th- 76th week, or a good 17 months

"He found vomiting nasty. He had vomited in his bed and kept saying 'bah,' even after it had been cleaned up."

> Jim's mom, 80th week, or a good 18 months

"The crow of the rooster, as well as spiders, horses, dogs. It was new. I think that this is part of his newfound autonomy."

> Gregory's mom, 80th -81st week,
> or approaching 18½ months

"After his bath he always goes and sits down to pee. He tried so hard that this time a turd came out. He found that odd."

> Robin's mom, 82nd week, or approaching 19 months

"She has a wind-up Bert for her bath, but Bert's nose is loose and if the nose is lying in the water or Bert is lying there without a nose, then she is really scared and pulls herself back in a corner."

> Josie's mom, 83rd week, or 19 months

"He's been frightened of the vacuum cleaner for a while. He used to get on top of it when I turned it on. Now, he gets well out of the way in a corner until the cleaning is done."

> Steven's mom, 85th week, or 19½ months

"He keeps showing his father the 'troll king' he saw at the amusement park. Dad has to tell him a story about him. At the amusement park he was a bit frightened of the 'troll king.'"

> Thomas' mom, 86th week, or approaching 20 months

"He was afraid of a goat that came toward him at the petting zoo."

> Frankie's mom, 87th week, or 20 months

"Flies, mosquitoes and wasps scare her."

> Eve's mom, 87th week, or 20 months

"He was afraid of a spider in the garden and of flies."

> Harry's mom, 88th week, or a good 20 months

After the Leap

After 79 weeks or a good 18 months most toddlers become a little less troublesome than they were, although their budding notion of self and a tendency to want get their own way and the struggle for power are not making it any easier. However, those behaviors make them troublesome in a different way. They are not difficult in the sense of **the three C's:** CRYING, CLINGINESS and CRANKINESS. They are occasionally just

♫ Top Games for This Wonder Week

Here are games and activities that most 17-20 months old tod-dlers like best now and that help elaborate the new ability into many new skills:

- Playing silly together by pronouncing words differently and making silly movements
- Play wrestling
- Recognizing people
- Standing on his head, scrambling about, practicing balance
- Drawing
- Blowing bubbles
- Jumping and balancing on walls (up to 5 feet)
- Playing the fool
- Tickling and physical play
- Playing physical with Dad and joking around
- Playing outside
- Playing with other children
- Playing ball games
- Feeding the dog
- Ghost games
- Twirling around getting dizzy
- Playing circus
- Riding horse game
- Tag
- Hide and seek
- Reading stories
- Tongue games: Mother pushes her tongue against the inside of her cheek. Your toddler pushes your cheek in, whereby you stick your tongue out.

plain irritating. The trick is to place yourself above it all. Stop and count to ten, remember that your little darling is progressing and do your best to manage the situation. After all, this is a very good opportunity to phase in some rules of conduct for your toddler so he learns that the world doesn't revolve around him, and that he must take others into account as well.

Top Toys for This Wonder Week

Here are toys and things that most 17-20 months old toddlers like best now and that help elaborate the new ability into many new skills:

- Cars
- Clay
- Children's TV
- Children's books
- Small trinkets, things that belong together
- Garage with cars
- Toy airport
- Drawing on paper
- Bucket with sand and water
- Push car
- Plastic chair
- Ball
- Bicycle
- Stuffed animals, bears and dolls
- Stickers
- Sandbox
- Digging in the yard
- Sesame Street music
- Slide
- Coloring pencils
- Tractor trailer trucks
- Blowing bubbles
- Pinocchio
- Trains
- Swings
- Rocking horse
- Puzzles (up to 20 pieces)
- Clicker for the bike

Be careful with the following:

- The toilet
- The garbage cans

It is good to know that for adults, thinking and reasoning or logic are not the highest attainable goals, as some people like to think. Logic belongs in the world of programs and is subordinate to the worlds of principles and systems. If you really want to make a change, you will have to change your principles, and in order to change your principles, you will first have to change the accompanying system.

The problem is that concepts at system level are not easily changed in adults. That is in part due to the fact that every change at the system level has far reaching effects for all levels under the world of systems. And that doesn't happen without a struggle. History has taught us that such upheaval often brings with it revolution or war using words and even arms. A scientist will not quickly become a mystic nor will a Muslim quickly become a Christian.

Concepts at the system and principle level are more easily formed than that they are changed. Children learn them by observing their surroundings and then start to use them themselves. Sometimes adults place emphasis on certain system concepts. This is a textbook example of socialization and upbringing.

Your toddler is, of course, new to the show. His world is still very small and close to home. It will be many years, until after his childhood, before he has developed what we adults call an outlook on life, but a tender start has been made.

However tender this start may be, it is important and has far-reaching consequences. Among other things, a beginning is made with forming a conscience and learning norms and values. If a poor start is made here, the negative consequences will be most noticeable a few years down the road. If you give it all your attention, it will be a very good in-depth in-vestment. It will save you, your child and everyone around him a lot of misery.

The importance of this early start applies, of course, to all the other areas in the world of systems. Whether your tyke likes music, likes to build, talk, play with physical phenomena or practice body control, give this rising star a chance. You will be amazed at the pleasure you will have together.

postscript

Countless Wonders

By now you know that every mom will, at some time, have to deal with a baby who is tearful, cranky, or fussy; a baby who is difficult to please; a baby who, in fact, just needs to touch base.

It's our hope that when you find yourself coping with behaviors like these from your baby, you will now understand that you are not alone. Every mother is facing problems like these. All mothers experience worries and irritations when their infants reach certain ages. All mothers forget— or would like to forget—these trying times as soon as possible; as soon as the difficult period is over, in fact. It's human nature to play down the misery we have to go through, once the dark clouds have parted.

Now that you understand that your child's difficult behaviors and your own anxieties and irritability are all part of a healthy and normal development as your infant struggles towards independence, you can feel more secure and confident. You know what you're doing.

Even without an instruction manual, you know that your baby will explore each "new world" in her own individual way. You know that the best thing you can do is to "listen" to your baby, in order to help him on his way. You know how to have fun with him. You also know that you are the person who understands him best, and the person who can really help him unlike any other. We hope that the information and findings

we've shared with you about the Wonder Weeks that mark developmental stages will make it easier for you to understand and support your baby during these traumatic times. In a research project our Dutch parental support and education program "Hordenlopen" ["Leaping Hurdles"] was evaluated. That program was based on "The Wonder Weeks." It was shown that understanding and supporting your baby in this way makes a huge, positive difference for the parents themselves and for the later development of their babies. So your baby's development is in your hands, and not in those of your family, neighbors, or friends. Their babies may have been completely different. We have made this abundantly clear in this book and we hope that we have empowered parents to be immune to unwelcome and conflicting advice from others.

We have shown that every baby is "reborn" ten times in the first twenty months, or the so-called sensorimotor period. Ten times her world was turned upside down by a "big change" in her brain. Ten times she was bewildered and did everything in her power to cling to mommy. Ten times she touched base. And ten times she made a "mommy refill" before making the next leap in her development. Obviously, your toddler still has a long way to go.

More Wonders Await

Research of the development of brain waves (EEG) of children aged one-and-a-half to sixteen years has shown that major changes occur at the transition between well known stages in their mental development. The beginning of puberty is one such leap at a later age. For a long time it was common knowledge that the onset of puberty was triggered by surging hormones. But recent discoveries have shown that big changes in the brain also co-occur with the onset of puberty. These are not only changes in brain waves (EEG), but also sudden and extremely rapid increases in the volume of certain parts of the brain. For the umpteenth time these youth enter a new perceptual world, enabling them to gain a new insight that they could not possibly have developed at an earlier age. Teenagers are not keen to admit this, because they think they are on top of the world already. As parents we cannot help but smile at the thought that babies are of the same opinion.

Even teenagers still have a long way to go. Further leaps occur several more times before they become fully independent. There are even indications that adults experience these phases, too.

As the Colombian author and journalist Gabriel Garcia Marquez wrote in *Love in the Time of Cholera,*

> People are not born once and for all on the day that their mother puts them on to the Earth, but . . . time and again, life forces them to enter a new world on their own.

further reading

Readers who want to know more about the scientific literature behind the book *The Wonder Weeks* may consult the literature listed below.

Bell, M., & Wolfe, C.D. (2004). Emotion and cognition: An intricately bound developmental process. *Child Development*, 75, 366-370.

Bever, T.G. (1982). *Regressions in mental development: Basic phenomena and theories.* Hillsdale, NJ: Erlbaum.

Cools, A. R. (1985). Brain and behavior: Hierarchy of feedback systems and control of input. In P. P. G. Bateson & P. H. Klopfer (Eds.), *Perspectives in Ethology* (pp. 109-168). New York: Plenum.

Feldman, D.H. & Benjamin, A.C. (2004). Going backward to go forward: The critical role of regressive moment in cognitive development. *Journal of Cognition and Development*, 5(1), 97-102.

Heimann, M. (Ed.). (2003). *Regression periods in human infancy.* Mahwah, New Jersey: Erlbaum.

Horwich, R.H. (1974). Regressive periods in primate behavioral development with reference to other mammals. *Primates,* 15, 141-149.

Plooij, F. (1978). Some basic traits of language in wild chimpanzees? In A. Lock (Ed.), *Action, gesture and symbol: The emergence of language* (pp. 111-131). London: Academic Press.

Plooij, F. (1979). How wild chimpanzee babies trigger the onset of mother-infant play and what the mother makes of it. In M. Bullowa (Ed.), *Before speech: the beginning of interpersonal communication* (pp. 223-243). Cambridge, England: Cambridge University Press.

Plooij, F. (1984). *The behavioral development of free-living chimpanzee babies and infants*. Norwood, N.J.: Ablex.

Plooij, F. (1987). Infant-ape behavioral development, the control of perception, types of learning and symbolism. In J. Montangero (Ed.), *Symbolism and Knowledge* (pp. 35-64). Geneva: Archives Jean Piaget Foundation.

Plooij, F. (1990). Developmental psychology: Developmental stages as successive reorganizations of the hierarchy. In R. J. Robertson (Ed.), *Introduction to modern psychology: The control-theory view* (pp. 123-133). Gravel Switch, Kentucky: The Control Systems Group, Inc. distributed by Benchmark Publ., Bloomfield NJ

Plooij, F. X. (2003). The trilogy of mind. In M. Heimann (Ed.), *Regression periods in human infancy* (pp. 185-205). Mahwah, NJ: Erlbaum.

Plooij, F.X. (2010). The 4 WHY's of age-linked regression periods in infancy. In Barry M. Lester & Joshua D. Sparrow (Eds.), *Nurturing Children and Families: Building on the Legacy of T. Berry Brazelton*. Malden, MA: Wiley-Blackwell.

Plooij, F., & van de Rijt-Plooij, H. (1989). Vulnerable periods during infancy: Hierarchically reorganized systems control, stress and disease. *Ethology and Sociobiology*, 10, 279-296.

Plooij, F., & van de Rijt-Plooij, H. (1990). Developmental transitions as successive reorganizations of a control hierarchy. *American Behavioral Scientist*, 34, 67-80.

Plooij, F., & van de Rijt-Plooij, H. (1994). Vulnerable periods during infancy: Regression, transition, and conflict. In J. Richer (Ed.), *The clinical application of ethology and attachment theory* (pp. 25-35). London: Association for Child Psychology and Psychiatry.

Plooij, F., & van de Rijt-Plooij, H. (1994). Learning by instincts, developmental transitions, and the roots of culture in infancy. In R. A. Gardner, B. T. Gardner, B. Chiarelli & F. X. Plooij (Eds.), *The ethological roots of culture* (pp. 357-373). Dordrecht: Kluwer Academic Publishers.

Plooij, F., & van de Rijt-Plooij, H. (2003). The effects of sources of "noise" on direct observation measures of regression periods: Case studies of four infants' adaptations to special parental conditions. In M. Heimann (Ed.), *Regression periods in human infancy* (pp. 57-80). Mahwah, NJ: Erlbaum.

Plooij, F., van de Rijt-Plooij, H. H. C., van der Stelt, J. M., van Es, B., & Helmers, R. (2003). Illness-peaks during infancy and regression periods. In M. Heimann (Ed.), *Regression periods in human infancy* (pp. 81-95). Mahwah, NJ: Erlbaum.

Plooij, F. X., van de Rijt-Plooij, H., & Helmers, R. (2003). Multimodal distribution of SIDS and regression periods. In M. Heimann (Ed.), *Regression periods in human infancy* (pp. 97-106). Mahwah, NJ: Erlbaum.

Powers, William T. (1973). *Behavior: The control of perception.* Chicago: Aldine. Second edition (2005), revised and expanded, Bloomfield NJ: Benchmark Publications.

Sadurni, M., & Rostan, C. (2003). Reflections on regression periods in the development of Catalan infants. In M. Heimann (Ed.), *Regression periods in human infancy* (pp. 7-22). Mahwah, NJ: Erlbaum.

Trevarthen, C. & Aitken, K. (2003). Regulation of brain development and age-related changes in infants' motives: The developmental function of regressive periods. In M. Heimann (Ed.), *Regression periods in human infancy* (pp. 107-184). Mahwah, NJ: Erlbaum.

van de Rijt-Plooij, H., & Plooij, F. (1987). Growing independence, conflict and learning in mother-infant relations in free-ranging chimpanzees. *Behaviour,* 101, 1-86.

van de Rijt-Plooij, H., & Plooij, F. (1988). Mother-infant relations, conflict, stress and illness among free-ranging chimpanzees. *Developmental Medicine and Child Neurology*, 30, 306-315.

van de Rijt-Plooij, H., & Plooij, F. (1992). Infantile regressions: Disorganization and the onset of transition periods. *Journal of Reproductive and Infant Psychology,* 10, 129-149.

van de Rijt-Plooij, H., & Plooij, F. (1993). Distinct periods of mother-infant conflict in normal development: Sources of progress and germs of pathology. *Journal of Child Psychology and Psychiatry,* 34, 229-245.

Woolmore, A., & Richer, J. (2003). Detecting infant regression periods: weak signals in a noisy environment. In M. Heimann (Ed.), *Regression periods in human infancy* (pp. 23-39). Mahwah, NJ: Erlbaum.

www.livingcontrolsystems.com (Living Control Systems Publishing)
For those who are interested in further information on the Perceptual Control Theory (PCT) concerning the functioning of the human brain that inspired much of the thinking behind *The Wonder Weeks*, this resource site features books, introductions and commentary, simulation programs for your computer, and more.

index

Underscored page references indicate boxed text.

A

Adapting to baby's responses, <u>33</u>, <u>53</u>, 65-66
Aggravation. *See* Anger, parental
Aggression, avoiding, 90-91, 117-18, <u>142</u>, 158, 193, 210, 247, 283, 323, 351
Anger, parental
    week 8 developmental leap, 64-65
    week 12 developmental leap, 87
    week 19 developmental leap, 118
    week 26 developmental leap, 158
    week 37 developmental leap, 193, 209-10
    week 46 developmental leap, 245-46
    week 55 developmental leap, 282-83
    week 64 developmental leap, 323-24
    week 75 developmental leap, 391, 405
Annoyance. *See* Irritability, parental
Antics, physical, 334-36
Appearance of newborn, 34–35
Appetite, loss of
    week 8 developmental leap, 58
    week 12 developmental leap, 86
    week 19 developmental leap, 114
    week 26 developmental leap, 153
    week 37 developmental leap, 206
    week 46 developmental leap, 240
    week 55 developmental leap, 277
    week 64 developmental leap, 316
    week 75 developmental leap, <u>375</u>

Architecture, basic, 382, <u>389</u>, 427-28
Arguments, parental
    week 26 developmental leap, 158
    week 37 developmental leap, 209-10
    week 46 developmental leap, 246
    week 55 developmental leap, 282
    week 64 developmental leap, 322
    week 75 developmental leap, 377
Art, 380, 383, <u>388</u>, 390, 422-24, <u>424</u>
Attention, demand for
    appearance and, 34
    newborn's, 34
    week 8 developmental leap, 58
    week 12 developmental leap, 86
    week 19 developmental leap, 113
    week 26 developmental leap, 151
    week 37 developmental leap, 202
    week 46 developmental leap, 236
    week 55 developmental leap, 274
    week 64 developmental leap, 311-13, 318
    week 75 developmental leap, <u>375</u>, 378

B

Babyish behavior
    week 37 developmental leap, 206
    week 46 developmental leap, 240
    week 55 developmental leap, 277

week 64 developmental leap, 316-17

week 75 developmental leap, 375

Baby-proofing home, 133, 174, 221

Baby talk, 121

Balancing games, 187–88

Baths, 79, 185

"Big change" of developmental leaps

    mental development and, 12-13

    nervous system changes and, 13

    overview, 12

    phases of, common, 17

    sign of, major, 12-13

    week 5, 45-46, 48

    week 8, 66-67, 67, 71

    week 12, 93, 93, 96-97

    week 19, 119-21, 126-27

    week 26, 159, 164-66

    week 37, 221-13, 213

    week 46, 247, 253-54

    week 55, 284-85, 289

    week 64, 324-30, 330

    week 75, 377-82, 382

Body movement

    games, 177, 186-89, 264-65, 334-36, 364, 394-95

    investigative behavior and, 105–6, 128-30, 172-73, 221-22, 396

    nakedness and, 130, 393, 398-99

    walking, 179, 205, 240, 272, 334-36, 379, 393, 396-98, 430

    week 12 developmental leap, 105-6

    week 19 developmental leap, 128-30

    week 26 developmental leap, 166, 176-80

    week 64 developmental leap, 334-35

    week 75 developmental leap, 394-95

Body postures, 76

Boredom, alleviating, 33, 297

Brain changes

    week 5 developmental leap, 46

    week 8 developmental leap, 67

    week 12 developmental leap, 93

    week 19 developmental leap, 121

    week 37 developmental leap, 213

    week 55 developmental leap, 285

    week 64 developmental leap, 330

    week 75 developmental leap, 382

Breathing reflex, 32-34

C

Caretaking time for babies, 97

Clinginess

    week 5 developmental leap, 40

    week 8 developmental leap, 59

    week 12 developmental leap, 86

    week 19 developmental leap, 111

    week 26 developmental leap, 152

    week 37 developmental leap, 184–86

    week 46 developmental leap, 234-35

    week 55 developmental leap, 273-74

    week 64 developmental leap, 307, 309-10, 320-21

    week 75 developmental leap, 373, 374, 375, 376-77, 439

Comforting baby

    in good and bad moods, 23

    importance of, 49-50, 66

    slings for, 43

    tips, 43

Concern, parental

    week 5 developmental leap, 40-43

    week 8 developmental leap, 61-65

    week 12 developmental leap, 87-92

    week 26 developmental leap, 157

    week 75 developmental leap, 376

Conscience, 378, 384, 390-92, 442

Confidence in handling newborn, 20-23

Consistency, importance of, 228, 362-63, 390

Control, maintaining, 118, 142, 158, 210-14

Copycat games, 224–25

Crankiness, 10

    week 5 developmental leap, 39

    week 8 developmental leap, 57

    week 12 developmental leap, 85

week 19 developmental leap, 114

week 26 developmental leap, 149, 152, <u>154</u>

week 37 developmental leap, 199, <u>205</u>, 208

week 46 developmental leap, 237

week 55 developmental leap, 275

week 64 developmental leap, 313, <u>320</u>,

week 75 developmental leap, 374, <u>375</u>,
376, 439

Crawling, 130, 172-74

Creativity, <u>297</u>, 352, 359, 422-24, 434-35

Crying

in fussy phases, 2, 10, 13, 16

gender differences, <u>98</u>

newborn's, for attention, 21-22, <u>23</u>, 24, 27,
31, 34

week 5 developmental leap, 39-43, <u>43</u>, 48,
<u>49</u>, 53

week 8 developmental leap, 57, 61-62

week 12 developmental leap, 85, <u>88</u>

week 19 developmental leap, 111-14, <u>115</u>

week 26 developmental leap, 149, 151,
153, <u>154</u>

week 37 developmental leap, 199-200, <u>205</u>, 206

week 46 developmental leap, 233, 237, <u>242</u>

week 55 developmental leap, 272, 274,
276, <u>280</u>

week 64 developmental leap, 307-8, 313-15,
<u>320</u>

week 75 developmental leap, 374, <u>375</u>, 439

Cuddling. *See* Comforting baby; Physical contact
needs

D

Daydreaming, <u>205</u>, <u>242</u>, 276, <u>375</u>

Defensiveness, parental, in week 8 developmental
leap, 64

Demanding baby, 77, 80, 85, 87, 111-13, 145,
149, 151, 155, 158, 200, 202, 233,
236, 271, 275

Demolishing games, <u>218</u>

Developmental leaps. *See also specific weeks*

age categories of, determining, 13, 15

"big change" of, 10

fussy phases of, general, 11–12

future, 444-45

new skills in, general, 15-16

overview, 5–7, 12-13

parental roles in, general, 16–18

period after, general, 18

phases of, common, 17

understanding, 2–3, 443-44

week 5, 45-46, 48

week 8, 66-67, 71

week 12, 93, 96-97

week 19, 109, 114-15, 121

week 26, 147, 164-66

week 37, 211-13

week 46, 247, 253-54

week 55, 284-85, 289

week 64, 325-30, <u>330</u>

week 75, 378-82, <u>382</u>

Diaper change, refusing

week 26 developmental leap, 153

week 37 developmental leap, 204

week 46 developmental leap, 239

week 75 developmental leap, 402

Diary

week 5 developmental leap, <u>47</u>

week 8 developmental leap, <u>61</u>, <u>68-70</u>,

week 12 developmental leap, <u>88</u>, <u>94-95</u>

week 19 developmental leap, <u>115</u>, <u>122-25</u>

week 26 developmental leap, <u>154</u>, <u>160-63</u>

week 37 developmental leap, <u>205</u>, <u>214-15</u>

week 46 developmental leap, <u>242</u>, <u>248-52</u>

week 55 developmental leap, <u>280</u>, <u>286-88</u>

week 64 developmental leap, <u>320</u>, <u>332-33</u>

week 75 developmental leap, <u>375</u>, <u>384-89</u>

"Difficult" baby, <u>15</u>, 62

"Difficult" toddler, 439-40

Distancing, fear of, 167-70, 172, 311

Dreaming. *See* Daydreaming; Nightmares

Dressing games, <u>222-23</u>, <u>262</u>

E

Eating. *See* Appetite, loss of; Fussy phases
Empathy, 379, <u>385</u>, 408
Entertainment, demand for, 275, 311-12, <u>320</u>, 362, <u>375</u>
Examining. *See* Investigative behavior
Excitement, curbing to avoid injury, 143
Exhaustion. *See* Fatigue, parental
Expectations, raising, 183
Experimentation
    week 46 developmental leap, 255-56
    week 55 developmental leap, 296-97
    week 64 developmental leap, <u>332-33</u>, 334, 337, 343-44, 354, 359, <u>364-67</u>
    week 75 developmental leap, 382, 400, 426
Exploring. *See* Investigative behavior

F

Family, 373, 380-81, 383, <u>386</u>, 390, 412-15
Fantasy play, 377, 409-10, <u>424</u>
Farm, children's, <u>189</u>
Fatigue, parental
    week 19 developmental leap, 116
    week 26 developmental leap, 155
    week 37 developmental leap, 208
    week 46 developmental leap, 244
    week 55 developmental leap, <u>297</u>
Fear
    of distancing, 167-70, 172
    irrational, 213–14, 300, 361-62, 438-39
    Moro reflex and, 32
    understanding, <u>261</u>
Feedback, giving, 259-60, 355
Feeding games, <u>263</u>, <u>287-88</u>
Feel
    of fabrics, as game, <u>103</u>
First hours, newborn's, <u>21</u>
First sentences, 121, 380, <u>389</u>, 428, 432, 436-37
First steps, baby's, <u>179</u>, <u>250</u>

First words, baby's, <u>181</u>
Frustrations, understanding, <u>259</u>, 346
Fussy phases
    crying in, 2
    "difficult" baby and, <u>13</u>
    eating and, 190-1, 193
    of developmental leaps
        general, 11–12
        week 5, 39-40
        week 8, 57-61
        week 12, 85-87
        week 19, 112-16
        week 26, 149-55
        week 37, 199-204, 206-7
        week 46, 233-41, 243
        week 55, 272-79, 89
        week 64, 307-19
        week 75, 374-75
three C's and, 10
timing of, 13

G

Games
    Acting silly, <u>365-66</u>, <u>440</u>
    Airplane, <u>102</u>
    Baby's Own Cupboard, <u>189</u>
    balancing, <u>187-88</u>, <u>440</u>
    Ball games, <u>440</u>
    Bells and Switches, <u>222</u>
    Blowing bubbles, <u>440</u>
    body movement, <u>186-87</u>, <u>264-65</u>
    Calling, <u>365</u>
    Cartoons and monsters, <u>366</u>
    Chase, <u>225</u>
    Cooking, <u>366</u>
    Copycat, <u>224–25</u>
    demolishing, <u>218</u>
    Doing Dishes, 298, <u>367</u>
    Doing Housework, <u>262</u>
    Do This, <u>224</u>, <u>367</u>
    Double Hiding, <u>299</u>

454 **Index**

Drawing, 440

Dressing, 222-23, 262

exploring, 222-23

Falling, 189

Feeding, 263, 440

Feeling Fabrics, 103

Flying, 188

Ghost games, 440

Giddy-Up, Giddy-Up, Little Rocking Horse, 186

Giving the Doll a Bath, 298

Grooming, 262-63

Happy Talk, 136

helping out, 262-63, 298-99

Hide-and-Seek, 184-85, 225, 265, 299, 367, 440

Hiding Toys, 185

Household, 366

independence, 298-99

Joking, 366

Jumping and Bouncing, 103, 440

Kidding around, 365

Looking at Pictures, 136, 185

Making, 387, 421

Mirror, 137, 224

Naming, 223, 263

Nibbling, 103

outdoor, 189, 222, 364

Pat a Cake, 225, 264

Peek-a-Boo, 137, 184-85, 367

Pendulum, 102–3

Physical antics, 364, 440

Playing circus, 440

Playing outside, 440

Playing the fool, 440

Playing with other children, 440

Playwrestling, 440

Pointing Out and Naming, 263, 365

Pull-Up, 79

Reading stories, 440

Recognizing people, 440

Rhyming, 365

Riding horse, 440

Rocking Horse, 103

role switching, 225

Row, Row, Row Your Boat, 265

Scrambling about, 440

Singing, 136, 186-7, 365

Sitting, 187

Skillfulness, 364

Slide, 102

song and movement, 136, 186-7, 264-5

Sound, 299

Standing, 188

Standing Baby on Head, 188, 440

Tag, 440

talking, 185

This Is the Way the Lady Rides, 186-7

This Is Your Nose, 263

Tickling, 137, 440

Tongue games, 440

with toys, 188-89

Under the Cup, 265

Unpacking and Putting Away Groceries, 299

Unwrapping a Parcel, 265

Using hands and feet, singing and rhyming, 365

Vacuuming, 367

week 8 developmental leap, 78-79

week 12 developmental leap, 102-3

week 19 developmental leap, 136-7

week 26 developmental leap, 184-89

week 37 developmental leap, 222-25

week 46 developmental leap, 262-65

week 55 developmental leap, 280-81

week 64 developmental leap, 364-67

week 75 developmental leap, 440

With emotions, 367

What Happens Next, 136

Where's the Baby, 185

Whispering, 186

word, 223-4

Gender differences and,
  caretaking time, 98
  crying, 98

parental feelings, _171_

physical contact needs, _152_

sleeping, _98_

Getting to know newborn, 24-25

Giftedness, 80, _297_

Grabbing objects

week 19 developmental leap, 110, 120, 131, 141-42

week 26 developmental leap, 155

week 55 developmental leap, 278

week 64 developmental leap, 322

Gripping reflex, 32–33

Grooming games, _262-63_

Growth spurts, 2, 10-11

Habits, breaking old, 18, _297_, 362-63, 440

Hand control, 93, 131-34, 179

Head circumference changes

week 5 developmental leap, _46_

week 8 developmental leap, _67_

week 12 developmental leap, _93_

week 19 developmental leap, _121_

week 37 developmental leap, _213_

week 55 developmental leap, _285_

Head support, 113

Hearing

investigative behavior and, 52, 75

newborn's, _25_

reflex to turn toward sound and, 32, 93

sound relationships and, 165

week 5 developmental leap, 52

week 8 developmental leap, 75

week 12 developmental leap, 93

week 19 developmental leap, 140-41

week 26 developmental leap, 182

Helping baby. _See_ Parental roles

Helping behavior, _295_, 327, _333_, 341, 357-59, 399

Helping out games, _262-63_, _298-99_, _366_

Human contact. _See_ Physical contact needs

Imitation, 75, 121, _163_, _214_, _224-25_, _248_, _251-52_, 292, 303, 327, _332_, 339-42, _366-67_, 372, 381-82, _384_, _389_, 391, 397, 399, 409, 430, 437

Impatience, curbing, 142

Independence

games promoting, _298-99_

Investigative behavior and, 257, 289-91

week 8 developmental leap, 77

week 46 developmental leap, _258_

week 55 developmental leap, 289-91

week 64 developmental leap, 309, 313, 318

week 75 developmental leap, 395-402, 409

Individuals, differences between, _385_, 407-8

Insecurity, parental

week 5 developmental leap, 40

week 37 developmental leap, 207

week 46 developmental leap, 244

week 55 developmental leap, 281

Intelligence, first appearance of, 212

Investigative behavior

body movement and, 105–7, 120-30

body postures and, 76

creativity and, _297_

examination and, 131-134

experimentation and, 255-57, 296-97

exploring games and, _222-23_

hearing and, 52, 75

independence and, 257, 289–91

language and, 138, 140, 180-82, 293-95

manipulation and, 131-34

music and, 138, 140, 180-82, 293-95

play-acting and, 226, 229

space for, 220-21

touch and, 52, 73-75, 100, 101, 120

toys and, 292-93

vision and, 51, 73, 135

week 37 developmental leap, 216-21

week 55 developmental leap, 296-97

week 64 developmental leap, 334-43

week 75 developmental leap, 394-400, 411, 415, 424-27

Irritability, parental
week 8 developmental leap, 64
week 12 developmental leap, 87
week 19 developmental leap, 117
week 26 developmental leap, 159
week 37 developmental leap, 192-93
week 46 developmental leap, 230
week 55 developmental leap, 266-67
week 64 developmental leap, 321-22
week 75 developmental leap, 376-77, 391, 429, 440

J

Jealousy
week 46 developmental leap, 237
week 55 developmental leap, 275
week 64 developmental leap, 312-313
week 75 developmental leap, 375

Language skills
- baby talk, 121
- first sentences, 121, 380, 389, 428, 432, 436-37
- first words, 181
- Investigative behavior and, 138, 140, 180-82, 293-95, 339-40, 431-33, 435
- sound recognition and, 121
- talking games and, 185
- thinking skills and, 211
- week 19 developmental leap, 138, 140
- week 26 developmental leap, 180-82
- week 37 developmental leap, 198, 212, 214, 223-24
- week 46 developmental leap, 260-61
- week 55 developmental leap, 293-94

- week 64 developmental leap, 321, 339-40
- week 75 developmental leap, 382, 389, 424, 428-437
- word games and, 223-24

Laughter, generating baby's, 52, 99, 100, 103, 104, 132, 136-37, 168, 174, 177, 215, 259, 266, 352, 366-67, 384, 391-92, 407, 412, 431

Learning. See New skills

Listlessness
- week 12 developmental leap, 87
- week 19 developmental leap, 115-16
- week 26 developmental leap, 153
- week 37 developmental leap, 204
- week 46 developmental leap, 238
- week 64 developmental leap, 324
- week 75 developmental leap, 375

Living creatures, other, 410-12

M

Manipulating objects, 131-34, 164, 174-75, 216-20, 253, 255-56, 259, 292-93, 296-97, 332-33, 336-38, 382, 388-89, 419-21, 425-28

Map of surroundings, mental, 415-17

Massage, 36

Mental development
"big change" and, 12-13
milestones in, 12
studies on, 10

Mimicry, 379, 385, 409

Mischievous behavior
week 46 developmental leap, 243
week 55 developmental leap, 278-79
week 64 developmental leap, 318-19
week 75 developmental leap, 375

Moodiness
week 19 developmental leap, 114
week 37 developmental leap, 208
week 46 developmental leap, 237

week 55 developmental leap, 275

week 64 developmental leap, 313-14, 324

week 75 developmental leap, 375

Moro reflex, 32

Motion. *See* Body movement

Movement. *See* Body movement

Music

    investigative behavior and, 138, 140,
180-82, 293-95, 422-24

    recognizing, 121

    song and movement games, 136, 186-87,
264-65, 294-96, 299

    week 19 developmental leap, 138, 140

    week 26 developmental leap, 180-82

    week 37 developmental leap, 225

    week 46 developmental leap, 255, 264-65,
267

    week 55 developmental leap, 294-96, 299,
301

    week 64 developmental leap, 328, 365

    week 75 developmental leap, 380, 383,
388, 422-23, 424, 441, 442

N

Nakedness, body movement and, 130, 393,
398-99

Newborn

    appearance as attention-getter, 34

    boredom of, alleviating, 33

    confidence in handling, 20-23

    crying for attention, 34

    discovery process, 20

    first hours of, 21

    getting to know, 24-25

    hearing, sense of, 29

    physical contact and, need for, 36

    reflexes of, 32-33

    smell, sense of, 29-30

    taste, sense of, 30

    touch, sense of, 30

    understanding, 24-25

    vision of, 28-29

    world of, 26, 31

New skills

    acknowledging, 49

    in developmental leaps, general, 15-16

    week 5, 39, 49

    week 8, 56-57, 64-66, 68, 71, 72, 75, 80

    week 12, 84, 85, 92-93, 94-95, 97, 99, 101

    week 19, 110-11, 118-19, 122-25, 127,
141

    week 26, 148-49, 159, 160, 165, 166-67,
176, 183, 190-91, 192

    week 37, 198-99, 210, 213, 214-15, 222-
23, 229

    week 46, 232-33, 247, 248-52, 253-55,
261, 266

    week 55, 270, 272, 283, 285, 286-88,
289, 297

    week 64, 306, 307, 324, 330, 331, 331-
33, 334-40, 364-67

    week 75, 372, 373, 377, 380, 382-83,
383, 384-89, 440-41

    old habits and, breaking, 18, 183, 297

    rest breaks in learning, 53, 72

    sharing discoveries and, 71

Nice behavior

    week 37 developmental leap, 203

    week 46 developmental leap, 241

    week 55 developmental leap, 278

    week 64 developmental leap, 311, 317,
320, 331, 332-33, 341, 346, 349,
353

    week 75 developmental leap, 375, 376,
385, 408

Nightmares, 150, 203, 238, 280, 315, 320,
375, 437

Norms and values, 327, 362, 378, 381, 390-
92, 442

O

Old habits, breaking, 18, 183, _297_, 362-63, 440

Outdoor games, _189_, _222_, 336, _364_, 410-11, 415-16, 427, _440_

Out of sight is not out of mind, _384_, 406-07, 410, 417

P

Parental experiences of developmental leaps
    growth spurts and, 10-11
    stress, _49_
    understanding, 2–3
    ups and downs of, 10
    week 5, 40-43
    week 8, 61–65
    week 12, 87-92
    week 19, 116-18
    week 26, 155-59
    week 37, 207-10
    week 46, 244-46
    week 55, 281-83
    week 64, 321-24
    week 75, 376-77
    with newborn, common, 1

Parental roles in developmental leaps
    general, 16-18
    week 5, 49
    week 8, 72-73
    week 12, 97-101, 104-06
    week 19, 127-28, 138-40
    week 26, 167-183, 190-91, 193
    week 37, 216-21, 226, 228-29
    week 46, 255-61, 266-68
    week 55, 289-97, 300
    week 64, 331, 334-63
    week 75, 390-439

Patience, virtue of, 141-43, 266, 266-68

Personality of baby
    week 5 developmental leap, 48
    week 8 developmental leap, 71
    week 12 developmental leap, 96-97
    week 19 developmental leap, 127
    week 26 developmental leap, 166
    week 37 developmental leap, 213
    week 46 developmental leap, 254
    week 55 developmental leap, 271
    week 64 developmental leap, 331
    week 75 developmental leap, 383

Phobias, 229, 300

Physical contact needs
    gender differences, _153_
    meeting, 36
    newborn's, 36
    week 5 developmental leap, 40
    week 8 developmental leap, 59
    week 12 developmental leap, 86
    week 19 developmental leap, 113
    week 26 developmental leap, 152
    week 37 developmental leap, 201-02
    week 46 developmental leap, 235
    week 55 developmental leap, 274
    week 64 developmental leap, 309-11
    week 75 developmental leap, _375_

Physics, basic, 381-82, _388-89_, 425-27

Play-acting, 226, 229, 275, _333_, 341-43, 409-10

Playtime, setting aside, _17_

Pressure, parental, 91-92

Progress through raised expectations, 87

Puzzles, 387, 419-21, 428, _441_

Q

"Quality time", _17_

Quarreling. _See_ Arguments, parental

Quiet baby, _77_

R

Reaching for objects. _See_ Grabbing objects

Reflexes, newborn's, 32-33

Relationship, building, 159, 164-66

Resentment, parental, 117-18

Respect, teaching, _296_

Rest breaks, _53_, _72_, 426

Role switching games, _225_, 342-43

Rolling over, _105_, 128-30

Rules, learning new, _297_, 350, 357, 362-63, 380, _387_, 390, 417, 421, 440

S

Safety issues

    baby-proofing home, _133_, _174_, _221_

    toys, _192_, _227_, _267_, _301_, _368_, _441_

Schedules, feeding and sleeping, 43

Self, notion of, 373, 377-78, 380, _384_, _388_, 392-407, 439

Senses. _See_ Hearing; Smell; Taste; Touch; Vision

Sequences, recognizing, 253, 270-71, 283-84, 421

Shaking baby, avoiding, _65_, _91_

Sharing discoveries of baby, 71, 96-97, 127, 166, 213, 254, 289, 331, 383

Shyness

    week 8 developmental leap, 58

    week 12 developmental leap, 86

    week 19 developmental leap, 112

    week 26 developmental leap, 151

    week 37 developmental leap, 201

    week 46 developmental leap, 235

    week 55 developmental leap, 274

    week 64 developmental leap, 310, _320_, 343, 344

    week 75 developmental leap, _375_

Sight. _See_ Vision

Sleeping

    gender differences and, 98

    nightmares and, 150, 203, 238, _280_, 315, _320_, _375_, 437

    schedules, 43

    tips for inducing, _45_

    week 8 developmental leap, 60

    week 12 developmental leap, 87

week 19 developmental leap, 112

week 26 developmental leap, 150

week 37 developmental leap, 202-03

week 46 developmental leap, 237

week 55 developmental leap, 276

week 64 developmental leap, 313-14, _320_, 321, 369

week 75 developmental leap, _375_, 392, 425-26

Slings, making, _43_

Smell, newborn's sense of, _29-30_

Song and movement games, _136_, _186-87_, _264-65_

Sound. _See_ Hearing; Language

Speech. _See_ Language

Standing, 177-78, _188_

Stress, parental, _49_, 116, 155, 157, 207-10, 244-46, 281-83, 321-24, 376-77

Sucking reflex, 32

Sucking thumb, 87

Surroundings, exploring, 172-76, _221_, 266, _364_, 380, _386_, 415, 442. _See also_ Investigative behavior

Sweet behavior. _See_ Nice behavior

Swimming, 183, _189_, 261, 266, 362

T

Taste, newborn's sense of, _30_

Teenaging Toddler, 376-77, 380

Teething, _156_

"Temperamental" baby, _15_, 62

Temperature, newborn's sense of, _30_

Temper tantrums, 158, _205_, 209, _242_, 245, 258, 279, _280_, 281-83, 285, 302-03, 319, _320_, 322, 346-47, 352, _366_, _375_, 377, 402, 406

Thinking skills, _211_

Three C's, 10, 374. _See also_ Clinginess; Crankiness; Crying

Thumb sucking, 87

Time, sense of, 377, 380, <u>388</u>, 425

Touch

investigative behavior and, 52, 73-75, 93, <u>94</u>, 100-01, <u>103</u>, 104, 120, <u>123</u>, 131-32, 142, <u>161</u>, 180, 193, 216-19, <u>222</u>, <u>263</u>, <u>279</u>, 325

massage, <u>36</u>

newborn's sense of, <u>33</u>, <u>36</u>

week 5 developmental leap, 52

week 8 developmental leap, 73-75

week 12 developmental leap, 93, <u>94</u>, 100-01, <u>103</u>, 104

week 19 developmental leap, 120, <u>123</u>, 131-32, 142

week 26 developmental leap, <u>161</u>, 180, 193

week 37 developmental leap, 216-19, <u>222</u>

week 46 developmental leap, <u>263</u>

week 55 developmental leap, 279

week 64 developmental leap, 325

Toys

games with, <u>188-89</u>

investigative behavior and, 292-93

safety issues, <u>192</u>, <u>227</u>, <u>267</u>, <u>301</u>, <u>368</u>, <u>441</u>

week 8 developmental leap, <u>80</u>

week 12 developmental leap, <u>105</u>

week 19 developmental leap, <u>139</u>

week 26 developmental leap, <u>192</u>

week 37 developmental leap, <u>227</u>

week 46 developmental leap, <u>267</u>

week 55 developmental leap, <u>301</u>

week 64 developmental leap, <u>368</u>

week 75 developmental leap, <u>441</u>

Trapped, parental feelings of, 117

U

Understanding baby, 24-25, 27, 53, 89, 100, 148, 167-68, <u>171</u>, 207, 212, 229, <u>258</u>, 260, <u>261</u>, 271, 284, 294, 300, 308, 348, 358, 361, 391, 410, 431-33, 435, 438

V

Vision

eye turning and, 93

investigative behavior and, 51, 73, 135

newborn's, <u>28-29</u>

week 5 developmental leap, 46, 48, 51

week 8 developmental leap, <u>69-70</u>, 73, <u>77</u>, <u>78-79</u>, 81

week 12 developmental leap, 93, <u>95</u>, 97, 104

week 19 developmental leap, <u>124</u>, 127, 130-31, 135, <u>136-37</u>

week 26 developmental leap, 160-63, 167, 173, 175, <u>184</u>, <u>189</u>, 191, 194

week 37 developmental leap, 198, <u>224</u>

week 55 developmental leap, <u>288</u>, 289, 293-94, 296, <u>299</u>, 303

week 64 developmental leap, 328, 358-59

week 75 developmental leap, 406, 410, 421, 427-28, 438

W

Walking, <u>160</u>, 178-79, <u>179</u>, 220-21, <u>222</u>, <u>225</u>, 229, 240, <u>250</u>, 254, 257, 281, 290, 296, 302, 310, 330, <u>332-33</u>, 334-36, 338, 341-43, 345, 348, 353, 355-56, 362, <u>364-65</u>, 379, 393-98, 430

week 5 developmental leap

"big change," 45-46, 48

clinginess, 40

concern of parents, 40-43

crankiness, 39

crying, 39

diary, <u>47</u>

fussy signs, 39-40

glucose metabolism changes, <u>46</u>

head circumference changes, <u>46</u>

hearing, 52

insecurity of parents, 40

new skills, _39_, _49_

overview, 38

parental experiences, 40-44

parental roles, 49–53

period after, 54

personality, 48

physical contact needs, 40

touch, 52

vision, 51

week 8 developmental leap

  anger of parents, 65

  appetite, loss of, 58-59

  attention, demand for, 58

  "big change, " 66-67, 71

  body postures, 76

  brain wave changes, _67_

  clinginess, _59_

  concern of parents, 62-65

  crying, 60

  defensiveness of parents, 64

  diary, _61_, _68-70_

  fussy signs, 57-61

  games, 78-79

  head circumference changes, _67_

  hearing, 75

  independence, _77_

  irritability of parents, 64

  new skills, _57_, 65-66

  overview, 56-57

  parental experiences, 61–66

  parental roles, 72-73

  period after, 81-82

  personality, 71

  shyness, 58

  sleeping, 60

  touch, 73-75

  toys, _80_

  vision, 73

week 12 developmental leap

  anger of parents, 87

  appetite, loss of, 86

  attention, demand for, 85

"big change, " 93, 96-97

body movement, 105-06

clinginess, 86

concern of parents, 87-92

diary, 88, _94-95_

fussy signs, 85–87

games, _102-03_

head circumference changes, _93_

hearing, 98-100

irritability of parents, 87

listlessness, 87

new skills, _85_, 92

overview, 84–85

parental experiences, 87-92

parental roles, 97-98, 98-106

period after, 107-08

personality, 96-97

shyness, 86

sleeping, 87

touch, 100-01, 104

toys, _106_

week 19 developmental leap

  appetite, loss of, 114

  attention, demand for, 113

  "big change, " 119-21, 126-27

  body movement, 128-30

  brain wave changes, _121_

  clinginess, 111

  crankiness, 114

  diary, _115_, _122-25_

  fatigue of parents, 116

  fussy signs, 112-16

  games, _136-37_

  grabbing objects, 110, 120, 131, 141-42

  head circumference changes, _121_

  language, 138, 140

  listlessness, 115-16

  moodiness, 114

  music, 138, 138-40

  new skills, 118-19

  overview, 110-11

  parental experiences, 116-18

Index

parental roles, 127-28, 138, 140

period after, 144-46

personality, 127

resentment of parents, 117-18

shyness, 112

sleeping, 112

toys, 139

trapped feeling of parents, 117

vision, 135

week 26 developmental leap

    appetite, loss of, 153

    arguments of parents, 158-59

    attention, demand for, 151

    "big change, " 159, 164-66

    body movement, 166, 176-80

    clinginess, 152

    concern of parents, 157

    diaper change refusal, 153

    diary, 154, 160-63

    fatigue of parents, 155

    fussy signs, 149-55

    games, 184-89

    grabbing objects, 152

    irritability of parents, 159

    language, 180-82

    listlessness, 153

    music, 180-82

    new skills, 159

    overview, 148-49

    parental experiences, 155-59

    parental roles, 167-83, 190-91, 193

    period after, 194-95

    personality, 166

    shyness, 151

    sleeping, 150

    toys, 192

week 37 developmental leap

    anger of parents, 208-09

    appetite, loss of, 206-07

    arguments of parents, 209-10

    attention, demand for, 202

    babyish behavior, 206

    "big change, " 211-13

    brain wave changes, 213

    clinginess, 200-02

    diaper change refusal, 204

    diary, 205, 214-15

    fatigue of parents, 208

    fussy signs, 199-204, 206-07

    games, 222-225

    glucose metabolism changes, 213

    head circumference changes, 213

    insecurity of parents, 207

    investigative behavior, 216-21

    listlessness, 204

    mischievous behavior, 243

    new skills, 210

    nice behavior, 203, 241

    overview, 198-99

    parental experiences, 207-10

    parental roles, 212–14, 216-21, 226

    period after, 230

    personality, 213

    play-acting, 226, 229

    shyness, 201

    sleeping, 202-03

    toys, 227

week 46 developmental leap

    anger of parents, 245

    appetite, loss of, 240

    arguments of parents, 246

    attention, demand for, 236

    babyish behavior, 240

    "big change, " 247, 253-54

    clinginess, 234-35

    crankiness, 237

    diaper change refusal, 239

    diary, 242, 250-54

    experimentation, 255-56

    fatigue of parents, 244

    feedback, giving, 259-60

    fussy signs, 233-41, 243

    games, 262-65

    independence, 257

insecurity of parents, 244

jealousy, 237

language, 260-61

listlessness, 238

mischievous behavior, 243

moodiness, 237

new skills, 247

overview, 232-33

parental experiences, 244-46

parental roles, 255-61, 266-68

period after, 266-68

personality, 254

physical contact needs, 235

shyness, 235

sleeping, 237

toys, 267

week 55 developmental leap

anger of parents, 281-82

appetite, loss of, 277

arguments of parents, 282

attention, demand for, 275

babyish behavior, 277

"big change, " 284-85, 289

brain wave changes, 285

clinginess, 273-74

crankiness, 275

daydreaming, 276

diary, 280, 286-88

entertainment demands, 275

experimentation, 296-97

fussy signs, 272-79, 281

games, 298

glucose metabolism changes, 285

grabbing objects, 278

head circumference changes, 285

independence, 289-92

insecurity of parents, 281

investigative behavior, 296-97

jealousy, 275

mischievous behavior, 278-79

moodiness, 275

new skills, 283

nice behavior, 278

overview, 270-73

parental experiences, 281-83

parental roles, 289-97, 300

period after, 302-03

personality, 285

physical contact needs, 274

shyness, 274

sleeping, 276

toys, 301

week 64 developmental leap

anger of parents, 321-24

appetite, loss of, 316

arguments of parents, 322-24

attention, demand for, 311-12

babyish behavior, 316-17

"big change," 325-31, 330

brain changes, 330

clinginess, 309-11

crankiness, 313

daydreaming, 315-16

diary, 320, 332-33

entertainment demands, 311-12

experimentation, 306, 332-33, 334, 337,
343-44, 354, 359, 364-67

fussy signs, 307-19

games, 364-67

grabbing objects, 317-18

independence, 309, 325

investigative behavior, 334-43

jealousy, 312-13

mischievous behavior, 318-19

moodiness, 313-14, 324

new skills, 306, 307, 324, 330, 331, 331-
33, 334-40, 364-47

nice behavior, 311, 317, 320, 331, 332-33,
341, 346, 351, 355

overview, 306-07

parental experiences, 321-24

parental roles, 331, 334-63

period after, 368-70

personality, 331

physical contact needs, 311

shyness, 310, _320_, 343-44

sleeping, 313-14, _320_, 321, 369

toys, _368_

week 75 developmental leap

anger of parents, 391, 405

appetite, loss of, _375_

arguments of parents, 377

attention, demand for, _375_, 378

babyish behavior, _375_

"big change," 377-82, _382_

brain changes, _382_

clinginess, _373_, 374, _375_, 376-77, 439

crankiness, 374, _375_, 376, 439

daydreaming, _375_

diary, _375_, _384-89_

entertainment demands, _375_

experimentation, 382, 400, 426,

fussy signs, 374-75

games, _440_

independence, 395-402, 409

investigative behavior, 394-400, 411, 415,
    424-27

jealousy, _375_

mischievous behavior, _375_

moodiness, _375_

new skills, 372, _373_, 377, 380, _382-83_,
    383, _384-89_, _440-41_

nice behavior, _375_, 376, _385_, 408

overview, 372-74

parental experiences, 376-77

parental roles, 390-439

period after, 439-40, 442-43

personality, 383

physical contact needs, _375_

shyness, _375_

sleeping, _375_, 392, 425-26

toys, _441_

Word games, _223-24_

World of newborn, 26, 31

Worry. _See_ Concern, parental

Wriggling around naked. _See_ Nakedness, body
    movement and

internet

You may be interested to know that *The Wonder Weeks* is available in several languages and that there is plenty of supporting information on childhood development available on the Internet. A convenient way to access information on the Internet is to go to the website that is designed to support the English edition.

www.thewonderweeks.com

This website provides a great deal of additional information, including scientific research, the many languages into which *The Wonder Weeks* has been translated, how to order the book in any of these languages, and how to find blogs, forums, and other web pages with comments about *The Wonder Weeks* around the world in any language by searching the Internet using either the title or the ISBN number.

You can also subscribe to a free email service called *Leap Alarm*. See page 8.

Made in the USA
San Bernardino, CA
29 October 2012